19.95
2-5
292

THE
UNITED NATIONS
AT THE
CROSSROADS
OF REFORM

STUDIES IN INSTITUTIONAL ECONOMICS

THE
UNITED NATIONS
AT THE
CROSSROADS
OF REFORM

Wendell Gordon

M.E. Sharpe
Armonk, New York
London, England

Library of Congress Cataloging-in-Publication Data

Gordon, Wendell Chaffee, 1916–
The United Nations at the crossroads of reform / by
Wendell Gordon.
p.   cm.   —   (Studies in institutional economics)
Includes bibliographical references and index.
ISBN 1-56324-400-4.   —   ISBN 1-56324-401-2
1. United Nations. 2. International cooperation.
3. International relations. I. Title. II. Series.
JX1977.G676   1994
341.23—dc20   94–19451
CIP

Printed in the United States of America

The paper used in this publication meets the minimum requirements of
American National Standard for Information Sciences—
Permanence of Paper for Printed Library Materials,
ANSI Z 39.48-1984.

BM (c)   10   9   8   7   6   5   4   3   2   1
BM (p)   10   9   8   7   6   5   4   3   2

With great appreciation
to
an extraordinarily decent man

CLYDE EAGLETON

for many years
Professor of Government
New York University
Proponent of an effective
United Nations

Table of Contents

Part II: The Ingredients in the Pattern

Preface

The argument used in this work is in the framework of the institutionalism of Thorstein Veblen, John Dewey, John Kenneth Galbraith, Gunnar Myrdal, John R. Commons, J. Fagg Foster, Clarence Ayres, Allan Gruchy, Marc Tool, and Warren Samuels, no one of whom will entirely approve of the special slant of this writer. Involved is understanding the *process* of change: the nature of the process by which knowledge (particularly technical knowledge) is accumulated, impacts on institutions such as the United Nations, and calls for change in the workings (institutionalized behavior norms) of those institutions, and of all people.

I wish to acknowledge a special debt to Warren Samuels, the editor of the M.E. Sharpe, Inc., Studies in Institutional Economics series.

I am greatly indebted to Carolyn Ayers and Pat Wheeler for patiently typing and retyping the manuscript and to Jill Mason and Christine Florie for their most constructive contribution to the editing.

And I must express thanks to James R. Roach of the Department of Government at the University of Texas for critical and intelligent comments about the manuscript, comments which stimulated my efforts. I also have a similar debt to Richard D. Bartel, the editor at M.E. Sharpe, Inc., for critical but constructive comments.

Time will tell if the resulting manuscript is passable and worthwhile.

Wendell Gordon
July 1994

THE
UNITED NATIONS
AT THE
CROSSROADS
OF REFORM

Introduction

The Setting

The United Nations was established "to maintain international peace and security. . . ." It was also "to achieve international co-operation in solving international problems of an economic, social, cultural or humanitarian character, and in promoting and encouraging respect for human rights and for fundamental freedoms for all without distinction as to race, sex, language, or religion. . . ." Yet the nations of the world who charged the UN with these great missions never permitted it to acquire the resources it needed to fulfill them.

Thus, the UN is generally condemned as being incapable of carrying out its missions. In its efforts to prevent war and counteract aggressive invasions it is viewed as generally botching the job. This seems to be the case in the United States, where the presidency frequently deprecates the UN, both political parties in Congress welcome the chance to withhold funds from the UN, and condemnation of the UN is frequently heard from the general population. This attitude notwithstanding, it was the United States that was most influential at the San Francisco conference in 1945 in determining the precise role and powers of the UN. The organization did not create itself. It was created by the victors of World War II, meaning most particularly the United States, and was the result of their vision of an organization that could oversee the postwar world.

The authors of the charter were aware that it might have flaws, it might need revision. Consequently, they provided in Article 109 of the charter for "A General Conference of the Members of the United Nations for the purpose of reviewing the present charter." Moreover, they were sufficiently aware of the likely need for general change in the structure and functions of the UN that they further provided for the necessity of having such a conference. In paragraph 3 of Article 109 it was stated that: "If such a conference has not been held before the tenth annual session of the General Assembly following the coming into force of the present Charter, the proposal to call such a conference shall be placed on the agenda of that session of the General Assembly."

Inconsistently, despite the criticism of the UN that has been common, no such conference has been called. Yet it is surely most important that there be serious and general discussion in a prestigious meeting of the nations of the world of change in the structure and functions of the United Nations.

The Process of Change and Institutionalism

In discussing reform of the United Nations, one quickly becomes involved with the question as to just what goes on in the process of change. Society is made up of institutions such as organized religions, families, social groups and clubs, and governmental organizations such as the United Nations. The reform of the United Nations would be an example of institutional change. Institutionalism, the approach of this book, is that special field in the social sciences that emphasizes study of the process of institutional change.

The organization of this book is as follows: Chapters 1 through 10 describe the operation of the UN as an institution in terms of the chief units in the system: the General Assembly, the Security Council, the Secretary-General and the Secretariat, the Economic and Social Council and its innumerable subsidiary organs, the International Court of Justice, and the Trusteeship Council. In chapters 11 through 14 the substantive work of the

UN is analyzed in terms of the technology, institutions, environment, and people categories of institutionalism. Chapter 15 presents a discussion of the nature of possible desirable changes in the structure and functioning of the UN.

Some Background History

Organized, thoughtful efforts on the part of world society to prevent war began before the end of World War I and the establishment of the League of Nations. But such efforts were powerfully stimulated by those events. It is not surprising that this first serious effort on a worldwide scale to control war was not an instantaneous complete success. The use of war as an instrument of policy was too ingrained an institutionalized habit to be dispensed with readily. And a world of sovereign nation states where each recklessly pursues its own interests as it perceives those interests is not helpful in creating a civilized world.

The Covenant of the League of Nations was approved as an aspect of the peace treaties ending World War I in 1919. Article II of the Covenant provided: "Any war or threat of war, whether immediately affecting any of the Members of the League or not, is hereby declared a matter of concern to the whole League, and the League shall take any action that may be deemed wise and effectual to safeguard the peace of nations." Later articles provided additional detail as to possible types of action the League might take. On the whole, the text was sufficiently general so that, if there had been the will on the part of the leaders of the great powers, the use of strong, effective force to stop fighting was well within the purview of the Covenant.

But the United States defected. President Woodrow Wilson became ill and was not able to lead the effort to obtain ratification of the World War I peace treaties in the Senate. Leading Republican Senators William E. Borah and Henry Cabot Lodge led an effort that aborted ratification, and the United States people in the 1920s seemed generally to have endorsed this manifestation of isolation.

Geneva, Switzerland, was designated as the headquarters of the League. The organization consisted of an assembly with representatives of all the member nations. But the assembly could only make recommendations; meaningful decisions were left to a council, which consisted of representatives of the great powers: England, France, Italy, and Japan, and later Germany and the USSR (but not the nonmember United States), plus representatives of a sample of nonpermanent members from the other member countries.

Action in the council required a unanimous vote of all members. Thus, every council member, not just the great powers, had a veto. It followed that, from the beginning, there were limits on the ability of the League to take meaningful action in difficult situations. Obtaining unanimity is not easy.

There were also a secretariat and associated organizations such as the Permanent Court of International Justice at The Hague and the International Labour Organization in Rome.

Without the participation of the United States the League did a fair job of handling international crises during the 1920s, but it was frustrated by the greater problems of the 1930s. Especially disastrous was the inability of the League to handle the Japanese offensive in China (1937–45), the Italians in Ethiopia (1936), the Spanish Civil War (1936–39), or even the Chaco War between Paraguay and Bolivia (1932–35), but above all Adolf Hitler after 1933. The absence of the United States from the councils of the League played a significant role in its ineffectiveness, and the Neutrality Acts of the 1930s passed by a Democratic Congress, but with enthusiastic Republican support, underlined the point that world peace and world problems were not a major concern of the United States.

Come the United Nations

Then came World War II in 1939, and in 1941, with the help of the Japanese, the United States became involved. As World War II progressed, the allied powers, then calling themselves "the united nations," began to think in terms of a postwar political organization, an organization that they hoped would work better than the League of Nations. A series of conferences and discussions culminated in a conference in San Francisco in 1945 at which the victorious allies agreed on the charter of a successor organization to take the place of the League. They decided to call the organization the United Nations.

Part I

The Organization and Functioning of the United Nations

1

The United Nations and
Its Membership

The charter of the United Nations states: "We the peoples of the
United Nations determined to save succeeding generations from
the scourge of war, which twice in our lifetime has brought untold sorrow to mankind, and . . . to establish conditions under
which justice and respect for the obligations arising from treaties
. . . can be maintained . . . have resolved to combine our efforts to
accomplish these aims." The charter also refers to "fundamental
human rights," equal rights for all "nations large and small," the
promotion of "social progress and better standards of life in
larger freedom," and the employment of "international machinery" to accomplish such goals.

The United Nations became operative as the successor organization to the League of Nations on October 24, 1945, on the basis of
the charter signed at San Francisco on June 26 of that year.[1] In May
1946 the League of Nations formally dissolved itself and transferred
its assets, property, and buildings to the new United Nations.

Against the background of the League's inability to handle the
mess of the 1930s, the leaders of the Allies, particularly Franklin
Roosevelt and Winston Churchill, had begun early during World
War II to plan for a more effective worldwide organization to
keep the postwar peace. To this effect there were an Inter-Allied
Declaration signed June 12, 1941, at St. James's Palace in London; an Atlantic Charter, agreed to by Roosevelt and Churchill

on a battleship in the North Atlantic on August 14, 1941; a "Declaration by United Nations" on New Year's Day, 1942; declarations at conferences in Moscow, October 3, 1943, and Tehran, December 1, 1943. Concrete plans were first drawn up at a mansion in Washington called Dumbarton Oaks in the fall of 1944. There followed the notorious conference at Yalta involving Roosevelt, Churchill, and Joseph Stalin, in February 1945. The charter of the United Nations was then formally adopted at the conference in San Francisco. Enough ratifications were received to justify the United Nations' formal existence beginning October 24, 1945. The organization began to function with the opening of the first General Assembly on January 10, 1946, in London. On February 14 the General Assembly voted to accept the United States' invitation to locate the permanent headquarters there. Temporary headquarters were first located at Hunter College in New York City, (the Bronx) and then at Lake Success on Long Island. The decision to locate permanently on Manhattan's East Side was made December 14, 1946. Occupancy of the headquarters building began in August of 1950.

The principal organs of the new organization were the General Assembly, Security Council, Economic and Social Council (ECOSOC), Trusteeship Council, International Court of Justice, and Secretariat, all headed by a secretary-general. There were and are innumerable auxiliary, subsidiary, related, autonomous, specialized, and associated organizations, some antedating the United Nations and even the old League of Nations. The ties that bind are quite strong in some cases, weak in others. Some are dependent on the United Nations budget for financing; others are more or less financially independent, such as the International Monetary Fund.

Membership

It is not automatic that all countries are members. The initial members were the countries that participated in the United Nations Conference on International Organization that convened in San Francisco on April 25, 1945, plus Argentina, Denmark,

Byelorussia, the Ukraine, and Poland, making a total of fifty-one. The original membership was basically the victors in World War II.

By 1994 the membership was 184. The membership fluctuates, however (see Figure 1.1). One might believe that it is simple and straightforward to identify a nation, argue that all nations should be members of the United Nations, and automatically recognize the membership of all such identifiable nations. The situation is, however, not quite so simple for several reasons, in part because of difficulties associated with the concept of sovereignty, in part because of questions involved in identifying the personnel of a government entitled to speak for a country. And there are other problems.

Palestine is illustrative of the difficulties. Is Palestine or should Palestine be recognized as an independent country? Should the Palestine Liberation Organization be recognized as the government or legitimate representative of that country? The changes made in 1994 seem not to have resolved these issues. What is the proper role of such a country? What is the proper role of a country such as Monaco, which handles its own internal affairs and gambling casino as an ostensibly independent and sovereign country but whose foreign affairs are managed by the French government? Monaco became a member of the UN in 1993.

Admission to the UN involves an initial recommendation by the Security Council and a subsequent final decision by the General Assembly. The Security Council may move with speed or very slowly, sometimes taking years to respond to applications for admission. The General Assembly has typically acted promptly after the Security Council makes a recommendation. Procedures are also provided in Article 5 of the charter for the temporary suspension or expulsion of members following recommendations of the Security Council and action by the General Assembly.

Disproportion in Size of Countries

The one-country, one-vote system prevailing in the General Assembly might be acceptable if the countries were about the same

Figure 1.1 **Members of the United Nations** (as of May 1993)

Country	Date of Admission	Country	Date of Admission	Country	Date of Admission
Afghanistan	19 Nov. 1946	Botswana	17 Oct. 1966	Cyprus	20 Sep. 1960
Albania	14 Dec. 1955	Brazil	24 Oct. 1945	Czech Republic	19 Jan. 1993
Algeria	8 Oct. 1962	Brunei Darussalam	21 Sep. 1984	Democratic People's Republic of Korea	17 Sep. 1991
Angola	1 Dec. 1976	Bulgaria	14 Dec. 1955	Denmark	24 Oct. 1945
Antigua and Barbuda	11 Nov. 1981	Burkina Faso	20 Sep. 1960	Djibouti	20 Sep. 1977
Argentina	24 Oct. 1945	Burundi	18 Sep. 1962	Dominica	18 Dec. 1978
Armenia	2 Mar. 1992	Cambodia	14 Dec. 1955	Dominican Republic	24 Oct. 1945
Australia	1 Nov. 1945	Cameroon	20 Sep. 1960	Ecuador	21 Dec. 1945
Austria	14 Dec. 1955	Canada	9 Nov. 1945	Egypt	24 Oct. 1945
Azerbaijan	2 Mar. 1992	Cape Verde	16 Sep. 1975	El Salvador	24 Oct. 1945
Bahamas	18 Sep. 1973	Central African Republic	20 Sep. 1960	Equatorial Guinea	12 Nov. 1968
Bahrain	21 Sep. 1971	Chad	20 Sep. 1960	Eritrea	28 May 1993
Bangladesh	17 Sep. 1974	Chile	24 Oct. 1945	Estonia	17 Sep. 1991
Barbados	9 Dec. 1966	China	24 Oct. 1945	Ethiopia	13 Nov. 1945
Belarus	24 Oct. 1945	Colombia	5 Nov. 1945	Fiji	13 Oct. 1970
Belgium	27 Dec. 1945	Comoros	12 Nov. 1975	Finland	14 Dec. 1955
Belize	25 Sep. 1981	Congo	20 Sep. 1960	France	24 Oct. 1945
Benin	20 Sep. 1960	Costa Rica	2 Nov. 1945	Gabon	20 Sep. 1960
Bhutan	21 Sep. 1971	Côte d'Ivoire	20 Sep. 1960	Gambia	21 Sep. 1965
Bolivia	14 Nov. 1945	Croatia	22 May 1992	Georgia	31 July 1992
Bosnia and Herzegovina	22 May 1992	Cuba	24 Oct. 1945		

Country	Date of Admission	Country	Date of Admission	Country	Date of Admission
Germany	18 Sep. 1973	Jordan	18 Sep. 1955	Marshall Islands	17 Sep. 1991
Ghana	8 Mar. 1957	Kazakhstan	2 Mar. 1992	Mauritania	27 Oct. 1961
Greece	25 Oct. 1945	Kenya	16 Dec. 1963	Mauritius	24 Apr. 1968
Grenada	17 Sep. 1974	Kuwait	14 May 1963	Mexico	7 Nov. 1945
Guatemala	21 Nov. 1945	Kyrgyzstan	2 Mar. 1992	Micronesia	
Guinea	12 Dec. 1958	Lao People's		(Federated States of)	17 Sep. 1991
Guinea-Bissau	17 Sep. 1974	Democratic Republic	14 Dec. 1955	Monaco	28 May 1993
Guyana	20 Sep. 1966	Latvia	17 Sep. 1991	Mongolia	27 Oct. 1961
Haiti	24 Oct. 1945	Lebanon	24 Oct. 1945	Morocco	12 Nov. 1956
Honduras	17 Dec. 1945	Lesotho	17 Oct. 1966	Mozambique	16 Sep. 1975
Hungary	14 Dec. 1955	Liberia	2 Nov. 1945	Myanmar	19 Apr. 1948
Iceland	19 Nov. 1946	Libyan Arab Jamahiriya	14 Dec. 1955	Namibia	23 Apr. 1990
India	30 Oct. 1945	Liechtenstein	18 Sep. 1990	Nepal	14 Dec. 1955
Indonesia	28 Sep. 1950	Lithuania	17 Sep. 1991	Netherlands	10 Dec. 1945
Iran (Islamic Republic of)	24 Oct. 1945	Luxembourg	24 Oct. 1945	New Zealand	24 Oct. 1945
Iraq	21 Dec. 1945	Madagascar	20 Sep. 1960	Nicaragua	24 Oct. 1945
Ireland	14 Dec. 1955	Malawi	1 Dec. 1964	Niger	20 Sep. 1960
Israel	11 May 1949	Malaysia	17 Sep. 1957	Nigeria	7 Oct. 1960
Italy	14 Dec. 1955	Maldives	21 Sep. 1965	Norway	27 Nov. 1945
Jamaica	18 Sep. 1962	Mali	28 Sep. 1960	Oman	7 Oct. 1971
Japan	18 Dec. 1956	Malta	1 Dec. 1964	Pakistan	30 Sep. 1947

Country	Date of Admission	Country	Date of Admission	Country	Date of Admission
Panama	13 Nov. 1945	Seychelles	21 Sep. 1976	Turkey	24 Oct. 1945
Papua New Guinea	10 Oct. 1975	Sierra Leone	27 Sep. 1961	Turkmenistan	2 Mar. 1992
Paraguay	24 Oct. 1945	Singapore	21 Sep. 1965	Uganda	25 Oct. 1962
Peru	31 Oct. 1945	Slovakia	19 Jan. 1993	Ukraine	24 Oct. 1945
Philippines	24 Oct. 1945	Slovenia	22 May 1992	United Arab Emirates	9 Dec. 1971
Poland	24 Oct. 1945	Solomon Islands	19 Sep. 1978	United Kingdom of Great Britain and Northern Ireland	24 Oct. 1945
Portugal	14 Dec. 1955	Somalia	20 Sep. 1960	United Republic of Tanzania	14 Dec. 1961
Qatar	21 Sep. 1971	South Africa	7 Nov. 1945	United States of America	24 Oct. 1945
Republic of Korea	17 Sep. 1991	Spain	14 Dec. 1955	Uruguay	18 Dec. 1945
Republic of Moldova	2 Mar. 1992	Sri Lanka	14 Dec. 1955	Uzbekistan	2 Mar. 1992
Romania	14 Dec. 1955	Sudan	12 Nov. 1956	Vanuatu	15 Sep. 1981
Russian Federation	24 Oct. 1945	Suriname	4 Dec. 1975	Venezuela	15 Nov. 1945
Rwanda	18 Sep. 1962	Swaziland	24 Sep. 1968	Viet Nam	20 Sep. 1977
Saint Kitts and Nevis	23 Sep. 1983	Sweden	19 Nov. 1946	Yemen	30 Sep. 1947
Saint Lucia	18 Sep. 1979	Syrian Arab Republic	24 Oct. 1945	Yugoslavia	24 Oct. 1945
Saint Vincent and the Grenadines	16 Sep. 1980	Tajikistan	2 Mar. 1992	Zaire	20 Sep. 1960
Samoa	15 Dec. 1976	Thailand	16 Dec. 1946	Zambia	1 Dec. 1964
San Marino	2 Mar. 1992	The former Yugoslav Republic of Macedonia	8 April 1993	Zimbabwe	25 Aug. 1980
Sao Tome and Principe	16 Sep. 1975	Togo	20 Sep. 1960		
Saudi Arabia	24 Oct. 1945	Trinidad and Tobago	18 Sep. 1962		
Senegal	28 Sep. 1960	Tunisia	12 Nov. 1956		

size, but a situation in which five countries represent half of the population of the world and half of the countries represent only about 4.5 percent of the total population makes such a procedure a bit undemocratic. Also, in discussion in the General Assembly each nation is entitled to "equal time" to describe its position, a procedure that can be quite time consuming.

These considerations suggest a doubt as to the reasonableness of the criteria for identifying a country for UN membership. Or, perhaps, the membership criteria may be left as is if the rules on voting and podium time are changed. This issue is discussed further in the next chapter.

Location

Shirley Hazzard has reported that: "The United Nations Preparatory Commission, meeting in 1945, advocated that the United Nations should be so situated as to be free from any attempt at improper political control or the exercise of undesirable local influence." She also has mentioned that the 1946 *Yearbook of the United Nations* recorded that the organization "should not be located in the territory of one of the major powers, in particular one of the five permanent members of the Security Council."[2]

These precepts represented a concern that if the headquarters were located in the territory of a great power that power might use its position to influence the work of the United Nations, or merely to hamstring the organization.

But the power leverage of the United States in 1946 and the financial inducements provided in the offer of a site in New York City represented more pressure than the fledgling organization could resist. The headquarters came to the United States and to New York City and with the anticipated consequence, question as to whether the United States has misused its position.

Control of Access

The Headquarters Agreement between the United States and the United Nations, which was concluded in 1947, provided: "The federal, state or local authorities of the United States shall not impose any impediments to transit to or from the headquarters district of representatives of members or officials of the United Nations, or of specialized agencies or representatives of nongovernmental organizations recognized by the United Nations for the purpose of consultation." Other wording in the agreement strove to plug any possible loopholes in its meaning. The United States was not supposed to try to control access.

Despite this seemingly firm commitment, the United States government (Congress, the Executive, and assorted local governments) has interfered with the coming to New York of people on United Nations business. And the United Nations has allowed itself to be overridden or inconvenienced by such interference.

An example of such an incident occurred in late 1988 when the United Nations General Assembly was to be addressed by Yasir Arafat, the chairman of the Palestine Liberation Organization. The United States Secretary of State George Shultz, strongly encouraged by Jewish organizations, refused to grant Arafat the necessary visa to enter the United States in order to get to the UN compound, arguing that it was not good judgment to allow the head of a terrorist organization to enter the United States. The United Nations' reaction was to go to the expense of transferring the General Assembly to Geneva to hear an address by Arafat on December 13.

The United Nations might consider the appropriateness of moving its principal headquarters to a place where it can better control its own working arrangements. Geneva would be a possibility. Or perhaps a small country such as Luxembourg might see advantages to such a role and be more cooperative than the United States has been.

The General Assembly

The United Nations charter, in article 7, identifies "the principal organs of the United Nations" as: the General Assembly, Security Council, Economic and Social Council, Trusteeship Council, International Court of Justice, and Secretariat, six organs in all. It then proceeds to discuss the functions of the organs. The following chapters in part I deal with the organization and functions of the United Nations in terms of the work of those entities, beginning with the General Assembly.

Composition and Procedure

The General Assembly consists of delegations from each of the member countries (with up to five members in a delegation), each delegation having one vote. The delegations and their leaders are typically appointed by their heads of state and vote accordingly. The first meeting of the General Assembly opened on January 10, 1946, in London. Regular annual meetings now begin, generally but not always, the third Tuesday in September and are usually held at the headquarters in New York. Various procedures are available for calling special meetings.

The General Assembly plays a central role in the selection of the members of the Security Council, the International Court of Justice, and the Trusteeship Council, as well as the secretary-general. It is also assigned, in Chapters XII and XIII of the charter, functions in support of the trusteeship system and the International Court of Justice.

The six standing committees of the General Assembly are the First (Disarmament and International Security); Second (Economic and Financial); Third (Social, Humanitarian, and Cultural); Fourth (Special Political and Decolonization, formerly Trusteeship); Fifth (Administrative and Budgetary); and Sixth (Legal). This committee structure represents a modest organizational change initiated at the fall 1993 (forty-eighth) session of the General Assembly. The previous seven committee structure, which included one unnumbered committee, had been in existence for many years.

Much of the work in these committees involves reconsideration of reports that have already been processed in the Economic and Social Council or resolutions adopted at international conferences that the conference wishes to have endorsed by the General Assembly. The work of two of these committees, which has been summarized in the December 1992 *UN Chronicle*, will illustrate what went on at the fall 1992 session of the General Assembly.

On the work of the First Committee the *UN Chronicle* reported:

> The Committee will review 21 major items and some 30 subitems, ranging from reduction of military budgets to prevention of an arms race in outer space. Deliberations are expected to focus on the continuing spread of technologies of mass destruction and the need to find a balance between self-defense and acceleration of conventional arms supply. The Committee will recommend that the Assembly commend the Convention on the Prohibition of the Development, Production, Stockpiling and use of Chemical Weapons and on their Destruction. . . . New approaches to implementing a zone of peace in the Indian Ocean will be explored.

On the work of the Second Committee the *UN Chronicle* reported:

> The follow-up to the UNCED [United Nations Conference on Environment and Development of June 1992] in Rio will be highlighted in the Committee, although debate will take place in the plenary. A wide range of development issues, including operational activities, will be considered. These include the external debt crisis, interna-

tional cooperation for the eradication of poverty in developing countries, trade and development, and net transfer of resources between developing and developed countries. Special humanitarian and disaster relief assistance are also of critical concern.

Much of the meaningful work of the General Assembly occurs in these committees. The oratory occurs in the General Assembly itself, although extremely important votes occasionally occur in that body. Examples are the Uniting for Peace Resolution of 1950 (discussed in chapter 3) and the Universal Declaration of Human Rights of 1948 (discussed in chapter 14).

Areas of Activity

The General Assembly may sometimes appear as a forum in which most of the time is devoted to emotional speakers from underdeveloped countries who are bent on denouncing the Western temperate-zone powers. But this apparent froth overlies a good deal of substantive, if disorganized, functioning and gathering of information about world problems. And there has been a marked reduction in the amount of anti-Western oratory since the Soviet Union began to collapse following 1985.

Article 10 of the charter states that the General Assembly may discuss "any matters within the scope of the present Charter or relating to the powers and functions of any organs provided for in the present Charter, and, except as provided in Article 12, may make recommendations to the Members of the United Nations." Recommendations are not binding orders, and their influence may be great or minor depending on circumstances and personalities and also on the degree of esteem in which the General Assembly is itself held. This degree of esteem has had its ups and downs over the years.

Maintenance of International Peace and Security

The role of the General Assembly in the maintenance of international peace and security is an example of an area in which the assembly has come to exercise more influence relative to the

Security Council than seems to have been anticipated in the charter. For example, in article 12 the General Assembly is admonished that "while the Security Council is exercising in respect of any dispute or situation the functions assigned to it in the present Charter, the General Assembly shall not make any recommendation with regard to that dispute or situation unless the Security Council so requests." International peace and security were viewed, in the beginning, to be the primary concern of the Security Council, not the General Assembly.

Yet in the period from the Korean War in the early 1950s until the Persian Gulf War in the early 1990s, it was frequently the General Assembly that actually took meaningful, if weak, action as the United Nations attempted to deal with international disputes. (The details of this history are traced in chapter 4, "Peacemaking or Peacekeeping.")

The Question of Binding Legislation

The General Assembly cannot legislate in the sense of passing binding laws of the type commonly enacted by national legislatures, but this does not mean that its draft treaties and resolutions are without meaning. Draft treaties prepared by conferences called by the General Assembly may become effective law in the member countries when ratified by the national legislatures of those countries, and they may come to constitute international law in the relations between nations. Also, resolutions passed by the General Assembly in connection with which no action is taken by national legislatures, may become meaningful customary international law as a result of the respect shown to the provisions of those resolutions by the member nations.[1]

An example of this process is the Universal Declaration of Human Rights, which was a 1948 resolution of the General Assembly (see chapter 14). The *compelling* influence of the provisions of this document on the actual behavior of nations has been evident many times over the years.

That law may come into existence in this way is not grounds

for complacency about the adequacy of the procedures for creating international law. People concerned with the frequent inability of world society to control autocratic and oppressive governments may well continue to believe that some such organization as the United Nations General Assembly should have a measure of genuine lawmaking power.

The Economic and Social Role

Article 13 of the charter provides: "The General Assembly shall initiate studies and make recommendations for the purpose of: . . . promoting international cooperation in the economic, social, cultural, educational and health fields, and assisting in the realization of human rights and fundamental freedoms for all without distinction as to race, sex, language or religion." What is involved is spelled out in greater detail in the charter in Chapter IX, "International Economic and Social Co-operation," and Chapter X, "The Economic and Social Council." Much of the time and energy of the General Assembly goes into these activities as its committees originate programs and receive and review the reports of the various agencies working under its general supervision. The Economic and Social Council (see chapter 6) is its agent in much of this supervisory work. Yet, on the whole, what is involved is discussion and the filing of reports; little in terms of enforceable law has come out of this activity. But the UN as an organization is hardly to be censored for not making more effective use of the information it gathers. The member states who created the UN have not given it that power.

The Budget

Last but scarcely least, in article 17 the General Assembly is assigned responsibility for considering and approving the budget of the "Organization." Member nations have a treaty obligation to pay the share of the expenses of the organization that is apportioned to them by the General Assembly. The plain statement in the charter calls on them to do this without equivocation. They have no legitimate excuse for failure to pay as assessed. This does not mean, however, that they will do so. In fact, the United States has been one of the more notorious delinquents, frequently using this financial leverage to try to influence United Nations policy.

Voting

On important questions (such as those involving peace and security; the election of members to the Security Council, the Economic and Social Council, and the Trusteeship Council; the admission, suspension, and expulsion of member states; trusteeship and budgetary matters), passage requires a two-thirds majority of members present and voting. For other questions, a simple majority is the rule.

The two-thirds rule would seem to give some measure of protection to the few great powers against the possibility of being overwhelmed in the voting by the numerous small countries. However, as was indicated in chapter 1, the possibility is real that a measure may be passed by a two-thirds vote consisting of some 122 members who represent but 6 or 7 percent of the population of the membership. This may appear as excessive power in few hands, even to one who is also concerned with the "excessive power" of the permanent members in the Security Council.

This issue is important, since the national delegations in the General Assembly are automatically voting according to the instructions of their home governments in almost all circumstances. To make matters worse, many of the small countries are controlled by dictators. These conditions fortify an impression that the General Assembly is not geared to speak for the world's people in any democratically meaningful sense. Some system of weighted voting would seem desirable in order for the result better to represent the democratic opinion of the world's population.

Further Reforms

Also on democratic grounds, it would seem desirable to have a system for selecting the delegates to the General Assembly in a manner that would make them more representative of the people and less beholden to the executive branches and, frequently, dictators in their countries of origin.

Direct election of delegates should have adverse effects for dictators. As matters stand, the delegates from a country ruled by a dictator are handpicked by that dictator. They will likely defend and apologize for that dictator. But, if delegates are directly elected by the citizenry in free elections that are monitored for honesty by outside observers, the likelihood of the election of delegates unsympathetic to the dictator is surely increased. Thus the UN and the outside world may become better informed as to conditions in the country, possibly creating sufficient pressure on the dictator to cause an improvement in his or her ways. Beyond this, direct election might also be an influence facilitating the fall of the dictator.

_____3

The Security Council

The Security Council, which, on paper, has the power to order the use of force to compel nations to "make peace," is made up of representatives from fifteen of the member countries. It originally had eleven members, five permanent and six elected by the General Assembly. The expansion was implemented January 1, 1966. The five permanent places go automatically to the so-called great powers, the permanent members that dominated the writing of the original charter at San Francisco in 1945: the United States, Britain, France, China, and the Soviet Union (now Russia). The occupants of the other ten places are elected for two-year terms by the General Assembly.

The charter provides that, in the election, due regard shall be paid "to the contribution of Members of the United Nations to the maintenance of international peace and security and to the other purposes of the Organization, and also to equitable geographical distribution." Area representation is implemented in a procedure that allocates the ten seats as follows: five for Asia and Africa, one for Eastern Europe, two for Latin America, and two for Western Europe and other states. It is less clear how the proviso to allocate seats according to contribution to the maintenance of peace and security can be implemented, except that the policy may provide leverage for blackballing troublemakers, though it does not seem to have been used in that way up to the present time.

Purpose

The Security Council of the United Nations has the power to make decisions that all member states are legally obligated under the charter to implement. To this end the charter has been ratified by the appropriate authorities in all the member countries. The United States Senate, for example, approved the charter by a two-thirds vote in the same way it ratifies treaties, as provided by the U.S. Constitution.

The charter places "on the Security Council primary responsibility for the maintenance of international peace and security," and the member nations "agree to accept and carry out the decisions of the Security Council." It is correct and important to note that none of the members have taken this latter obligation seriously. They "accept and carry out" when they decide that it is in their interest to do so. But the United Nations, if it is to be taken seriously, has to have the power to enforce its will directly without being dependent on the cooperative spirit of individual members. Even the United States does not have the right to pick and choose and implement only those policies approved by this country. It is obligated to take the bitter with the sweet, as are all member countries.

The Veto

Before it can ask for the aid of the member states in enforcing its desire, the Security Council has to express itself by a vote. According to the charter: "Decisions of the Security Council . . . shall be made by an affirmative vote of nine members including the concurring votes of the permanent members." The latter phrasing expresses the provision that has come to be called the big power veto, although the word veto does not appear in the wording. This is an improvement by comparison with the covenant of the League of Nations, which gave each country a veto; that is to say, a vote had to be unanimous.

The provision that all of the five permanent members must

cast concurring votes seems to say that mere failure to participate in a vote by a permanent member defeats a motion. This
interpretation seems not, however, to have been applied. The
vote making the Korean War a United Nations operation was
cast in the absence of the Soviet delegation, and the Chinese
abstained on some council votes during the Persian Gulf War
situation. Nevertheless, those actions were ruled to be formally
endorsed.

In any event, the ability of the Security Council to maintain
peace is compromised by the ability of the most powerful to
legally frustrate the process. Even if a permanent member is a
clear-cut aggressor and votes against sanctions, the United Nations is debarred under chapter VII of the charter from applying
force against that country.

This situation has frequently been rationalized by "realists"
on the ground that anyone with common sense knows that the
strongest powers in the world are not going to permit themselves to be bound by a vote dominated by small countries.
Furthermore, since it is most important to have an international
organization such as the United Nations, a provision such as
the great power veto is a price that must be paid if the UN is to
include the great powers, which is virtually to say, if it is to
exist at all.

On the other hand, it might be argued that smaller, would-be
aggressors are going to feel justified in disregarding restraints
that are not respected by the great powers. The result is then a
proliferation of limited wars among the smaller countries. Why is
the idea so unthinkable that world society should have the leverage to force even great powers to abide by majority rule or some
other reasonable voting rule?

The great powers also have a stake in worldwide law and
order, which means they should appreciate, in their own interest,
the importance of all members abiding by the general decision. If
the members of a community are to cooperate with genuine good
will, all (except possibly a few misanthropes) must have a feeling
that there is genuinely shared responsibility.

Peacemaking and Peacekeeping Procedures

Article 1 of the charter says, "The Purposes of the United Nations are: 1. To maintain international peace and security, and to that end: to take effective collective measures for the prevention and removal of threats to the peace, and for the suppression of acts of aggression or other breaches of the peace. . . ." And article 2, paragraph 5, states, "All Members shall give the United Nations every assistance in any action it takes in accordance with the present Charter, and shall refrain from giving assistance to any state against which the United Nations is taking preventive or enforcement action." In discussing the functions and powers of the Security Council, the charter reads in article 24: "In order to ensure prompt and effective action by the United Nations, its Members confer on the Security Council primary responsibility for the maintenance of international peace and security, and agree that in carrying out its duties under this responsibility the Security Council acts on their behalf."

Is all this just wordiness or does it mean something?

The United Nations Charter was ratified as a treaty by the appropriate legal procedures in each of the member states, and thus observance of its precepts became a legal obligation of the presidents, legislative bodies, governments, and people of each member.

The specific procedures provided for in the charter for the implementation of peace are laid out in chapters VI, VII, VIII, and XII, probably in too much detail. Short and flexible constitutions seem more likely to work in the long run.

Chapter VI is titled "Pacific Settlement of Disputes." This chapter admonishes disputants to use a wide range of procedures to solve problems on their own initiative, especially before actual fighting begins. It also authorizes the Security Council to investigate troublesome disputes and make recommendations to the parties concerning appropriate procedures for reconciling disputes, including, if appropriate, referral of the dispute to the International Court of Justice at The Hague. It permits the General Assembly to consider and make recommendations concerning threats to international peace and security, except for the proviso in article 12 to the effect that: "While the Security Council is exercising in respect of any dispute or situation the functions assigned to it in this present Charter, the General Assembly shall not make any recommendation with regard to that dispute or situation unless the Security Council so requests." Thus, the charter places primary responsibility, but not necessarily all responsibility, for the pacific settlement of disputes with the Security Council.

The power to deal more forcefully with serious disputes (that is to say; disputes once they become violent) is ostensibly completely vested in the Security Council. The charter gives the General Assembly no role in decisions to use force to compel peace. This matter is dealt with in chapter VII, "Action with Respect to Threats to the Peace, Breaches of the Peace, and Acts of Aggression." Article 41 of chapter VII also provides for the possible use of measures not involving armed force that may be employed at the discretion of the Security Council to pressure disputants and aggressors to behave. Such measures "include complete or partial interruption of economic relations and of rail, sea, air, postal, telegraphic, radio and other means of communication, and the severance of diplomatic relations." In the case of the Persian Gulf War of 1990–91, the Security Council made extensive use of such measures before authorizing the use of armed force. Whether continued and more determined use of these measures might have brought a result more desirable than the military action that was generated, no one can say for certain—and more desirable from whose point of view? Similarly, in the Yugoslav troubles of 1992, the Security Council established a naval blockade of Serbia in November of that year.

Next Article 42 introduces the possibility of the use of military force: "Should the Security Council consider that measures provided for in Article 41 would be inadequate or have proved to be inadequate it may take such action by air, sea or land forces as may be necessary to maintain or restore international peace and security." Note that nothing is said here to indicate that this procedure is not to apply if the offender is a great power. Surely that is the situation above all others where the procedure of article 42 should apply if the whole procedure is to be meaningful and respected in all countries great and small. Yet, if the great power is itself the aggressor, it can protect itself by the use of the veto.

The Military Staff Committee

Articles 39 through 51 (chapter VII) of the charter stumble through messy answers to the question as to where a United Nations force would come from. The answers given at San Francisco in 1945 depended upon meaningful cooperation among the United States, the United Kingdom, France, the Soviet Union, and China. The delegates, especially including the United States delegation, who assumed such cooperation merit no rewards as prophets. Perhaps neither does President Roosevelt, although it should be remembered that he was gravely ill during the latter part of the war and died in the spring of 1945, before the San Francisco Conference met.

Meaningful cooperation was envisaged by article 46: "Plans for the application of armed forces shall be made by the Security Council with the assistance of the Military Staff Committee." Article 47 goes on to say: "There shall be established a Military Staff Committee to advise and assist the Security Council on all questions relating to the Security Council's military requirements for the maintenance of international peace and security, the employment and command of forces placed at its disposal, the regulation of armaments, and possible disarmament." But then comes the joker: "The Military Staff Committee shall consist of the Chiefs of Staff of the permanent members of the Security Council or their representatives." Further, "the Military Staff Committee shall be responsible under the Security Council for the strategic direction of any armed forces placed at the disposal of the Security Council. Questions relating to the command of such forces shall be worked out subsequently." The senior military

officers of the great powers were, thus, to control the mobiliza-
tion and use of the armed forces assembled under the United
Nations banner. That is, a committee composed of the chiefs of
staff of the Soviet, American, British, French and Chinese armies
was, cooperatively, to control the procedures involved in the use
of force.

Article 43 begins: "All members . . . undertake to make available to the Security Council, on its call and in accordance with a
special agreement or agreements, armed forces, assistance and
facilities. . . ." It concludes: "The agreement or agreements shall
be negotiated as soon as possible . . . and shall be subject to
ratification by the signatory states in accordance with their respective constitutional processes." Article 45 states: "The
strength and degree of readiness of these contingents and plans
for their combined action shall be determined, within the limits
laid down in the special agreement or agreements referred to in
Article 43, by the Security Council with the assistance of the
Military Staff Committee."

The United States and the Soviet Union immediately disagreed
on the criteria to be used in developing these policies. The United
States wanted a large, mobile (land, sea, and air) force in readiness to fight anywhere. Contributions to this force were to be
related to the size and character of the armed forces of each of
the great powers. The Soviet Union "wanted a relatively smaller
force, equality of contributions by the permanent members, and a
clear definition of the conditions under which the force might be
used."[1] And the Soviet Union did not want the United Nations to
maintain its own permanent, military bases. The Cold War was on.

No agreement has ever been arrived at to provide for the permanent existence of a meaningful force available at the disposal
of the United Nations, though to this day, the Military Staff Committee has regular meetings. When crises have developed that
called for the creation of United Nations forces, those forces have
had to be created ad hoc, and their existence has been dependent
on the willingness of a member country to provide forces under
the prevailing circumstances. Troops subject to United Nations

control are not automatically there when the United Nations Security Council votes to counter aggression with force. As was the case in Korea and the Persian Gulf, at least one great power has to be motivated to lead the effort to counter aggression if anything is to happen. The result is that, to a significant degree, the action appears to be more the work of the leading great power than the work of the United Nations.

Both Korea and the Persian Gulf, for example, were effectively United States actions, endorsed by the United Nations. They were not actions controlled by the United Nations. The generals in command in Korea and the Persian Gulf were American. The forces were largely American. The equipment was largely American. Decisions seem largely to have been American-made, although it is not possible for an outsider (or possibly an insider) to indicate the degree to which non-Americans actually influenced decisions.

One may well believe that if reform of the United Nations in the 1990s occurs, and if it involves the implementation of various long dormant clauses in the UN charter, many countries will be offended. The clauses providing for a permanent UN force organized under the Military Staff Committee are an important example. It is reasonable to guess that the other 175 (or so) countries are not going to be pleased to provide the armies for peacemaking when the troops they provide will be controlled by a committee consisting of the chiefs of staff of the American, Russian, British, French, and Chinese armed forces.

The Cabal

In the days of the Cold War between the USSR and the United States, the result of the big power veto was, in most cases, to immobilize effective peacemaking. The only effective peacemaking action of the UN before 1990 occurred after the invasion of South Korea by North Korea in 1950, when the Security Council was able to authorize United Nations action because of the absence of the Soviet delegation. (The Congo episode in 1960–64 may be considered an exception to this generalization. But more on both of these issues in chapter 4, "Peacemaking or Peacekeeping.")

About 1990, power relations changed. Soviet power disintegrated, and the USSR government of Mikhail Gorbachev proved willing to cooperate with the United States in United Nations action against Iraq in the face of that country's invasion of Kuwait. The Soviet Union wanted United States aid, economic and otherwise, in this remarkably transformed world. The communist government of China, which had long since replaced Taiwan as the Chinese government occupying the corresponding permanent seat on the Security Council, was sufficiently desirous of conciliating United States public opinion after the Tiananmen Square massacre of 1989 to be willing to abstain on the crucial Persian Gulf War votes, thus permitting avoidance of a permanent member veto.

Yemen and Cuba, elected members of the Security Council at that time, did vote against the United States on many of the Persian Gulf War issues. But votes of, more or less, 12 for, 2 against, 1 abstention, and no great power veto, supported the United States agenda in the Persian Gulf.

The preliminary discussions prior to the Security Council votes on these Persian Gulf resolutions occurred in a setting where the representatives of the other great powers met with the United States in what might be called a cabal and worked out the details of the resolutions. The United States was the initiator, it seems, of virtually all the resolutions. Great Britain generally strongly backed the United States position; the French were cooperative; the Russians, burdened with their own troubles, were also cooperative. And the Chinese had decided not to make trouble. The great powers then presented the full Security Council with a resolution that was more or less automatically approved by that council. There was no meaningful discussion in the full Security Council.

The result was an official United Nations action into which the countries that were not great powers had virtually no input. President Bush heaped praise on the United Nations for its role in the

Persian Gulf War, but it does not follow from this that the war was conducted according to a United Nations agenda. On the contrary, it was conducted according to a United States agenda via "the cabal" procedure.

The same procedure was used in connection with the inception of the armed intervention in Somalia to facilitate the delivery of relief supplies to the starving population in the winter of 1992–93. In November 1992, the United States volunteered to provide the United Nations with up to thirty thousand troops to implement the intervention. But it insisted on United States, not United Nations, command of the operation, which was also to involve the troops of other nations. The United States pressured a reluctant Boutros Boutros-Ghali, secretary-general of the United Nations, to endorse the United States command. The United States then obtained endorsement from the other permanent members of the Security Council, the cabal, before the resolution was presented to the full Security Council, which went along. But there were murmurs of discontent with the procedure by which the great powers were implementing their view of appropriate procedure in the Security Council.

Increasingly, the substantive discussion of Security Council resolutions seems to occur only among the five permanent members of the Council, without much contribution by other countries. It is not surprising that Germany and Japan are pressing to become permanent members, and the small countries are not happy with the procedure. But this may well not be an enduring situation. Recently in Somalia and in Yugoslavia, Rwanda, and Haiti cabal and United States leadership seems to have become largely negative. Does the old saying "Nature abhors a vacuum" carry a message to the present generation of great powers?

Relation to General Assembly and Uniting for Peace

In 1950, on the urging of the United States, the General Assembly adopted the Uniting for Peace Resolution, which provides that on occasions when the Security Council, "because of lack of unanimity of the permanent members," fails to act in a case of aggression, the General Assembly can recommend action. This step was taken because of realization that effective Security Council action could not have been taken in the Korean War situation if the Soviet Union had attended the crucial session. The United States initiated the Uniting for Peace Resolution in order to have an alternative channel for use in problem situations in which Security Council action was frustrated.

The action that the General Assembly is authorized to recommend does not include the application of military force. It permits sending troops to a troubled area, but the troops can be only lightly armed and can fire only in self-defense. They are not authorized to use force to stop fighting. They are not authorized to practice, in the jargon, *peacemaking*, or peace enforcement. They are allowed to practice *peacekeeping*, meaning that it is hoped that the mere presence of such troops between two belligerent armies will inhibit hostilities. They can only be sent if authorized by the country on whose soil they would be stationed, and they must be withdrawn at that country's request.

The United Nations action in establishing a truce between Egypt and Israel (and Britain and France) in 1957 during the hostility over the control of the Suez Canal followed the format of the Uniting for Peace initiative. The peacekeeping force placed on the truce line represented General Assembly action taken on Egyptian soil with the permission of Egypt and in the face of the refusal of Israel to cooperate. As such, the force proved helpless when Egypt decided it wished the United Nations force to leave in 1967. In the face of such a request, and on the basis of a decision by U Thant, UN secretary-general at the time, the United Nations peacekeeping force packed up and left, and war promptly began between Egypt and Israel.

Except for the complicated Congo episode (1960–64), virtually all of the United Nations measures to deal with wars and hostilities between the Korean War of the early 1950s and the Persian Gulf War of 1990–91 were of the ineffective peacekeeping variety. And the fairly helpless peacekeepers occasionally proved tempting targets to the troops of one or another of the hostile armies.

Policy Recommendation

The great power veto should be abolished, and, if the practice of having permanent members on the Security Council is continued, Germany, Japan, and perhaps India should be added to the list.

Both Germany and Japan are economically stronger than at least two of the present permanent members, the United Kingdom and France; and India has the second largest population in the world. Having been defeated or nonexistent as an independent nation during World War II should not be grounds, after fifty years, for exclusion from the select group of permanent members, who were initially all victors in the war.

However, a more general reform of the Security Council and the United Nations, such as suggested in chapter 15, "Reform of the United Nations," could make this a moot issue.

4

Peacemaking or Peacekeeping

In January 1992, the Security Council requested the secretary-general to prepare an analysis of and recommendations on ways of strengthening and making more efficient the capacity of the United Nations for preventive diplomacy, for peacemaking and for peacekeeping. The Boutros-Ghali report was issued June 17, 1992, and was entitled "An Agenda for Peace." The term *peacemaking*, on the basis of paragraphs 20 and 34–45 of the report, includes both "the pacific settlement of disputes" in the sense of chapter VI of the charter and the use of force as provided for in chapter VII of the charter. Force, or enforcement, may include measures such as embargoes and the use of military troops in combat.

Peacekeeping is a concept not found in the charter. It was endorsed in the Uniting for Peace Resolution adopted by the General Assembly in 1950 and first applied to implement the truce at the end of the Suez War in 1956. Peacekeeping involves the insertion of lightly armed forces between armies that have already agreed to an armistice. This is done with the permission of at least one of the opposing armies, and the peacekeepers are expected to withdraw if asked by the contestant who has given them permission to be there.

There follows a brief history of the peacemaking and peacekeeping efforts to which the United Nations has been a party since World War II.[1]

Palestine and Israel to 1950

Jews have been interested in returning to Palestine for centuries. Some were able to return during the nineteenth and early twentieth centuries, when Palestine was a part of Turkey, but during World War I Great Britain promised the area to the Arabs in exchange for their assistance in fighting the Turks. However, in the Balfour Declaration of 1917, Great Britain also endorsed establishing a national home for the Jews in Palestine. In 1920 the League of Nations assigned the mandate for Palestine and Trans-Jordan (now Jordan) to Great Britain, and Palestine was designated to become a Jewish national home, but with "due regard" for the rights of non-Jewish Palestinians, who constituted most of the population.

Under the British mandate, between the two World Wars Jewish migration to Palestine continued, accelerating after Hitler came to power in 1933. The Jewish settlers acquired land and established settlements, but they were periodically attacked by the Palestinians. In 1936 the British proposed a geographical division of the country between Jews and Arabs, but in 1939, they issued a White Paper announcing their intention to create a single independent state in the region. British policy remained ambivalent. For a time the British limited Jewish immigration to Palestine to 1,500 persons a month; in 1944 they cut it off altogether. The British also limited the areas in Palestine where Jews might acquire land. In 1939 in Palestine there seem to have been about 900,000 Moslems, 400,000 Jews, and 100,000 Arab Christians.

During World War II both the Palestinians and the Jews supported the British (the Allied side), both apparently hoping to obtain British support thereby. Trouble was in the making at the end of World War II. Ambivalence as a policy had not solved the problem.

Matters came to a head in 1947 when the British mandate under the League of Nations was coming to an end. The British wished to remove themselves from a central role in working out the problem and did not want a United Nations trusteeship to follow their League mandate. Britain brought the problem before the General Assembly (not the Security Council) in April 1947. The result: "A Special Committee appointed by the Assembly to make recommendations for the future status of Palestine proposed in a majority plan the partition of the Territory into an Arab State and a Jewish State, with an international regime for Jerusalem."[2] That plan, at the time, was acceptable to the Jews and rejected by the Arabs.

Meanwhile, there was sporadic serious fighting between the Jews and the Arabs, and on April 23, 1948, the Security Council established a Truce Commission for Palestine, composed of the consular representatives of Belgium, France, and the United States, to supervise the implementation of a cease-fire that the Council had called for.

On May 14, 1948, several things happened at once. The General Assembly decided to appoint a United Nations mediator for Palestine, and Count Folke Bernadotte of Sweden was given this task. On the same day, the United Kingdom relinquished its mandate over Palestine, the Jewish Agency proclaimed the existence of the state of Israel, and the United States (followed by the Soviet Union on May 17) recognized the existence of the new state. The area involved in the new state was presumably that assigned to Israel in the partition of Palestine proposed by the special committee of the UN. But identification of such an area quickly became irrelevant.

The next day, the Palestinian Arabs, assisted by the Arab states, opened hostilities against Israel. The United Nations mediator, Folke Bernadotte, was given the assistance of several military observers. Thus came into being in May or June 1948, "the first United Nations peacekeeping operation, the United Nations Truce Supervision Organization (UNTSO)" with its team of military observers.[3] On June 11, a truce went into effect, but it was followed by more fighting, a second cease-fire, and more fighting. On September 17 Bernadotte was assassinated by Jewish terrorists.

Ralph Bunche, an American diplomat, was appointed by the

United Nations to take the place of Bernadotte, and armistice conditions were finally worked out in January 1949 between Israel and the Arab League. By then Israel occupied half again as much territory as had been included in the initial state of Israel. No offsetting Palestinian state had been established. Jordan annexed territory along the Jordan River, and Egypt occupied a strip of southern Palestine along the coast, which came to be called the Gaza Strip. These were lands that would have been in the share of the Palestinian Arabs if the UN-proposed partition of Palestine had occurred. Other areas of these lands were in limbo.

Thus, when the armistice went into effect in January 1949, the Jews had a country, the state of Israel, a functioning government, and effective control of substantially more territory than had been assigned to them in the original United Nations partition plan of April 1947. Also, since large numbers of the Palestinian Arabs had fled during the fighting, the Jews were in a position to occupy and permanently appropriate considerable private land without paying compensation.

Governance of the areas in Palestine that had not been taken over by Jordan or Egypt was in chaos. There was no organized government effectively in position to espouse the interests of the Palestinians living in those areas. Contributing to this situation was the failure of Egypt, Jordan, and the other Arab League countries to take any interest in their plight. The Arab League countries, and especially Egypt, were not hospitable to Palestinian refugees. They preferred to have them concentrated in squalor in camps in such places as the Gaza Strip. There they were more of a threat to the Israelis than would have been the case if the bordering Arab countries had welcomed them.

At all events, in early 1949, there was a United Nations presence in the area. It consisted of a United Nations Truce Supervision Organization and associated United Nations Military Observers (UNMO). Their headquarters were set up at Government House in Jerusalem. From the beginning, the military observers were lightly armed or unarmed individuals.

UNTSO did provide, through many years, a continuity to

United Nations peacekeeping efforts. It was the only such organization with a continuing existence, unlike many other United Nations organizations or forces, which have come into being to deal with particular situations here and there over the world and then disappeared after the crisis has been resolved or swept under the rug. UNTSO, in fact, proved a useful training ground for personnel who later served on other missions. For example, Canadian Major-General E.L.M. Burns, who was the chief of staff of UNTSO in Jerusalem in 1956, became the chief of the first United Nations Emergency Force, the peacekeeping force hurriedly organized to supervise the armistice between Israel and Egypt during the Suez crisis of that year.

The Korean War

On June 25, 1950, the North Korean army, which had been trained by the Russians, invaded South Korea. On the same day, the Security Council acted; it identified the invasion as a breach of the peace, called for a cessation of hostilities, and asked member nations to "render every assistance to the United Nations in the execution of this resolve." The Soviet representative was not present to cast a veto because the USSR was boycotting the Security Council to protest the fact that the Chinese seat on the Security Council had not been taken from the Chiang Kai-shek government and turned over to the communist government which had gained control of mainland China.

The United States interpreted the Security Council call to "render every assistance" to justify direct military response by the United States, and on June 26, the American government ordered its military forces to assist South Korea. On June 27, a Security Council resolution recommended that members "furnish such assistance to the Republic of Korea as may be necessary to repel the armed attack and to restore international peace and security in the area."[4] On July 7, the Security Council authorized a "unified command under the United States."

General Douglas MacArthur of the United States was the commander of all the forces of the unified command, which included Korean troops plus forces of varying size from about sixteen countries, and had the right to fly the United Nations flag. This arrangement was generated on very short notice. Clearly, there was no time for serious consideration as to whether it was appropriate.

In his book, *International Government*, Clyde Eagleton described the result: "The channels of authority and even of communication above [General MacArthur] were not made clear; there was, indeed no organ of the United Nations which could give him political direction, much less military direction. Communication went awkwardly through the Secretary-General to the United States Mission to the United Nations, and from it through American agencies to the command in Korea. The United States directly negotiated agreements with each state contributing forces. In general, the function of command was about the same as if all the forces had been United States forces; the need of a single authority for military purposes was recognized."[5]

How similar to the Persian Gulf War situation in 1990–91!

Eagleton also commented, "Political direction, however, did not work so well. . . . In October 1950 Communist China entered the fray, thereby making the military task and the political problems much greater. The Soviet representative had returned to the Security Council and his veto rendered the Council impotent. The United States therefore turned to the General Assembly. . . . This was not a United Nations action, in the sense of decision and order having come from the Security Council; it was rather a joint venture by a small group of its Members, though acting under the recommendation of the Council."[6]

The United States government in 1950 was acutely aware that fortuitous circumstances had justified the Korean War as being a United Nations operation. Consequently, the United States decided to sponsor the Uniting for Peace Resolution, which was adopted by the Assembly November 3, 1950 (see chapter 3). The possible usefulness of this ambiguous approach was untested until the Suez Canal troubles of 1956. In the meantime, the Korean situation settled into a long-drawn-out armistice-stalemate with South Korea surviving as an independent state. At best this was a mixed success, or failure, from all points of view.

Suez

The Suez crisis of 1956 involved a serious great-power confrontation and clarification of the latitude for action or power that the United Nations possessed in a crisis. In the early 1950s Egypt began to restrict Israeli shipping through the Suez Canal and the Strait of Tiran at the entrance to the Gulf of Aqaba. This activity was "in contravention of a decision of the Security Council."[7] Also, sporadic fighting between Israel and Egypt had continued in the Gaza Strip area.

On July 19, 1956, the United States withdrew its financial support for the Aswan dam project on the Nile River. This step expressed U.S. support for Israel and opened Egypt to Soviet influence. It was followed a week later by the announcement of Egyptian President Gamal Abdel Nasser of the nationalization of the Suez Canal Company, an enterprise jointly owned by the British and French since the Suez Canal Convention of 1888. Part of the justification given by Nasser for the nationalization was that the Suez Canal dues could be used to finance the Aswan dam construction.

On September 23, 1956, France and Britain requested that the Security Council consider the "situation created by the unilateral action of the Egyptian Government in bringing to an end the system of international operation of the Suez Canal. . . ." The next day Egypt requested that the Council "consider actions taken by some powers, particularly France and the United Kingdom, which constitute a danger to international peace and security. . . ." The Council met on September 26, and, as a result of that meeting, Dag Hammarskjöld, the UN secretary-general, worked out a compromise that was unanimously adopted by the council on October 13, 1956. Note that the Russians voted for this compromise, which provided for:

1. free and open transit through the canal,
2. respect for the sovereignty of Egypt,
3. insulation of the operation of the canal from the politics of any country,
4. fixing of the canal tolls and charges by agreement between Egypt and the users,
5. use of a fair proportion of the dues for Egyptian development, and
6. settling by arbitration any disputes involving the canal and the Egyptian government.[8]

But then Israel, with reason to believe it had French and British support (and perhaps even tacit United States consent), suddenly attacked Egypt in a major offensive on October 29, 1956.

At this point the United Nations Truce Supervision Organization team, which had been in place since the Palestinian armistice of 1949, called on Israel to pull back its forces to the Israeli side of the border. The chief of staff of the UNTSO group was Major-General E.L.M. Burns of Canada. The active role of Canada in trying to foster peaceful settlement of the dispute was promoted by the Canadian secretary for external affairs, Lester Pearson, who later won a Nobel Peace Prize for his efforts.

On October 30, the British and French governments presented an ultimatum "impartially" to Israel and Egypt calling on both sides to cease hostilities and withdraw their forces to a distance of ten miles from each side of the canal. The ultimatum was accepted by Israel, whose troops in any event were far from the canal, and rejected by Egypt, whose national territory was actually involved.[9]

Also on October 30, the United States submitted a draft resolution to the Security Council calling upon Israel to withdraw its armed forces to behind the 1949 armistice lines. The resolution was vetoed by the British and French, who, on October 31, themselves invaded Egypt near Port Said. At the time, the British prime minister was Anthony Eden and the French premier, Guy Mollet. This action apparently involved a prearrangement of the

British, French, and Israelis to which the United States (President Eisenhower) was not a party.[10]

The British and French vetoes in the Security Council resulted in a transfer of the matter to the General Assembly in accordance with the procedure endorsed in the Uniting for Peace Resolution. The transfer occurred as a result of a formal proposal by Yugoslavia. However, the charter did not authorize the General Assembly to order the use of armed force in a peacemaking operation. It did endorse the discussion of the crisis in the General Assembly. There followed the establishment by the General Assembly of a peacekeeping force to be posted along the to-be-created armistice line with the permission of Egypt and with the understanding that the force would be withdrawn when so requested by Egypt.

A proposal to this effect was made by Canada and adopted by the General Assembly on November 4, 1956, providing "for the setting up, with the consent of the nations concerned, of an emergency United Nations Force to secure and supervise the cessation of hostilities." The Canadian General Burns was appointed on an emergency basis as the chief of the command. He was authorized to recruit from the Military Observer group attached to UNTSO "a limited number of officers who were to be nationals of countries other than those having permanent membership in the Security Council, and further authorized . . . in consultation with the Secretary-General, to undertake the recruitment directly from various Member States other than the permanent members of the Security Council, of the additional number of officers needed. . . ."[11]

Thus was born the first United Nations peacekeeping force (the first UN Emergency Force, UNEF). It had a basis in UNTSO, which had existed in Jerusalem since 1948 and in the Uniting for Peace Resolution of Korean War days. Its weakness was that, as a creation of the General Assembly rather than the Security Council, it could not use effective force to stop the fighting. It was lightly armed, and its presence was conditioned by the whim of the government on whose territory its troops were stationed. Thus, in 1956, Israel refused to permit the presence of the UNEF on the side of the Suez Canal controlled by Israel. Egypt permitted its presence for eleven years on the western side of the canal, until shortly before Egypt decided to resume fighting with Israel in 1967. At that time, the UNEF was withdrawn from the western side of the canal, on Egypt's request, and shortly thereafter the 1967 war was begun by Egypt.[12] It has been much debated whether United Nations Secretary-General U Thant should have complied with Egypt's request to withdraw the peacekeeping force. At any rate he did, and a precedent was set.

The Congo

Belgium granted independence to the Congo on June 30, 1960, having previously done virtually nothing to prepare the backward, poor, exploited country for the trials and tribulations that go with independence. A hastily convened Parliament had elected Joseph Kasavubu as President and Patrice Lumumba as prime minister.

On July 5, the Belgian-led army mutinied, and Belgian administrators and technicians fled the country. Lumumba attempted to gain control of the situation by reconstituting the army with Congolese in command: Victor Lundula as commander and Joseph Mobutu as chief of staff. The Belgian officers were dispensed with, and Ralph Bunche, the United Nations man on the scene, requested the Belgians not to bring in fresh Belgian army troops. In spite of this, the Belgians sent in fresh troops on July 11. Under the protection of Belgian troops, Moïse Tshombé declared the independence of the rich copper-producing province of Katanga in the southern Congo. The international copper companies were protecting their interests. The country was in an uproar. On the night of July 13–14, 1960, the Security Council voted to authorize the secretary-general to provide the government of the Congo with military assistance. The United States and the USSR, it may be noted, both voted in favor of this resolution. (There were no negative votes, but there were three abstentions.) It also should be noted that what this initial United Nations action authorized was peacekeeping in the sense of the Uniting for Peace Resolution, not peacemaking. The force at its peak strength involved twenty thousand troops.

On September 5, 1960, President Kasavubu tried to dismiss Prime Minister Lumumba. For the next eleven months there was no legal government in the Congo.[13] There were "four opposing camps, each with its own armed forces." And the UN forces were suffering many casualties but trying not to take sides in the struggle. Lumumba was arrested in November by troops under the control of General Mobutu. On January 17, 1961, he apparently was killed in Katanga province; by whom, on whose authority, seems not to be clear.

On February 21, 1961, after long debate, the Security Council authorized the UN troops (ONUC: Opération des Nations Unies au Congo) to use force to prevent civil war in the Congo.[14] Thus, the operation in the Congo became an effort at peacemaking. On August 2, 1961, President Kasavubu constituted "a Government of national unity" headed by Prime Minister Cyrille Adoula, "which was unanimously approved by both Chambers" of the legislature.[15] The Adoula government was internationally recognized and the UN considered that there was a government in the Congo that ONUC could legitimately support.

The chief remaining trouble was with the secessionist province of Katanga. There, the Belgian copper-mining company, Union Minière du Haut-Katanga, was supporting the Tshombé government. Foreign mercenaries and Belgian military personnel had been effectively mobilized, although without the public endorsement of the Belgian government. Dag Hammarskjöld, the UN secretary-general, was striving to effect the withdrawal of the foreign mercenary and Belgian military personnel. Then, on a flight to Ndola in Northern Rhodesia to meet Tshombé, he was killed along with seven other UN staff members and the Swedish crew in an airplane crash on September 17, 1961.

Steady and well-handled UN and ONUC pressure, over the course of the next year, led to the end of Katanga secession.

Also, the Union Minière Belgian copper company agreed to pay its taxes to the central government of the Congo. The authority of the central government was consolidated, and on June 30, 1964, the UN force in the Congo withdrew from the country, leaving behind a program of technical assistance. The application of a judicious mixture of peacekeeping and peacemaking, as of 1964, could be reckoned a success.

The sequel is less encouraging. In 1965 General Mobutu, apparently with United States support, gained dictatorial control of the government of the Congo (now Zaire), control that he was still exercising in 1994.

Meanwhile, before 1990, the United Nations had to deal with many other international crises, in India-Pakistan, Lebanon, West New Guinea (West Irian), Yemen, Cyprus, the Dominican Republic, El Salvador, Afghanistan, Angola, Southwest Africa (Namibia), and more. A typical pattern involved a period of armed conflict followed by a United Nations negotiated truce and the insertion of a lightly armed peacekeeping force between the contestants. Several such stalemates then lasted for years, with the contestants occasionally shooting at members of the peacekeeping forces when things got dull along the front.

The Persian Gulf

Iraq invaded Kuwait on August 2, 1990. The United Nations Security Council on August 2 in Resolution 660 condemned the Iraqi invasion and demanded an immediate troop withdrawal, threatening economic sanctions if Baghdad did not comply. The vote in the Security Council was 14–0, with Yemen not participating. Then President Bush suddenly took the initiative by backing up and amplifying the United Nations action. There resulted a situation with parallels to the Korean War inception. The recent collapse of the communist regime in Moscow resulted in Russia's cooperation, or at least absence of opposition, to United States leadership in handling the Iraqi invasion of Kuwait. Also, the Chinese, although ostensibly remaining stoutly communist, were desirous of international acceptance and wished to live down the Tiananmen Square massacre. They decided to compromise by abstaining on crucial votes where United States domination of the scene might have run into trouble if it had faced a Chinese veto. So it developed that the United States, during the fall of 1990, was able to obtain support for President Bush's increasingly tough positions by votes in the neighborhood of 12 for, 1 abstention, and 2 against.

Resolution 660 of August 2, 1990, immediately after the Iraqi invasion of Kuwait, seems to have involved spontaneous condemnation of the action and a demand that Iraq withdraw immediately and unconditionally all its forces to the positions in which they were located on August 1, 1990. No particular United States pressure was involved. But the quick success of the Iraqi invasion of Kuwait and the movement of Iraqi troops to the Saudi Arabian border, offering the threat of an invasion of Saudi Arabia, with oil fields the prize, led President Bush to order the movement of United States troops to Saudi Arabia. This initial sending of American troops to Saudi Arabia was United States action, independent of UN sponsorship.

On August 6, and involving United States urging, the Security Council imposed mandatory economic sanctions against Iraq. Resolution 665 of August 25 called for a naval embargo of shipments to Iraq, which the United States Navy, with modest support from other Security Council members, proceeded to implement with vigor. Action included controlling ships going to neutral ports from which goods might move overland to Iraq. Especially involved was the Jordanian port of Aqaba.

After several months, President Bush decided that the role of the American forces in Saudi Arabia should change from the merely defensive prevention of an Iraqi takeover of Saudi Arabia to a military offensive. Security Council endorsement of this major change in approach was obtained in the slightly ambiguous wording of Resolution 678 on November 29, 1990. The resolution provided for "a pause of goodwill" to allow Iraq a final opportunity to withdraw from Kuwait, while authorizing member states to "use all necessary means" to implement Resolution 660 if Iraq had not complied by January 15, 1991. Authorization of the use of military force was not specifically mentioned, just "all necessary means." Was this delicate use of language necessary to get the resolution passed? Probably not. But it may have made a difference of a few votes in the margin of passage and thus helped to validate the claim that the action to be taken enjoyed general worldwide support.

Meanwhile, debate continued as to whether the economic sanctions, if allowed to operate, could ultimately be successful, avoiding the need for what might be a bloody war. Since there was considerable sentiment in the United States for giving economic sanctions more chance, President Bush decided that it was expedient to obtain the prior approval of Congress for the use of armed force involving United States troops. After considerable debate, Congress gave President Bush his mandate on January 13, 1991, just two days before the UN resolution granted permission to use "all necessary means." The congressional action stated: "The President is authorized . . . to use United States Armed Forces pursuant to United Nations Security Council Resolution 678 (1990) in order to achieve implementation of Security Council Resolutions: 660, 661, 662, 664, 665, 666, 667, 669, 670, 674, and 677."

The bombing of Iraq began promptly on January 16. Ground operations began on February 24, 1991, and involved initially a major push directly into Iraq, bypassing Kuwait, as well as a direct invasion of Kuwait. After a quick, highly successful campaign, President Bush ordered a suspension of "offensive combat operations" on Wednesday, February 28. An armistice agreement was signed a few days later.

In that agreement the American general Norman Schwarzkopf agreed to permit the Iraqis to continue to fly their military attack helicopters. He remarked with regard to the granting of this permission that he was convinced by the argument that, since his aircraft had destroyed so many bridges, the Iraqis needed to be able to use helicopters to supplement ground transportation if the country was to be satisfactorily administered after the armistice.

Apparently one reason President Bush was willing to stop the fighting so quickly without first forcing Saddam Hussein from office was due to confidence that internal forces in Iraq would accomplish this result. President Bush also believed it was desirable for Iraq to retain its territorial integrity. This meant that he did not desire effectively to support the Shiite revolt against Saddam around Basra in southern Iraq or the Kurd revolt in the north. He was counting on a palace coup in Baghdad and apparently the continuation in power of the elite who had supported Saddam in power—minus Saddam.

The attack helicopters that the Americans had permitted the Iraqis to continue to use, then, facilitated their putting down the Shiite revolt around Basra. After that was accomplished, enough of the Iraqi troops were available to put down the Kurdish revolt in the north. Furthermore, since no palace coup occurred in Baghdad, President Bush found that the man he had denounced so strongly between August 1990 and February 1991 remained in power. Iraqi aggressiveness had been set back by the war, but much of their military power remained.

The New World (Dis)Order

In 1991 we saw an ephemeral defeat for the Iraq of Saddam Hussein, the collapse of the Soviet Union as the leader of half of a bipolar world, and, early on, much comment by President Bush on the subject of a New World Order. Prophets were speaking of the "American century" about to begin and of a Pax Americana to compare with the Pax Britannica of the nineteenth century. There would be a grand international consensus to inaugurate this New World Order. The United Nations would be available to validate the policy decisions of the United States. No particular reform of the United Nations was needed for it to play this helpful role. A Golden Age was at hand to be guided by a benevolent Uncle Sam.

Nondemocratic countries and non-market-system economies

were to shift over to democratic, market systems by a sudden, inspired transformation, and the deed would be done. A substantial number of nondemocratic, non-market-system countries took a pledge to proceed apace with this transformation, expecting some United States largess as a quid pro quo. Poland became a sort of bellwether, setting an example in following this script.

But then things began to go wrong. The efficient Germans had trouble digesting East Germany. Civilized Czechoslovakia broke into two countries. Hungary, despite a head start in reforming, developed problems. These may be regarded as temporary glitches in an otherwise promising scenario, but there have been more serious problems in Liberia, Lithuania, Armenia, Georgia, Azerbaijan, Lithuania, Moldova, Ukraine, and Tajikistan, and Russia itself. Then came Somalia, Yugoslavia, and Rwanda.

Somalia (1992–93)

At the beginning of World War II the area that is now Somalia was divided into two parts: British Somaliland in the north, facing the strategic Bab el Mandeb Strait at the entrance of the Red Sea, and Italian Somaliland, a larger southern area facing the Indian Ocean. A third area, French Somaliland (Djibouti), has not become part of Somalia.

The British conquered Italian Somaliland during World War II and granted independence to Somalia in 1960. Since World War II the region has been the scene of rivalry between the United States and the Soviet Union. In 1977 Somalia expelled its Soviet advisers and in 1980 granted the United States permission to establish military bases. The United States had thus been active in Somalia before 1992, when President Bush intervened to protect the famine relief.

A general, Muhammed Siad Barre, had seized power in 1969. On January 26, 1991, the government of Siad Barre was overthrown after weeks of bloody fighting, but no organized government proved capable of taking over, and the country was plunged into chaos. Rival warlords fought among themselves.

Starvation became an increasingly serious problem. International agencies, trying to provide famine relief, found themselves harassed and their supplies stolen by gangs of toughs. The American press vigorously covered the deteriorating situation, and pressure increased to do something about it.

The UN was involved in the efforts to provide relief supplies to the country (along with the International Red Cross and several other organizations), making major efforts to be helpful against frustrating conditions, theft of supplies, and violence. In April 1992 the UN provided for the establishment of a small military force to protect the delivery of relief supplies in Somalia. This was called the UN Operation in Somalia (UNOSOM). Initially it consisted of a battalion of about five hundred Pakistani troops and some fifty UN observers. About 3,500 troops of various nationalities in addition to the Pakistanis (Canadians, Belgians, Egyptians, and Nigerians) were projected for the operation, which was to be of the peacekeeping variety. By November this activity remained a futile gesture so far as giving effective protection to the delivery of relief supplies was concerned. The secretary-general's representative in Somalia, Ismat Kittani, reported helplessly on his efforts to implement relief.

At that time, after the November election in the United States, in the waning days of his presidency, President Bush became interested in providing substantial United States forces to assure the safe distribution of relief supplies. Boutros-Ghali and the UN were interested in having such support, but an issue that arose during the Persian Gulf War arose again. Boutros-Ghali wanted the UN flag to fly over the operation and a general answering to UN authority to command the operation. President Bush wanted the United States flag to fly over the operation and an American general responsible to the United States government to command it. Fortunately for the viability of the operation, a substantial proportion of the troops involved were from other nations whose governments did not refuse to allow their troops to be commanded by an American. Boutros-Ghali and the UN and the other nations yielded to United States sensitivities, and the *Hous-*

ton Post headline reported the result: "The U.N.'s Flag Will Not Fly over American Troops."

The United Nations was thus deprived of an opportunity to acquire experience in running such operations, experience it needs. An American Marine lieutenant general, Robert B. Johnston, commanded the combined forces, and political decisions involved in implementing the operation in Somalia were made by a United States Department of State official getting his instructions from Washington, Robert B. Oakley.

On December 9, 1992, the American and the associated forces moved into Somalia to try to ensure the distribution of the relief supplies to the Somali population by conciliatory working with the warlords rather than by overruling them and "neutralizing" them by force. President Bush also was aware that, in order to get American support for what he was doing, he needed to be extremely solicitous about the safety of the American troops involved and to make sure that they would not become involved in an interminable operation. In consequence, much planning went into arranging for the early withdrawal of the American forces and the turning of the operation over to United Nations control.

In January of 1993, Bill Clinton was inaugurated as president of the United States. The transfer of control of the forces in Somalia occurred on May 4, 1993, and General Cevik Bir of Turkey became the UN commander of what became a UN force. At that time President Clinton agreed that about four thousand United States troops (support troops rather than combat troops) would remain in Somalia under the command of General Bir, which was a potentially significant development. United States opposition to having U.S. troops fighting under UN command was at least no longer absolute.

The situation in Somalia seemed to improve. Famine was no longer a serious problem, and the economy, especially away from Mogadishu, was reviving. But the country still had no government. A clan leader named Mohammed Farah Aidid began giving the UN forces trouble in the southern part of Mogadishu. Fighting erupted, and there were casualties. United States combat troops, who had been sent back to Somalia, suffered casualties. In this setting President Clinton announced that all United States troops would be withdrawn from the country by the end of March 1994. Withdrawal of virtually all of the American forces occurred on schedule and other countries reduced their troop strength. But the UN maintained a token force in the country while establishment of an effective government was delayed and the country disappeared from the headlines.

Yugoslavia

Yugoslavia, the land of the South Slavs, has a population that is fairly uniform ethnically except for Albanians in Kosovo and a hodgepodge of Turks, Albanians, Serbs, Romanians, Greeks, and Bulgarians in Macedonia. The Slavs of Slovenia are generally Roman Catholic, use the Roman alphabet, and speak a Slavic language of their own. The Slavs of Croatia are Roman Catholics and use the Roman alphabet, but their language is Serbo-Croatian. The Slavs of Serbia are Eastern Orthodox, use the Cyrillic alphabet, and speak Serbo-Croatian, the same language as the Croats. The Muslims of Bosnia are ethnic Slavs who were converted to Islam after the Slavs were defeated by the Ottoman Turks in 1389, but there are also Eastern Orthodox Serbs in Bosnia. The Albanians are ethnically distinct and have lived in the southwestern Balkans north of Greece since before the Slavs came. They have a unique language and are predominantly Muslim.

Complicated though they may be, these facts do not explain why a country that seemed to be functioning fairly coherently under Marshal Tito from World War II until Tito's death in 1980 should suddenly tear itself apart. Of course, desire for independence did dominate a lot of areas at the time of the collapse of the Soviet Union, but it takes more than desire for independence to explain the brutality and killing and fighting in Yugoslavia. Some people fall back on ancient feuds as an explanation. At any rate, the carnage in the former Yugoslavia has been a fact of life.

Slovenia was first in asserting independence successfully in 1989 after a brief period of fighting with Yugoslav (chiefly Serb) troops. Croatia came next, and the fighting with the Serbs was long drawn out and bitter before the region asserted its independence. Bosnia came next and fairly quickly established a government dominated by Muslims but containing some cooperating Bosnian Serbs. Slovenia, Croatia, and Bosnia, all three, as independent nations, became members of the United Nations. But then Serbian nationalists from both Bosnia and Serbia began asserting themselves in Bosnia, and the fighting became brutal. The UN, NATO (North Atlantic Treaty Organization), the European Union, various European governments, and the United States have played ineffective roles in trying to resolve the dispute. But the Security Council with its cabal of permanent members, including the United States, has shied away from taking a strong peacemaking initiative.

What to Do about It

Implementation of the terms of the charter as they have stood, unimplemented, since 1945 would be an improvement over present practice. The charter provides in chapter VII and particularly in article 47 for the establishment of an armed force under the control of the United Nations that would be authorized to effect peacemaking with force. Effort to exercise this mandate was frustrated during the late 1940s by the surfacing of the bipolar world and the Cold War between the Soviet Union and the United States and the consequent inability of the Americans and Russians on the Military Staff Committee to agree on the terms of reference of the UN force.

In any effort to establish a more effective United Nations force under chapter VII, there is at least one important change that should be made. The monopoly in command of the United Nations force in the hands "of the Chiefs of Staff of the permanent members of the Security Council" should be replaced by a command structure more palatable to the other 180 or so members of the international community. This will require revision of the charter.

Revision of the charter could also include a simple and straightforward procedure for financing a United Nations permanent force, organized and controlled by the United Nations. A basic provision, chipped in granite, in the charter would provide that each nation turn over to the United Nations a fixed percent, let us pick the figure 25 or 30 percent out of the air, of its armed forces budget. Such a provision would create the financial basis for a United Nations force that even a great power would have to respect. This arrangement would tend to frustrate any country trying to build up an armed force capable of dominating the world. It would also create a force capable of dealing with petty tyrants and self-centered, "chips-on-shoulder" patriots. In fact, a self-reinforcing machinery would be developed that would tend to inhibit armament programs and arms races. Where is the gain from an arms buildup if the power-hungry nation cannot create a dominating force but must continually contribute to a United Nations force? Also, the small-nation dictator would know that the United Nations force must be handled with respect. It might also give pause to battle-hungry perpetuators of ancient feuds such as those who have been destroying Yugoslavia.

Two things more should be said about this assessment involving a percentage of each country's military budget: As the threat of wars was lessened and national armies were scaled back, UN receipts from these assessments would be reduced and the size of the UN force itself would be reduced. Those concerned about the possible undesirable long-view implications of a permanent, powerful, functionless UN force will appreciate the usefulness of this automatic tendency to scale it back. Also, the receipts from the assessment against military budgets should always be available to finance nonmilitary UN expenditures when that seems appropriate.

Another measure that would quickly provide the permanent UN military force with much useful plant and equipment would be for NATO to turn over much of its plant and equipment to the

UN—much as did the League of Nations when it gracefully bowed out in 1945.

The problem of unemployed soldiers might be lessened if they were given the opportunity to join the UN military force. Sir Brian Urquhart, longtime high official in the UN Secretariat, has recommended the establishment of a permanent, small, international volunteer force: "All these [arguments] point strongly to the need for a highly trained international volunteer force, willing, if necessary, to fight hard to break the cycle of violence at an early stage in low-level but dangerous conflicts. . . ."[16]

The Secretary-General
and the Secretariat

In article 7 of the UN charter the Secretariat is listed as one of the principal organs of the United Nations. The secretary-general is the head of the Secretariat and the highest ranking official in the UN system. The Secretariat is the working personnel of the system, people of many nationalities and diverse skills.

The Secretary-General

Article 97 speaks of the role of the secretary-general, who is appointed by the General Assembly upon the recommendation of the Security Council. It says that: "He shall be the chief administrative officer of the Organization." The text continues: "The Secretary-General shall act in that capacity in all meetings of the General Assembly, of the Security Council, and of the Trusteeship Council, and shall perform such other functions as are entrusted to him by these organs." And "the Secretary-General shall make an annual report to the General Assembly on the work of the organization." Article 99 states that "the Secretary-General may bring to the attention of the Security Council any matter which in his opinion may threaten the maintenance of international peace and security." And in article 101: "The staff shall be appointed by the Secretary-General under regulations established by the General Assembly." The term of office of the secretary-general is five years; reelection for a second, but not a third, term is customary.

Initially one of the questions as to what this assignment actually meant involved whether the secretary-general should function as a more or less anonymous, "do what one is told" secretary or as a leader. As it has worked out, the secretaries-general have expended most of their time and energy as high-profile executives dealing with the great problems of war and peace. They have not been actively concerned with problems of staff morale and recruitment and Secretariat organization. Their activities in the areas of war and peace have been conditioned by the necessity to work cooperatively with both the Soviet Union and the United States.

The secretaries-general have been:

Trygve Lie, Norway (1946–53)
Dag Hammarskjöld, Sweden (1953–61)
U Thant, Burma (1962–71)
Kurt Waldheim, Austria (1972–81)
Javier Pérez de Cuéllar, Peru (1982–91)
Boutros Boutros-Ghali, Egypt (1992–   )

Many of the things secretaries-general have done have been condemned by one or another of the great powers. The Soviet Union was especially unhappy with Trygve Lie, the United States with U Thant. But neither was especially condemnatory of Kurt Waldheim, who later was seriously charged with an active Nazi past.

Crisis decisions by the Security Council and the General Assembly are generally hastily made and leave considerable latitude to the secretary-general in terms of implementation. For example, the manner of recruitment and the style of operation of the United Nations Emergency Forces has followed a pattern hurriedly developed by Dag Hammarskjöld at the time of the Egypt-Israeli War of 1956. Military units were arranged for by the secretary-general in hurried negotiations with the countries that could be induced to provide the troops. Questions of monetary and equipment support have been an important aspect of the work of the secretary-general, especially since many nations drag their feet in paying the assessments assigned to them for supporting the troops. The United States has long been delinquent in this matter. It will be remembered that the procedures provided for in the charter for obtaining the troops have never been worked out. Especially difficult in all these respects has been the problem of obtaining and financing the troops for the operation in Somalia.

Secretaries-general have, upon occasion, taken direct initiatives. Sometimes during crises the secretary-general may attempt to mediate disputes without authorization from the Security Council or the General Assembly. Sometimes this has been done with considerable success; in other cases the results have not been notably successful.[1]

As matters stand the secretary-general is in an ambiguous position in relation to the heads of state. Whether the secretary-general is a level above, equal to, or below a head of state in terms of some hierarchy of relative power or prestige is not always clear. The position lacks a meaningful police power to enforce "laws" with respect to nations or individuals, nor is there an army with an established loyalty to the UN or a legislative body that passes laws, in the ordinary sense, for a chief executive to enforce.

The secretary-general is in an anomalous but important position, lacking coercive power but being the crucial figure on the world scene who is not primarily concerned with the particular interests of a nation state. Yet the secretary-general is not in a position effectively to manage the United Nations and is even less well situated to be an effective world leader, not even being recognized as "the first among equals" by the leaders of the major powers. The secretary-general, since 1945, has become an increasingly important figure in dealing with peace and war, but even as recently as 1990–91 was not in position to be the leader in policy determination during the Persian Gulf War. The myriad economic and social organizations in the UN system are scarcely within the secretary's purview. And the secretary seems to some degree to have abdicated the power the charter has actually provided in connection with controlling the secretariat.

Up to the 1992 selection, the person to hold the office had to be endorsed by both the Soviet Union and the United States, a constraint that severely limited the field of candidates. The initial formal endorsement of the candidate was then made by the Security Council, and the definitive appointment was next promptly and cooperatively made by the General Assembly.

The selection of Boutros Boutros-Ghali in 1991 was the first made in a setting where the confrontation between the United States and the Soviet Union was not the initial conditioning ingredient. The selection process of the future would seem to be one where the initial choice is made by a Security Council consisting of representatives of the United States, Britain, France, Russia, and China and ten other countries on the council on a rotating basis, it being quite accidental which countries will be on the council at a given time. The extent to which the great-power cabal will dominate the process remains to be seen. What does not remain to be seen is that the Security Council representatives who make the selection are entirely controlled in their choices by their home governments in power.

A resolution adopted by the General Assembly on January 24, 1946, provided that "the *first* Secretary-General shall be appointed for five years, the appointment being open at the end of that period for a further five-year term." The five-year renewable term became the accepted practice. But in later years question has been raised about the practice. Brian Urquhart and Erskine Childers in a report to the Ford Foundation and the Dag Hammarskjold Foundation, published in 1990, expressed the opinion that "a single term of seven years would have many advantages. It would give a Secretary-General the opportunity to undertake far-reaching plans and to ignore undesirable pressures [especially those involved in running for re-election]. It would make possible a more orderly and considered process for selecting the best possible successor. In our view the seven-year, single term of office is the key to improving the whole process and should be established as soon as possible."[2]

Another suggested change has involved the possibility of direct popular election of the secretary general. But perhaps the world should be allowed to "settle down" a little bit before that innovative procedure is attempted. Meanwhile, designation by more democratically based Security Councils and General Assemblies would seem not too unsatisfactory a procedure.[3]

The Secretariat

The Size of the Staff

The secretary-general is the head of a bureaucracy that is quite small in terms of the size of bureaucracies of major nation states. The Secretariat proper in 1991 had 13,973 employees of whom 9,625 were paid from the regular budget and 4,348 were paid from sources outside the budget. Included in the total were 3,810 employees in the professional category.[4] Including employees of associated organizations such as the International Monetary Fund but not peacekeeping forces the figure would approximate 50,000. In comparison, the United States federal civilian employment at about the same time was over 3,300,000. Such a comparison makes the UN seem quite small indeed.

The Top-Level Staff

By 1991 a variegated organization involving about thirty under secretaries and heads of departments reported directly to the secretary-general. To put it mildly, organization was diffuse, and the secretary-general was at least nominally involved in everything. But the resulting situation was one where he actually concerned himself very little with most activities except threats to the peace and acts of aggression.

Just browsing through the "United Nations System of Organizations and Directory of Senior Officials" prepared in 1991 by the secretariat of the Administrative Committee on Coordination is an eye-opening experience because it is so complicated, but then, so is browsing through the *United States Government Manual*.

Promptly on taking office in January 1992 Secretary-General Boutros Boutros-Ghali implemented a major simplification of the administrative structure. The *UN Chronicle* of June 1992 reported his views: "My management policy will be to delegate and expect managers to manage. . . . The nature of administration must therefore change. I will, *inter alia*, do everything within my power to make administrative procedures simpler, more transparent and easier to follow."

Changes involved consolidation of departments and the creation of four new departments. The *UN Chronicle* reported the changes:

> Among the changes were:
>
> - two Under-secretaries-general—Vladimir Petrovsky of the Russian Federation and James Jonah of Sierra Leone—to oversee the work of a newly created, comprehensive department of Political Affairs, which incorporates the responsibilities of five former departments and offices;
> - a new Department of Peace-keeping Operations, headed by Under-Secretary-General Marrack Goulding of the United Kingdom;
> - the new Department of Economic and Social Development—encompassing the work of four now-defunct major UN units—headed by Ji Chaozhu of China, and
> - a fourth new department—created to deal with humanitarian affairs—led by Jan Eliasson of Sweden, who also has the title of Emergency Relief Coordinator.
>
> The Legal Department, headed by Under-Secretary-General Carl-August Fleischauer of Germany, will absorb the functions of the Office for Ocean Affairs and the Law of the Sea.
>
> Other new appointments included: Eugeniusz Wyzner of Poland . . . as Under-Secretary-General for Public Information and Richard Thornburgh (former United States Attorney General and two-time Governor of Pennsylvania) as Under-Secretary-General of an expanded Department of Administration and Management.

The Staff as a Whole

The staff in general, as distinct from the leaders, is a staff that the secretary-general ostensibly has a major role in creating. In addition to the core staff paragraph 2 of article 101 provides that: "Appropriate staffs shall be assigned to the Economic and Social Council, the Trusteeship Council, and, as required, to other organs of the United Nations. These staffs shall form part of the Secretariat." For the most part, the staffs of the "specialized agencies" such as the International Monetary Fund, and many other associated agencies and organizations, do not form part of the Secretariat proper. This distinction would seem to have some significance in terms of prestige, salary scales, membership in pension funds and employee organizations.

Further along in paragraph 3 of article 101 it is stated that "the paramount consideration in the employment of the staff and in the determination of the conditions of service shall be the necessity of securing the highest standards of efficiency, competence, and integrity." There follows the qualification that "due regard shall be paid to the importance of recruiting the staff on as wide a geographical basis as possible."

A problem has been presented by the circumstance that the increasing number of less developed countries in the UN, while claiming their geographical quotas, have not had well-qualified professional people to fill such positions. In consequence, the professional quality of the Secretariat may not have been as high as it might have been. It is noticeable to an outsider that there is a lag of increasing length in the issuance of various of the standard yearbooks and statistical works published by the United Nations. So there is an information gap of increasing size in the data on economic, social, and political conditions in the world. There does exist a civil service system that screens the new employees. And the salary scale of UN employees has been more or less comparable with the salary scales for government employees in the major member countries.

An example of the problems that have occurred is a situation in which the work an employee is doing is supposed to be done by someone on a higher level. Grievance procedures to handle such problems do not always work satisfactorily, and so on.[5] There is a union among the employees, the Federation of International Civil Servants' Associations (FICSA), of which Edward J. Freeman was the president in 1992. The general feeling in this organization seems to be that its relation with the UN officialdom is not on a particularly satisfactory footing. In 1992 it was petitioning the Fifth Committee of the General Assembly to agree to "maintain the competitiveness of General Service salaries and pensions, restore the competitiveness of professional salaries and pensions, and give [employees] the right to negotiate our conditions of service. . . ."[6] FICSA reports that it has thirty-two thousand members, perhaps three-fifths of the employees making up the whole United Nations system.

The Loyalty Question

In Article 100 of the charter, it is provided that: "In the performance of their duties the secretary-general and the staff shall not seek or receive instructions from any government or from any other authority external to the Organization. They shall refrain from any action which might reflect on their position as international officials responsible only to the Organization." And in support of this attempt to implement a genuinely independent international civil service, the obligation is placed on each of the member nations that: "Each Member of the United Nations undertakes to respect the exclusively international character of the responsibilities of the secretary-general and the staff and not to seek to influence them in the discharge of their responsibilities."

It was a major question, first with the League of Nations and then with the United Nations, as to whether it is appropriate to believe in the possibility of an international civil service whose members will work genuinely in the interest of the world rather than serving as instruments of the national policies of the nations of which they are citizens. The first secretary-general of the

League of Nations was Sir Eric Drummond, of Britain, who strongly believed in the concept "of a truly international civil service, which would owe its loyalty exclusively to the global system it was administering."[7]

It surely is appropriate, and necessary for the respectability of an organization, that its employees be concerned to serve the interest of that organization. In effecting this result it would seem appropriate that the United Nations be primarily itself responsible for selecting its employees rather than their being selected by the member governments. The charter clearly called for this independence. At the very beginning in 1946 and for a little while, it seemed that the United Nations might employ that approach and follow the example of the League of Nations. But that approach, if it was ever followed, was not followed for long. The United States and the Soviet Union quickly set bad examples by pressuring the United Nations to clear with them hiring of their nationals and to discharge and hire specific ones at their request. This practice went to the extent that countries could claim the right that their nationals would occupy particular strategic positions in the UN organization.

It would be difficult to assign primary responsibility between the United States and the Soviet Union for violation of the impartiality and competence codes. During the McCarthy era, the United States actively pressured the UN to clear its nationals with the government so as to purge American communists, or people who happened to be on one of Senator McCarthy's lists. "Astonishing as it may seem in retrospect, Secretary-General Lie permitted the FBI to set up shop in the UN building, explaining that it was for the convenience of the large number of personnel who were to be interrogated and fingerprinted."[8] This was as early as 1949.

In 1953, although the FBI had lost its offices at the UN headquarters, the practice of United States screening of U.S. citizens continued. "There is no doubt that both Trygve Lie and Dag Hammarskjöld were well informed on the trend of thinking in United States investigating agencies when they permanently accepted, in 1953, the official screening process for United States personnel at the United Nations; and were aware that there could scarcely have been a set of bodies more inimical to the concept of internationalism."[9]

As for the Soviet Union, that country succeeded in inducing the United Nations to hire Soviet citizens as Secretariat employees on the recommendation of the Soviet government from a very small panel that it presented. Also, the appointments were customarily for a time period such as five years, after which the individual was rotated back to a position in the Soviet government. These, therefore, were not career, professional appointments. An additional oddity was that the Soviet government required its citizens serving with the United Nations to turn over a portion of their salary to the Soviet government to compensate for the fact that UN salaries were higher than Russian government salaries.

In a twist on that practice, at least one government, the Japanese, seems to have provided salary supplements to Japanese government people taking jobs with the UN—to compensate them for UN salaries being lower than Japanese salaries. Japan also had an interest in being well and competently represented in the Secretariat.[10]

Criticism of the Efficiency of the Secretariat

These influences do not add up to the creation of a model, efficient, international civil service. The result has been described in a report made in 1988 for the United Nations Association of the U.S.A., called "United Nations Management and Decision-Making Project," by a committee headed by Elliott L. Richardson, a distinguished Republican former secretary of defense and former attorney general. The prose, in a section of the report, runs:

At the heart of this situation are the following basic problems:

- the absence of objective, uniform criteria guiding recruitment and management (promotion, termination, training, rotation, etc.) of U.N. employees

- the absence of an administrative environment that is conducive to the application of such criteria
- the lack of clarity about the mission of the Office of Personnel Services (OPS) and too little disposition on the part of the U.N.'s top leadership to ensure that OPS's function is clarified and fulfilled
- the tendency by the member states to give the Secretariat inappropriate and unproductive tasks to fulfill.

This situation has caused an erosion in the collective self-image of the U.N. staff and in the reputation enjoyed by the U.N. Secretariat among numerous member governments and sections of the international press and public as well. Among the consequences of the shortcomings listed above are:

- the considerable number of staff who are not well qualified for the positions they hold or the grade levels at which they are employed. (An advanced university degree for all entering professionals is a "policy objective" of OPS, but the available data reveals that more than half lack such a degree, while 12.5 percent of those at the Under-Secretary or Assistant Secretary-General level do not have Bachelor's degrees.)
- the large number of staff in management positions, including many at the most senior levels, who lack management skills, training, or previous management experience
- the extreme unevenness in the quality of the "outputs" of individual U.N. offices
- the disproportionately small number of women employed in the professional ranks and the extremely low representation of women at the senior levels
- the tendency for political considerations to exert a strong influence on recruitment at the level of P–3 and above
- the insufficient emphasis on fairness and objective, merit-based considerations in some promotions
- the frequent disregard for maintaining minimal standards of efficiency and competence, particularly after an employee has received a permanent contract
- the near impossibility of terminating an employee's service on the basis of unsatisfactory performance
- the generally low morale among the staff, reflecting a feeling that

promotion opportunities are not merit-based, and frustration over poor supervision and badly conceived work assignments—a situation that causes some of the U.N.'s most talented employees to leave its service.[11]

Beyond a doubt, the mess is not merely the result of inattentive secretaries-general and incompetence in the Secretariat. It results from the lack of a leadership among the member countries that is willing to look beyond national interest to the interest of all nations in common in an effective, impartial UN.

Recommendations on Personnel Policy

In a 1986 "Report of the Group of High-Level Intergovernmental Experts to Review the Efficiency of the Administrative and Financial Functioning of the United Nations" there was this general recommendation (Recommendation 41):

Personnel policy and management in the United Nations has suffered as a result of the considerable political and other pressures that have influenced the selection of staff. The secretary-general should exercise greater leadership in personnel matters and ensure that the selection of staff is done strictly in accordance with the principles of the charter. He should improve the management of human resources, protect the authority of the official in charge of personnel and instruct all other senior officials to refrain from influencing the selection of staff. The office responsible should be renamed "Office of Human Resources Management."[12]

The Economic and Social Council and the Subsidiary Organs

According to article 7 of the charter, the principal organs of the United Nations include the Economic and Social Council. Such subsidiary organs as may be found necessary may also be established. As it has turned out, many of these subsidiary organs are related to the United Nations through the channel of the Economic and Social Council (ECOSOC).

The Economic and Social Council

The Economic and Social Council is the coordinating body for most of the activities of the United Nations aside from the maintenance of international peace and security. Chapter IX of the charter deals with the general subject of international economic and social cooperation, and chapter X deals specifically with the organization and functions of ECOSOC. Article 55 of chapter IX reads:

> With a view to the creation of conditions of stability and well-being which are necessary for peaceful and friendly relations among nations based on respect for the principle of equal rights and self-determination of peoples, the United Nations shall promote:
>
> a. higher standards of living, full employment, and conditions of economic and social progress and development;

b. solutions of international economic, social, health, and related problems; and international cultural and educational co-operation; and

c. universal respect for, and observance of, human rights, and fundamental freedoms for all without distinction as to race, sex, language, or religion.

Article 60, with regard to international economic and social cooperation, reads: "Responsibility for the discharge of the functions of the Organization set forth in this Chapter shall be vested in the General Assembly and, under the authority of the General Assembly, in the Economic and Social Council, which shall have for this purpose the powers set forth in Chapter X." Thus, although ECOSOC is designated as a principal organ of the UN, it is essentially subordinated to the General Assembly.

The Economic and Social Council consists of fifty-four members "of the United Nations elected by the General Assembly," eighteen each year for three-year terms. "Fifty-four members" means one representative from the government of each of fifty-four countries. A retiring member is eligible for immediate re-election. This means that the United States and other great powers may be and are more or less automatically re-elected.

Articles 62 through 71 seem to make ECOSOC generally responsible for United Nations work in the "economic and social" field. The language is extensive and seems to cover everything. ECOSOC may study and make recommendations to the General Assembly on international economic, social, cultural, educational, health, human rights and fundamental freedoms, and related matters. It may prepare draft conventions for submission to the General Assembly. It may sponsor international conferences to concern themselves with such matters. It is the link between the central organization of the UN and most of the subsidiary organs.

There is a hodgepodge of subsidiary organizations created by the various principal organs of the United Nations. They may engage in research or report writing, or statistics gathering, or dealing directly with economic or social problems, or with sponsoring international conferences. They may prepare resolutions that may or may not be endorsed by the General Assembly. They may make some money selling Christmas cards.

It is worth looking at the range of activity of these organs. The range is impressive, even if these organizations are not all in commanding positions in the areas with which they are concerned. A lot of knowledge, experience, and frustration as to how the world works is being gathered. In any event, the UN is not just a Secretariat in a moderately tall building on the East Side of Manhattan.

Subsidiary Organs[1]

The subsidiary organs discussed here are part of the UN structure proper (Figure 6.1). Their expenditures are for the most part financed out of the regular UN budget. Their personnel or staffs are employees of the UN. These organizations, which are subsidiary to ECOSOC, include so-called "sessional committees," functional commissions, regional commissions, standing committees, expert bodies, and ad hoc bodies. Then there is also the inter-agency Administrative Committee on Coordination.

The sessional committees consist of temporary groups set up to deal with the special problems of any particular session of ECOSOC, plus those regular continuing committees: the First (Economic) Committee, the Second (Social) Committee, and the Third (Program and Co-ordination) Committee. What their work involves is primarily the screening of the reports of the various subsidiary organs reporting to ECOSOC

Functional Commissions:

- Commission for Social Development
- Commission on Human Rights: Chairman Pal Solt of Hungary (1992). This commission concerns itself with *apartheid*, the protection of minorities, detention, indigenous populations, the right to development, and involun-

Figure 6.1 The United Nations System

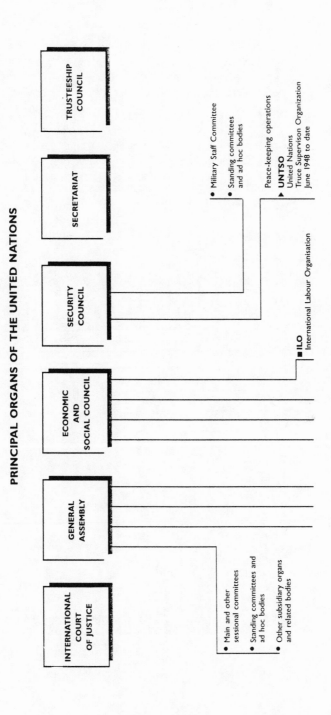

PRINCIPAL ORGANS OF THE UNITED NATIONS

INTERNATIONAL COURT OF JUSTICE

GENERAL ASSEMBLY

ECONOMIC AND SOCIAL COUNCIL

SECURITY COUNCIL

SECRETARIAT

TRUSTEESHIP COUNCIL

● Main and other sessional committees

● Standing committees and ad hoc bodies

● Other subsidiary organs and related bodies

■ ILO
International Labour Organisation

● Military Staff Committee

● Standing committees and ad hoc bodies

Peace-keeping operations

▶ UNTSO
United Nations
Truce Supervison Organization
June 1948 to date

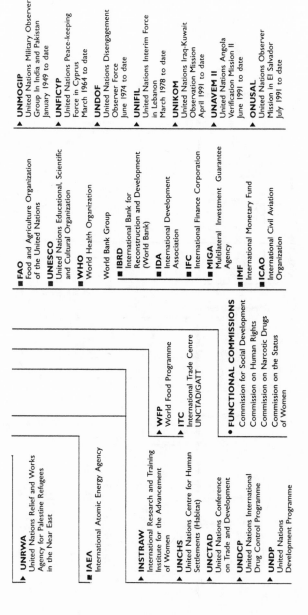

▶ **UNRWA**
United Nations Relief and Works Agency for Palestine Refugees in the Near East

■ **IAEA**
International Atomic Energy Agency

▶ **INSTRAW**
International Research and Training Institute for the Advancement of Women

▶ **UNCHS**
United Nations Centre for Human Settlements (Habitat)

▶ **UNCTAD**
United Nations Conference on Trade and Development

▶ **UNDCP**
United Nations International Drug Control Programme

▶ **UNDP**
United Nations Development Programme

▶ **WFP**
World Food Programme

▶ **ITC**
International Trade Centre UNCTAD/GATT

● **FUNCTIONAL COMMISSIONS**
Commission for Social Development
Commission on Human Rights
Commission on Narcotic Drugs
Commission on the Status of Women

■ **FAO**
Food and Agriculture Organization of the United Nations

■ **UNESCO**
United Nations Educational, Scientific and Cultural Organization

■ **WHO**
World Health Organization

World Bank Group

■ **IBRD**
International Bank for Reconstruction and Development (World Bank)

■ **IDA**
International Development Association

■ **IFC**
International Finance Corporation

■ **MIGA**
Multilateral Investment Guarantee Agency

■ **IMF**
International Monetary Fund

■ **ICAO**
International Civil Aviation Organization

▶ **UNMOGIP**
United Nations Military Observer Group In India and Pakistan January 1949 to date

▶ **UNFICYP**
United Nations Peace-keeping Force in Cyprus March 1964 to date

▶ **UNDOF**
United Nations Disengagement Observer Force June 1974 to date

▶ **UNIFIL**
United Nations Interim Force in Lebanon March 1978 to date

▶ **UNIKOM**
United Nations Iraq-Kuwait Observation Mission April 1991 to date

▶ **UNAVEM II**
United Nations Angola Verification Mission II June 1991 to date

▶ **ONUSAL**
United Nations Observer Mission in El Salvador July 1991 to date

UNEP
United Nations
Environment Programme

▲ **UNFPA**
United Nations Population Fund

▲ **UNHCR**
Office of the United Nations
High Commissioner for Refugees

▲ **UNICEF**
United Nations Children's Fund

▲ **UNIFEM**
United Nations Development
Fund for Women

▲ **UNITAR**
United Nations Institute
for Training and Research

▲ **UNU**
United Nations University

▲ **WFC**
World Food Council

Commission on Sustainable
Development

Population Commission

Statistical Commission

● **REGIONAL COMMISSIONS**

Economic Commission
for Africa (ECA)

Economic Commission
for Europe (ECE)

Economic Commission for
Latin America and the
Caribbean (ECLAC)

Economic and Social Commission
for Asia and the Pacific (ESCAP)

Economic and Social Commission
for Western Asia (ESCWA)

● **SESSIONAL AND STANDING
COMMITTEES**

● **EXPERT, AD HOC
AND RELATED BODIES**

■ **UPU**
Universal Postal Union

■ **ITU**
International
Telecommunication Union

■ **WMO**
World Meteorological Organization

■ **IMO**
International Maritime Organization

■ **WIPO**
World Intellectual
Property Organization

■ **IFAD**
International Fund for
Agricultural Development

■ **UNIDO**
United Nations Industrial
Development Organization

┈ **GATT**
General Agreement on
Tariffs and Trade

▲ **MINURSO**
United Nations Mission for the
Referendum in Western Sahara
September 1991 to date

▲ **UNPROFOR**
United Nations Protection Force
March 1992 to date

▲ **UNTAC**
United Nations Transitional
Authority in Cambodia
March 1992 to date

▲ **UNOSOM**
United Nations Operation in Somalia
April 1992 to date

▷ **ONUMOZ**
United Nations Operation
in Mozambique
December 1992 to date

▲ **UNOMUR**
United Nations Observer Mission
Uganda-Rwanda
22 June 1993 to date

▲ United Nations programmes and organs
(representative list only)

■ Specialized agencies and other autonomous
organizations within the system

● Other commissions, committees
and ad hoc and related bodies

tary disappearances. In 1992 it concerned itself with the former Yugoslavia and its ethnic cleansing and human rights violation problems.
- Commission on Narcotic Drugs
- Commission on Sustainable Development: Chairman Razali Ismail of Malaysia (1993)
- Commission on the Status of Women
- Population Commission
- Statistical Commission

Regional Commissions:

The regional commissions have their headquarters in the areas of the world with which they are primarily concerned rather than in New York. They are nevertheless parts of the basic UN structure and are included in the UN budget proper. They are principally research organizations that publish the results of their investigations.

- Economic and Social Commission for Asia and the Pacific (ESCAP)
- Economic and Social Commission for Western Asia (ESCWA)
- Economic Commission for Africa (ECA): Its headquarters are in Addis Ababa.
- Economic Commission for Europe (ECE): This commission has had a distinguished existence dating back to the 1940s when Gunnar Myrdal was its head.
- Economic Commission for Latin America and the Caribbean (ECLAC): This commission has two headquarters, one in Santiago, Chile, the other in Mexico City. It also has had a distinguished existence dating back to the 1940s when it was merely ECLA (the Economic Commission for Latin America). The then head of the organization, Raul Prebisch, was responsible for an influential group of reports, one of the themes of which was that there exist basic influences handicapping underdeveloped because there is a

tendency causing the long-run or secular terms of trade of underdeveloped countries to worsen, that is, alleging that the average price of their exports is falling relative to the average price of their imports.

Standing Committees:

- Commission on Transnational Corporations: Many reports have been written on transnational corporations and conferences held, but extremely important issues in connection with their roles, national loyalties (patriotism), behavior, and tax status remain. Policy planning in this area is important. The UN Center on Transnational Corporations is its secretariat and research arm.
- Committee on Program and Co-ordination (CPC). This committee is the principal subsidiary organ of the ECOSOC and of the General Assembly for planning, programming, and coordination, and it reports directly to both. It is concerned with UN planning in general.
- Committee on Natural Resources

Expert Bodies:

- Ad Hoc Group of Experts on International Co-operation in Tax Matters
- Committee for Development Planning
- Committee of Experts on the Transport of Dangerous Goods
- Committee on Crime Prevention and Control
- Intergovernmental Working Group of Experts on International Standards of Accounting and Reporting
- United Nations Group of Experts on Geographical Names

Ad Hoc and Other Related Bodies:

- Intergovernmental Committee on Science and Technology for Development
- (Office of the) United Nations High Commissioner for Refugees (UNHCR): High Commissioner, Mrs. Sadako

Ogata of Japan (1991). This is a high-profile, active organization dealing, hands on, with the major refuge problems of the world, and working at the task with resources inadequate to the job.

- United Nations Center on Transnational Corporations: Executive Director, Peter Hansen. This is the secretariat and research arm of the Commission on Transnational Corporations.
- United Nations Center for Human Settlements (UNCHS), that is to say, housing.
- United Nations Children's Fund (UNICEF): Executive Director, James P. Grant, of the United States (1980–). This organization is well known for its annual sale of Christmas cards through which it supplements the funds it has available to assist especially poor children in underdeveloped countries. UNICEF stands, actually, for United Nations International Children's Emergency Fund.
- United Nations Development Program (UNDP): Administrator James Gustav Speth of the United States (1993–). This organization concerns itself with the economic development of underdeveloped countries. It is the coordinating organization for much of the work in the economic development area.
- United Nations Environment Program (UNEP): Executive Director Mostafa Kamel Tolba (1976–). This organization reports to the General Assembly through ECOSOC. It has been active in efforts to protect the environment. In cooperation with the World Commission on Environment and Development, it was concerned with the high-profile 1992 conference in Rio de Janeiro on the subject of the environment and development. The problem of devising a development process that will be sustainable without injuring the environment has been a central aspect of the work of environmentalists, whose efforts deserve far more support than they have received in developed countries.
- World Food Program (WFP): Executive Director Catherine

Bertini of the United States (1992–). This organization reports annually to ECOSOC, the Food and Agriculture Organization, and the World Food Council. Catherine Bertini's appointment to the post of executive director in 1992 elicited a certain amount of newspaper publicity at the time due to the fact that the United States government spent a substantial sum of money to support her travels as she lobbied to obtain the position. Apparently, the United States was interested for political reasons in having an executive director who would favor American positions with regard to the relative amounts of food aid given various countries. Her previous position was as assistant secretary in the U.S. Department of Agriculture. Fairly substantial sums of money are involved, some $700 million in food aid in 1986, and the figures seem to be rising.

Administrative Committee on Co-ordination (ACC):

This committee, working under the personal chairmanship of the secretary-general of the UN, includes the executive heads or responsible officials of most of the subsidiary organizations of the UN system. It was established, at least in large part, in an effort to meet the United States' charges of inefficiency and waste in the system, which charges have been used as an excuse by the United States for delinquency in meeting its assessments. The United States' strong and repeated complaints on this score may seem somewhat overdone coming from a government experiencing considerable difficulty in keeping its own budget in order.

**Subsidiary, Ad Hoc, and Related Bodies
and Conferences Dependent Directly on
the General Assembly**

Many subsidiary organizations report to ECOSOC, which studies and digests their reports and makes appropriate reports and recommendations to the General Assembly. In other cases, initial reports are made to ECOSOC, but those reports, as such, are also passed on to the General Assembly to permit that body to consider them in their original form. In yet other cases, the subsidiary agency may report directly to the General Assembly without the intermediation of ECOSOC. What all this adds up to is a classification nightmare. At any rate, there follow the names of organs in the latter category.

Standing Committees, Other than the Six
Main Committees (of the General Assembly):

- Advisory Committee on Administrative and Budgeting Questions (ACABQ)
- Committee on Contributions

Other Subsidiary, Ad Hoc, and Related Bodies:

- Advisory Committee on the United Nations Educational and Training Program for Southern Africa
- Advisory Committee on the United Nations Program of Assistance in the Teaching, Study, Dissemination and Wider Application of International Law
- Board of Auditors
- Collective Measures Committee
- Committee for the United Nations Population Award
- Committee of Trustees for the United Nations Trust Fund for South Africa
- Committee on Applications for Review of Administrative Tribunal Judgments
- Committee on Arrangements for a Conference for the Purpose of Reviewing the Charter. This review which has been continually postponed since 1956 is long overdue. See article 109, paragraph 3, of the United Nations charter. All members of the UN are on this committee.
- Committee on Conferences. The possibility of a great many expensive conferences on innumerable subjects that fre-

quently result in well-meaning but never implemented resolutions indicates the desirability of having a committee in position to exercise some sort of limiting influence over the process.

- Committee on Information. This body reports to the General Assembly on the efficacy with which the UN keeps the public informed of its activities.
- Committee on Relations with the Host Country. Efforts by the United States to control access to the United Nations underline the desirability of such a committee.
- Committee on the Exercise of the Inalienable Rights of the Palestinian People
- Committee on the Peaceful Uses of Outer Space. An increasingly important subject.
- Disarmament Commission
- Global Environmental Facility (established in 1990). This organization was established jointly with the World Bank to channel money for environmental purposes from rich countries to poor countries.
- High-Level Committee on the Review of Technical Cooperation among Developing Countries
- Intergovernmental Committee on Science and Technology for Development. The working arm of this group is an Advisory Committee on Science and Technology for Development.
- International Civil Service Commission. The UN civil service has problems in the tenure and morale area that need attention.
- International Law Commission
- Investments Committee
- Joint Advisory Group on the International Trade Centre UNCTAD/GATT
- Joint Inspection Unit (JIU). The unit's eight inspectors, chosen from among members of the supervision or inspection bodies of member nations or people of similar qualifications, draw up suggestions, over their own signa-

tures, as to improvements in the way the UN system oper-
ates. It was established in 1967.

- Negotiating Committee on the Financial Emergency of the United Nations
- Special Committee against Apartheid
- Special Committee on Peace-keeping Operations
- Special Committee on the Charter of the United Nations and on the Strengthening of the Role of the Organization
- Special Committee on the Situation with Regard to the Implementation of the Declaration on the Granting of Independence to Colonial Countries and Peoples
- United Nations Administrative Tribunal
- United Nations Capital Development Fund
- United Nations Commission on International Trade Law (UNCITRAL)
- United Nations Conference on Trade and Development (UNCTAD): Secretary General K.S.S. Dadzie (1986–). A significant activity, originally fostered by Raul Prebisch.
- United Nations Institute for Disarmament Research (UNIDIR)
- United Nations Institute for Training and Research (UNITAR): Executive Director Michel Doo Kingué (1982–)
- United Nations Joint Staff Pension Board
- United Nations Population Fund (UNPF): Executive Director: Mrs. Nafis Sadik of Pakistan (1987–). This organization works under the guidance of the UN Development Program. It was formerly the United Nations Fund for Population Activities. Mrs. Sadik has been active in the advocacy of family planning.
- United Nations Relief and Works Agency for Palestine Refugees in the Middle East (UNRWA): Commissioner-General Ilter Turkmen (1991–)
- United Nations Scientific Committee on the Effects of Atomic Radiation
- United Nations Staff Pension Committee
- United Nations University: Rector, H.G. de Souza (1987–)
- United Nations Voluntary Fund for Indigenous Populations

- United Nations Voluntary Fund for Victims of Torture
- World Food Council: Executive Director, Gerald Trant (1986–). The World Food Program reports to this body.

Specialized Agencies

These organizations regularly report to ECOSOC. But the reporting procedure and the ECOSOC role may be quite nominal in the case of many of the organizations, such as the World Bank and the International Monetary Fund. The matter of reporting may be a more significant operation with other agencies. The details of these arrangements are worked out in agreements between ECOSOC and the specialized agency at the time the relationship is established.

The specialized agencies are, then, separate organizations with identities of their own, with special relationships to the United Nations. They were originally established, individually, by international treaties among the countries who chose to join that particular agency. They are financed, separately from the UN financing procedures, according to the provisions of those treaties, typically by assessments to be paid by the member countries. Their organizations are separate from the UN structure. Their personnel is not part of the UN Secretariat. A list of these agencies and their basic functions follows. See Table 6.1 for additional information.

Food and Agriculture Organization (FAO)

Basic Function: To increase production from farms, forests, and fisheries; improve distribution, marketing, and nutrition; better conditions for rural people.

Actually the United Nations has at least three organizations working in what might be called the food and agriculture area. There is the FAO itself; the World Food Program, which seems to be subordinated to the FAO; and the International Fund for

Table 6.1

Specialized Agencies

Agency	Date established	Headquarters	Agency head	Staff size	Member countries	Administrative budget	Lending and grants
Food & Agriculture Organization (FAO)	1943[a]	Rome	Edouard Saouma (1976—)	6,400 (1991)	161 (1991)	$647 mil[b] (1991)	Approx. $700 mil/year[c]
Genl. Agreement on Tariffs & Trade (GATT)	1948	Geneva	Peter Sutherland (1993—)	440 (1991)	110 (1993)	$107 mil (1991)	
Intl. Atomic Energy Agency (IAEA)	1957	Vienna	Hans Blix (1981—)	2,193 (1991)	112 (1991)	$192 mil (1991)	
Intl. Bank for Recon. & Devel./World Bank (IBRD)[d]	1946[e]	Washington, D.C.	Lewis T. Preston (1992—)	5,900 (1991)	170 (1992)	Exp. $574 mil, income $1,200 mil (1991)	$15 bil in FY 1990
Intl. Finance Corp. (IFC)	1956	Washington, D.C.	Head of IBRD	656 (1991)	141 (1991)	Exp. $529 mil, $166 mil in 1991	$2.2 bil in FY 1990
Intl. Development Assn. (IDA)[f]	1960	Washington, D.C.	Head of IBRD	140 (1991)	See note 6 below	Exp. $280 mil, $6 bil in 1991 income $286 mil (1986)	
Intl. Civil Aviation Org. (ICAO)	1944[g]	Montreal	Philippe Rochat	777 (1991)	164 (1991)	Exp. $130 mil (1990–92)	
Intl. Fund for Ag. Devel. (IFAD)	1977	Rome	Idriss Jazairy (1984—)	239 (1991)	145 (1990)	Exp. $45 mil (1991)	$280 mil (1991)
Intl. Labour Organisation (ILO)	1919[h]	Geneva	Michel Hansenne (1989—)	3,345 (1991)	152 (1991)	Exp. $330 mil (1990–91)	
Intl. Maritime Organization (IMO)	1958	London	W.A. O'Neil (1990—)	296 (1991)	135 (1991)	31 mil British pounds (1991)	
Intl. Monetary Fund (IMF)[i]	1946	Washington, D.C.	Jean-Michel Camdessus (1987—)	1,963 (1991)	170 (1992)	$476 mil (1993–94)	3,740 mil SDRs (1993)

Organization	Founded	Headquarters	Head (term)			Expenditure
Intl. Telecommunication Union (ITU)	1865[j]	Geneva	P.J. Tajanne (1989–)	736 (1991)	166 (1991)	Exp. $184 mil (1991)
UN Educational, Scientific & Cultural Org. (UNESCO)	1946	Paris	Federico Mayor (1987–)	2,771 (1991)	163 (1991)	$378 mil (1990–91)
UN Industrial Development Org. (UNIDO)	1986[k]	Vienna	Mauricio de María y Campos (1993–)	1,386 (1991)	154 (1991)	Exp. $180 mil (1990–91)
Universal Postal Union (UPU) Berne	1874[l], Adwaldo Cardoso Botto de Barros (1985–)	139 (1986)	168 (1991)	26 mil Swiss francs (1991)		
World Health Org. (WHO)	1948	Geneva	Hiroshi Nakajima (1988–)	4,694 (1991)	170 (1991)	Exp. $734 mil (1992–93)
World Intellectual Property Org. (WIPO)	1970[m]	Geneva	Arpad Bogsch (1973–)	402 (1991)	135 (1991)	Exp. $128 mil (1990–91)
World Meteorological Org. (WMO)	1951[n]	Geneva	G.O.P. Obasi (1984–)	229 (1991)	155 (1991)	Exp. 96 mil Swiss francs (1990–91)

Sources: Yearbook of the United Nations, 1986, 1991; *International Monetary Fund Annual Report, 1993: Focus, GATT Newsletter;* and other sources.
[a] Relation agreement with UN, December 1946.
[b] Total operating funds in 1991. Funded through assessed contributions of members and miscellaneous sources. Not included in regular UN budget.
[c] Much of actual funding is handled by the World Food Program.
[d] International Bank for Reconstruction and Development.
[e] Result of 1944 Bretton Woods conference.
[f] Operations are managed by IBRD.
[g] Became a UN specialized agency in 1947.
[h] Established specialized agency relation with UN in 1946.
[i] Lending and Drawings: SDR (Special Drawing Rights) 7.5 billion, approximately $8.5 billion (1991). Credit Outstanding: SDR 22 billion, approximately $26 billion.
[j] Present label, 1932; relation to UN, 1947.
[k] After being a unit within the UN secretariat since 1966.
[l] Established relation with UN in 1947.
[m] Became a specialized agency of the UN in 1974.
[n] Having been a nongovernmental organization since 1873.

Agricultural Development (IFAD), which seems to be on the same level as the FAO. The FAO has had a varied program that has, for example, included work in increasing grain production, which in 1970 earned a Nobel Prize for agronomist Norman E. Borlaug of the United States for work done in Mexico.

General Agreement on Tariffs and Trade (GATT)—Due to Become the World Trade Organization on January 1, 1995

Basic Function: To provide a forum for settling trade disputes and negotiating on tariff rates and other trade restrictions.

Three organizations were projected at the Bretton Woods Conference in 1944 to cover the major areas of international economic relations. The International Bank for Reconstruction and Development (IBRD) would handle international long-term lending and capital movements; the International Monetary Fund (IMF) would handle monetary matters and problems in the areas of foreign exchange rates and short-term finances; for its part, the International Trade Organization (ITO) would cover the field of commodity trade.

Final form for the charters of the IBRD and IMF was agreed on at Bretton Woods, but the ITO charter required further work. A series of conferences working to this end in the late 1940s culminated in a conference at Havana in 1948. The form of the charter was largely the work of the United States delegation. It seemed at the time that the establishment of the organization was close at hand, but for short-term tactical reasons President Truman did not submit the treaty to the Senate for ratification. Succeeding presidents have also failed to do so for varying reasons.

When it became obvious that there would be delay in establishing the ITO, several countries, including the United States, decided that it was desirable to go ahead with implementing some of the chapters in the ITO charter, without waiting for United States Senate ratification. United States participation in this activity was rationalized on the basis of authority allegedly granted by the successive Reciprocal Trade Agreements Acts enacted by Congress from the 1930s to date.

At any rate, out of this situation the General Agreement on Tariffs and Trade was born. This ostensibly temporary organization (pending ratification of the ITO charter) was consequently the principal functioning organization in the international trade field for over forty years. GATT has conducted a series of long-drawn-out conferences at which reductions in trade restrictions, principally tariffs, have been negotiated. Also resulting from GATT work have been a series of international raw-commodity control schemes, applicable to several widely traded raw materials (sugar, coffee, tin, etc.). Such agreements were frequent in the pre–World War II period, but they have been rather less frequent and influential since the 1940s.

Rules and tariff rates established by GATT have become influential in regulating some 80 percent of world trade.

Finally, January 1, 1995, it becomes the World Trade Organization (WTO) with expanded functions—rather than ITO.

International Atomic Energy Agency (IAEA)

Basic Function: To promote the safe, peaceful uses of atomic energy. It provides inspectors in the field to investigate compliance by countries with international agreements in the atomic field.

The IAEA is not formally designated as a specialized agency in the UN system, and yet it seems to correspond to most of the characteristics of such agencies. It was independently established by a multilateral treaty. Its activities are financed by its own assessments against its member governments. The chief clear-cut difference is that its UN relationship is with the General Assembly rather than with ECOSOC, and it reports regularly to the General Assembly. Also, it has engaged in much inspection work at the behest of the secretary-general.

The agency promotes the use of atomic energy for peaceful

purposes and assists in atomic research and the application of such research. It arranges for the exchange of information and specialists and of supplies of materials, equipment, and facilities. It applies safeguards against the diversion of materials to military use. It works under the provisions of the Treaty on Non-Proliferation of Nuclear Weapons. It offers technical aid and training and helps draft domestic laws and international conventions. It played a role in dealing with the problems arising as a result of the Chernobyl disaster in the Soviet Union in 1986. It provides inspectors in the effort to determine whether Iraq has been continuing to develop a nuclear weapons capability after the Persian Gulf War of 1990–91. It has been involved in trying to determine whether North Korea has a nuclear weapons program.

International Bank for Reconstruction and Development (IBRD)/World Bank

Basic Function: To provide loans and technical assistance for economic development projects in developing countries and encourage cofinancing.

International Finance Corporation (IFC):
   Basic Function: To foster growth of private sector in underdeveloped countries by lending. A subsidiary of the World Bank, listed above.

International Development Association (IDA):
   Basic Function: To offer low-interest, very long-term loans to finance infrastructure. A subsidiary of the World Bank, listed above.

All three of these institutions were established on the basis of ratified international agreements. The IFC and the IDA were proposed by the World Bank to meet special needs; they are housed in Washington with the World Bank and are subsidiaries of that organization. All report annually to ECOSOC and have a relationship with the United Nations, but actually the relation is quite nominal. These are major organizations, as can be seen from the magnitude of their lending. They receive no financial support from the UN.

There seems to be an institutionalized understanding that a United States citizen, nominated by the United States government, will automatically be the head of the World Bank, which means also the head of the IFC and the IDA. This arrangement may have undesirable results in terms of politicizing some or much of the lending of these institutions.

International Civil Aviation Organization (ICAO)

Basic Function: To concern itself with the orderly and safe growth of international civil aviation, that is to say with regulations and standards and questions as to whether those standards are being observed.

The coordination of criteria in these matters by the nations of the world is most important and desirable, but the possibility does exist that in evaluating fault in particular incidents the agency's judgment may be politicized. A somewhat atypical example of its work may be revealing. At an early stage in the review of the action of the American guided missile cruiser *Vincennes* in shooting down Iran Air Flight 655 over the Persian Gulf on July 3, 1988, killing all 290 people on board, the ICAO had occasion to express an opinion on the event. In its opinion it accepted the official United States view that the shooting was an accident and that the United States had therefore not violated any international conventions. This ruling did not become the last word in the matter, however. The case is still pending in the International Court of Justice.

International Fund for Agricultural Development (IFAD)

Basic Function: To provide funds for and assistance to agricultural development in the poorest countries, with especial emphasis on small farmers and the landless poor in the poorest food-deficient regions.

IFAD is financed by contributions from the Organization for Economic Cooperation and Development (OECD) and the Organization of Petroleum Exporting Countries (OPEC), organizations not affiliated with the UN, with additional financing obtained from miscellaneous organizations. The UN does not contribute substantially to its financing, but IFAD does report annually to ECOSOC. The United States is the only member of IFAD with a permanent seat on its executive board.

Despite the ostensible commitment to assist the poorest of the poor, emphasis in recent years has shifted somewhat from concessional loans at extremely low interest rates and long maturities to loans to middle-income countries under lending conditions more nearly approximating those of ordinary commercial loans.[2]

International Labour Organisation (ILO)

Basic Function: To promote employment and improve labor conditions and living standards. It has a vocational training program and engages in extensive research and publication.

The organization is financially independent of the UN but reports annually to ECOSOC. The ILO, as an organization, won the Nobel Prize in 1969.

International Maritime Organization (IMO)

Basic Function: To promote cooperation on technical matters affecting international shipping.

Matters studied by IMO include oil spills, the possibility of disposing of low-level radioactive waste at sea, and the safety of life at sea. It is not concerned with ocean freight and passenger rates nor with the regulation of fishing.

International Monetary Fund (IMF)

Basic Function: To monitor and regulate the international monetary system.

This is a major institution, established by its own international treaty and financially independent of the UN, with which it has a relationship agreement. It reports annually to ECOSOC.

The IMF works in the areas of international monetary relations, foreign exchange rates, balances of payments, and short-term lending to support or influence the exchange value of currencies. In exchange for its financial support it is prone to require from assisted governments commitments to conservative, budget-balancing finance, restrictions on the extension of new domestic credit, and espousal of a free-market, private-enterprise-oriented economic system. During 1992–93 it was actively dealing with Russia in those terms.

International Telecommunication Union (ITU)

Basic Function: To regulate international radio, telegraph, telephone, and space radio-communications. It allocates radio frequencies.

This is a low-profile, important organization whose work affects almost everyone. The United States has been very active in trying to induce the ITU to curtail costs, especially since 1981. There is temptation to say it has been excessively active in so doing, to the detriment of the work of the ITU.

United Nations Educational, Scientific and Cultural Organization (UNESCO)

Basic Function: To foster educational, scientific, and cultural work worldwide.

UNESCO's establishment was to a greater degree under direct UN sponsorship than was the case with most of the other specialized agencies. It has the characteristics of a specialized agency, nevertheless, being established by an international agreement and having a relationship understanding with the UN. Its budget is prepared by the UNESCO General Conference.

The United States became highly critical of the management and many facets of the work of UNESCO and especially of its long-time director-general Amadou M'Bow. In part, this attitude may have been a result of United States feeling that UNESCO was ideologically closer to the Soviet Union than the United States thought desirable. At any rate, the United States withdrew from UNESCO in 1984, as did the United Kingdom, though it continued to participate in some aspects of UNESCO work: the Man and the Biosphere Program, international activities in library and information service, the World Heritage Fund, combating the illicit international movement of cultural property, copyright activities sponsored by UNESCO, various Intergovernmental Oceanographic Commission activities, and the International Geological Correlation Program. The United States has continued to contribute small sums of money to support these particular activities.

The United States seems to feel that it is appropriate for it to pick and choose the UN activities in which it will participate. This attitude is not helpful to making the UN a coherently effective organization. Of course other countries may do the same thing, but the action of the United States has the greatest impact because of the large monetary assessment carried by this country.

United Nations Industrial Development Organization (UNIDO)

Basic Function: To promote and accelerate industrial development in developing countries and promote industrial cooperation and development on global, regional, national, and sectoral levels.

UNIDO is a specialized agency in the sense of being established by an international agreement among the member states, supplemented by a relationship agreement with the UN. The organization has serious organizational and financial problems, according to the United States, which has been active in monitoring its finances.[3]

Universal Postal Union (UPU)

Basic Function: To improve postal service. Concerns itself with the reciprocal exchange of postal services between nations.

Despite the small size of UPU, its work represents an important example of what the simplifying, useful results of a modicum of international cooperation can be.

World Health Organization (WHO)

Basic Function: To direct and coordinate international health work. It helps governments, at their request, in carrying out public health programs. It sets standards for drugs and vaccines, establishes guidelines and criteria in environmental health, and provides other technical services in international health. It also promotes medical research, especially now in relation to AIDS.

At the end of 1990 the United States was $27 million delinquent in its dues to this agency. Lagging support for this agency seems to be a result of United States opposition to the membership of the Palestine Liberation Organization in WHO.

World Intellectual Property Organization (WIPO)

Basic Function: To protect, through international cooperation, literary, industrial, scientific, and artistic works.

The international treaties asserting the rights that WIPO tries to protect date from 1883 and 1886. The United States has, since 1887, been a party to the Paris Convention (1883) dealing with industrial property. It did not adhere to the Berne Convention (1886) for the protection of literary and artistic works until 1989. Involved are sensitive issues involving patent protection and new technical knowledge in areas such as semiconductors.

World Meteorological Organization (WMO)

Basic Function: To promote international cooperation in collection, analysis, and exchange of information on the weather.

This is extremely important work.

World Trade Organization (WTO):
See General Agreement on Tariffs
and Trade (GATT)

Evaluation

Before Boutros Boutros-Ghali's tenure began in 1992, the United
Nations had not had a secretary-general who was seriously concerned with questions of organizational structure, coordination, and
effectiveness. Perhaps the most active, effective, and prestigious of
the secretaries-general has been Dag Hammarskjöld, but his activities were high profile in the area of peacekeeping, and he seems to
have directed little attention to the areas of effective administration
and organization. Boutros-Ghali, however, initiated some significant changes at the beginning of his term of office.

Despite the ostensible dominance of ECOSOC in supervising
activities in the economic and social field, there has been ongoing dissatisfaction among groups of professionals working in
such activity areas with what has been actually accomplished by
ECOSOC and its subsidiary organs. Consequently, interested
groups have taken independent action in stimulating the General
Assembly and the secretary-general to endorse the calling of international conferences, more or less independently of ECOSOC,
to deal with various economic and social problems. With the
autonomous conferences have come additional permanent organizations—secretariats, commissions, etc.—which frequently
have duplicated the work of the ECOSOC special agencies, and
which, not infrequently, have been resented by the relevant special agencies.

The foregoing discussion of the disorganization and proliferation of conferences and agencies dealing with economic and social matters in the United Nations may make it seem as though
bringing some order out of this administrative chaos is *the* important reform measure that the UN should take, that once that is
done there would result a trim, neat and efficient, even admira-
ble, United Nations. In fact, since the 1970s, the proliferation of

reports recommending such reform has been a nontrivial aspect of the United Nations work.

More or less permanent agencies whose principal task is watching over the efficiency of UN organization include an Administrative Committee on Coordination (ACC), a Committee for Program and Coordination (CPC), an Advisory Committee on Administrative and Budgetary Questions (ACABQ), and more.

The United Nations, thus, has responded to criticism of its administration and financing by proliferating organizations to study these problems. But there has been as yet little effective guidance and implementation of this process by administrators in high places.

It does seem to this opinionated writer that there is more involved than assuring that the UN is an efficiently operating shop, spending virtually no money. The overarching issue is whether world society wishes to permit individual countries to frustrate the group's decision as to how the organization should operate.

Yves Beigbeder, author of *Management Problems in United Nations Organizations*, says on this subject: "UN organizations have management problems in various degrees. Some organizations are dynamic, effective in their field, well administered. Others suffer from vague or over-ambitious objectives, poor leadership, lack of staff competence and motivation, politicization, and bureaucratization. . . . Administrative reform in UN organizations is necessary and it is possible, in spite of political obstacles and bureaucratic resistance to change."[4]

A point to bear in mind is that all of the UN activity in the social and economic areas has had as its chief, perhaps its only, constructive usefulness the creation of a substantial core of people who are knowledgeable as to the nature of world problems. These people can do little more than accumulate knowledge until such time as the UN is permitted by the member nations to enact meaningful, legally binding legislation in the social and economic areas. Meanwhile, the sum of money spent on this activity is fairly trivial beside the waste of money by the nations of the world on their own armed forces and in other ways—while they sanctimoniously starve the UN.

One may have other reservations with regard to the continuing criticism of UN efficiency, which one generally hears with most persistence from the developed countries that are in the process of losing some of their relative influence to the less developed countries. The less developed countries, as their voting strength in the General Assembly has risen, have endorsed many programs and expenditures that especially benefit the poorer countries. The wealthy countries have been losing a measure of their control over the largess or aid that developed countries are providing to underdeveloped countries. And they are not very happy about that.

An aspect of the effort by the United States to inhibit UN spending may be seen in the position that U.S. representatives frequently take in preliminary discussion of the budgets of various agencies. The United States frequently has pressed for the application of the principle of "zero real growth" as the chief criterion for determining the size of the total monetary appropriation change in any given year.[5] And the U.S. representatives are prone to insist on disassociating themselves from "consensus" approval of budgets that they allege do not represent zero real growth. It seems reasonable to question whether zero real growth is a desirable principle by which the UN should be forced to operate and whether the United States is serving its own interests by objections to decisions that would otherwise be approved by consensus.

Issues of this sort are further indication that a general conference is due at which the world will consider the nature of the United Nations and of the New World Order. These issues should be discussed in the open in a major forum. What sort of a world do we want? What sort of a UN, if any, do we want?

Financial Policy

The United Nations charter provides in article 17:

1. The General Assembly shall consider and approve the budget of the Organization.
2. The expenses of the Organization shall be borne by the Members as apportioned by the General Assembly.
3. The General Assembly shall consider and approve any financial and budgetary arrangements with specialized agencies referred to in Article 57 and shall examine the administrative budgets of such specialized agencies with a view to making recommendations to the agencies concerned.

The major responsibility in budget planning, the enactment of revenue-raising measures, determining the relative burden on the different member countries, and the apportionment of funds to the various money spending organs is thus vested in the General Assembly.

The practice that has been developed for preparing the budget seems to work somewhat as follows.[1] The secretary-general obtains departmental estimates of needs, which are worked over by the Budget Division of the Controller's Office. Once the secretary-general has a version of the budget with which he is satisfied, he defends it in testimony before the Advisory Committee on Administrative and Budgetary Questions of the General Assembly, which then submits its report to the General Assembly, where the whole matter is debated in the Assembly's Fifth Committee (Administrative and Budgetary). There the matter is looked on with pretty much the same attitude as was the case when the matter was before the Advisory Committee. The document is then submitted to the full General Assembly for final approval. This adds up to a long-drawn-out process so far as the Secretariat is concerned, in a setting where many of the delegates are not particularly sympathetic to much of what the Secretariat is doing. But what budget-preparing process is not long and drawn out?

Obligation to Pay

Article 17 of the charter carries the provision that "the expenses of the Organization shall be borne by the Members as apportioned by the General Assembly." And, since the charter of the United Nations has been endorsed by the treaty-making authorities in each of the member countries, this means that the member countries have a contractual obligation to pay to the United Nations the sums decided on by the General Assembly.

There is involved here one of the most important problems confronting the United Nations. Although the member countries have a contractual obligation to pay, the United Nations has no effective enforcement tool for compelling them to pay. Yet, nonpayment of assessments is a serious problem for the viability of the United Nations. Delinquents have included most of the members, rich and poor, small and large, including most of the great powers. Over the years, the Soviet Union was frequently a delinquent. More recently, the United States has been the major delinquent.

The United States has extensively and intensively used the method of threatening not to pay its assessment as leverage to force the UN to adopt policies it supports. An example of this practice should be cited: "The Bush Administration threatened today to cut off all American financing for the United Nations if this year's General Assembly agrees to any upgrading of the status of the Palestine Liberation Organization's observer mission at United Nations headquarters here."[2]

Some Financial History

The Korean War was financed by each nation providing troops for the UN force at its own expense. This might be called the voluntary contribution approach. Some later operations, for example peacekeeping in Cyprus, have also been financed by voluntary contributions. But the financing of most of the peacekeeping, beginning with Suez in 1956, has been by special assessment. These have not been the ordinary assessments that are part of the regular UN budget; they are special assessments applied to all the UN members to finance a specific peacekeeping project. The formula for establishing the special assessments is similar to but slightly different from the formula applied in the regular budget assessments. Payment of the special assessments is a legal obligation on all UN members in the same sense as the regular budget assessments.

This meant in the case of Suez that the United States and the Soviet Union, who had voted in the Security Council to condemn the Israelis, French, and British, as well as the French and British, who had vetoed the motion, were legally obligated to pay the special assessments. France and the Soviet Union refused to pay. The motivation of the Soviet Union in being unwilling to help finance an operation it had voted for seems to have been that that country was anticipating a situation in which it might be the condemned aggressor and be called on to finance troops mobilized against it.

At any rate France and the Soviet Union began to accumulate large unpaid obligations to the UN. Neither country paid the assessment made in connection with the Congo problem in 1960, either. As a result, the amount of their delinquencies was approaching a figure equal to two years of UN assessments.

The United States, at this point, decided that it was appropriate for the UN to enforce article 19 of the charter against the Russians and the French. That article states: "A Member of the United Nations which is in arrears in the payment of its financial contributions to the Organization shall have no vote in the General Assembly if the amount of its arrears equals or exceeds the amount of the contributions due from it for the preceding two years. The General Assembly may, nevertheless, permit such a Member to vote if it is satisfied that the failure to pay is due to conditions beyond the control of the Member." The matter had been coming to a head through the late fifties and early sixties, during the Eisenhower and Kennedy administrations and the beginning of the Johnson administration. During those years the United States had been reasonably reliable in paying its assessments and therefore had some right to be critical of the delinquents.

The attempt to formalize the procedure for enforcing article 19 began on December 20, 1961, when, on the suggestion of the United States, the General Assembly asked the International Court of Justice for an advisory opinion on the matter. The court replied with an expression to the effect that the assessment to finance the peacekeeping forces in Suez and the Congo constituted binding financial obligations on all the members, even though all were not automatically obligated to provide troops. So the situation stood in 1964.

Meanwhile, a notable change had occurred in the power structure in the General Assembly. The so-called Non-Aligned Movement (NAM) countries had come to dominate the General Assembly, which had grown to 115 members. The United States could no longer command an automatic majority in that body. And the majority was not prepared to enforce the penalty of deprivation of voting rights against the delinquent Russians and French. Up to that time the United States had found the General Assembly more cooperative than the Security Council; from 1964 onward the United States became increasingly soured in attitude toward the General Assembly and its underdeveloped-country majority.

At any rate, in 1964, the refusal of the General Assembly to penalize the Russians and French resulted in a stalemate in that body that involved *not voting on anything* during the year. The United Nations was in crisis. Various measures, including the budget, were agreed to by a laboriously worked out consensus. On issues where no consensus could be worked out, no action was taken. The UN could scarcely be called a functioning organization at that time.

But the United States was becoming less sure as to where its own interests lay. What if the time should come when it was the United States that objected to paying assessments to support actions of which it did not approve? So, the United States executed a historic reversal of position on August 16, 1965. It renounced its endorsement of enforcement of article 19 against nonpayers of assessments. On that day United States ambassador to the United Nations Arthur Goldberg stated: "If any Member can insist on making an exception to the principle of collective financial responsibility with respect to certain activities of the organization, the United States reserves the same option to make exceptions if, in our view, strong and compelling reasons exist for doing so."[3]

From that time onward it became increasingly popular for countries to hold out on the payment of UN assessments that they had an obligation, established by signing the UN charter, to honor. In the United States the practice of holding out on funds owed the UN became popular in the executive branch—regardless of who was president—popular in Congress with both political parties, and popular with the general public, at least with those who objected to paying taxes and those who were indignant about the prevalence of "United States bashing" in the General Assembly.

The changeover from a situation in which the United States could virtually command a General Assembly majority to one in which criticism of the United States was a prevailing theme produced quite a change in the attitude of United States ambassadors to the United Nations from the polite and thoughtful Adlai Stevenson of the earlier period to the caustic and scornful Jeane Kirkpatrick of the Reagan era. The United States increasingly held out against paying all of its regular assessment, but it also began using nonpayment as leverage to force United States-endorsed policies on the United Nations. The United States was in a favorable position for doing this because it was head and shoulders ahead of the other countries in terms of the size of its assessment quota. Nonpayment by the United States contributed to a threat that the United Nations would not be able to meet its next payroll. Meanwhile, the United States was also finding particular United Nations programs of which it disapproved, especially UNESCO.

By 1986, secretary-general Javier Pérez de Cuéllar, in his annual report to the General Assembly, was lamenting: "1986 has witnessed the United Nations subjected to a severe crisis challenging its solvency and viability. Precisely at the time when renewed efforts have been called for to strengthen the Organization, its work has been shadowed by financial difficulties resulting primarily from the failure of Member States to meet obligations flowing from the charter. It is essential to lift this cloud . . . ; to ignore this necessity is to imperil the future prospects of a better world."

In 1990 another major change in the attitude of the United States toward the United Nations occurred in connection with Iraq's invasion of Kuwait. After years of being supportive of the Iraqis and Saddam Hussein in the context of the Iran-Iraq War, President Bush decided to lead the resistance to the Iraqi invasion of Kuwait and very imaginatively proceeded to use the United Nations as the cover organization for that resistance. Many countries found it much more acceptable to participate in a United Nations action than a purely United States endeavor. And the United States sponsored resolutions that consistently passed the fifteen-member Security Council with only two or three negative votes or abstentions. Above all, the Soviet Union (with its deteriorating situation) found it comfortable to go along in support of this succession of resolutions. Most important was the resolution justifying the use of force to evict Iraq from Kuwait.

The United Nations ostensibly played a major role in the Persian Gulf War, but it was not a United Nations peacekeeping force that did the fighting. President Bush overtly rejected the suggestion that, even nominally, the United States forces involved should be considered as United Nations forces fighting under the United Nations flag. (The United States made a greater concession to the United Nations' role during the Korean War in 1950.)

Current Financial Situation

The financial arrangements of the United Nations are *sui generis*. Nothing like them has been seen before in the area of public finance. The UN levies no taxes, direct or indirect. The basic money-raising device is the compulsory assessment, which member nations assume the obligation of paying when they sign the UN charter. The UN General Assembly establishes the criteria to determine the size of the assessment set for each nation, as well as the total amount to be collected. It repeats this process with each new budget.

The formula that the General Assembly has applied in making its legally binding assessments has taken into account assorted factors, including per capita income and indebtedness. But the chief factor has been a ten-year average of the country's gross domestic product (converted into U.S. dollars at official exchange rates). Countries such as Russia, which have experienced a major decline in production in the last three or four years, are not happy with the ten-year average approach. They would prefer something like three years. The shorter period would make their assessment correspond better with their current ability to pay, which is changing rapidly.

Sources of funds to support the United Nations are of three types: assessments in the regular budget, assessments to support peacekeeping operations, and voluntary contributions. An appreciation of the magnitudes involved can be obtained from Table 7.1 presented later in this chapter, "1992 Budget for the UN and its Affiliated Programs, by Source of Financing." In the 1992 regular budget, the assessment each member nation was obligated to pay, stated as a percentage of the total regular budget, was as follows for the top ten contributors:

United States	25.00%
Japan	12.45
Russian Federation	9.41
Germany (including East Germany)	8.93
France	6.00
United Kingdom	5.02
Italy	4.29
Canada	3.11
Spain	1.98
Netherlands	1.50

A somewhat different formula is used for computing peacekeeping percentages, and assigns to the United States a 30 percent share of the total of those assessments.

It is interesting to note that two of the top five countries, Japan and Germany, are not among the five permanent members of the Security Council. No wonder they feel aggrieved and entitled to permanent seats on the Security Council.

Many, or most, of the subsidiary organizations in the UN system obtain much or all of their funding from voluntary contributions or other arrangements that are not included in the regular budget. Nations may be willing to make voluntary contributions because they especially approve of the work of a particular organization, such as, for example, the World Health Organization or the Universal Postal Union. Other organizations, such as the International Monetary Fund and the World Bank, which are affiliated with the UN system, nevertheless were established under separate treaty arrangements with their member governments, and the size of the government contributions may be legally set by these separate treaties. The sums involved are not included in any UN budget. An organization such as the International Monetary Fund, although it is handling huge sums of money, may not be any noticeable financial drain on its member countries because it is making money from its banking activities or some other way.

The "Status of Contributions to the United Nations' Regular Budget for 1994 as at 28 February 1994" was set out in United Nations, Secretariat (ST/ADM/SER. B/431) of March 8, 1994. The first column is current-year contributions (assessments) payable as of January 1, 1994. The second column is contributions outstanding and overdue as of February 28, 1994, for both current and prior years. The third column is contributions for prior years which are overdue.

Status of Contributions to Regular UN Budget, 1994 (in US$1,000)

	Current Year Contributions (Assessments) (Due January 1, 1994)	Total Overdue (as of February 28, 1994)	Prior Year Overdue
1. United States	$ 298,260	$ 530,919	$232,659
2. Japan	126,652	126,652	0
3. Russian Federation	68,260	68,260	0
4. Germany	90,844	45,422	0
5. France	61,037	61,037	0
6. United Kingdom	51,068	38,301	0
7. Italy	43,642	43,642	0
...	...	...	...
19. China	7,833	7,833	0
Totals (all members)	$1,061,853	$1,256,179	$401,184

These figures are really quite remarkable. The total regular budget assessments for 1994 scarcely exceeded one billion dollars.

A somewhat different table dealing with contributions to peacekeeping as of February 28, 1994, is as follows (figures again in US $1,000):

Status of Contributions to Peacekeeping and Totals

	Total cumulated contributions (Assessments) (Payable as of Jan. 1, 1994)	Total Outstanding and Overdue (as of Feb. 28, 1994)
1. United States	$ 350,952	$ 284,859
2. Japan	83,206	3,432
3. Russia	530,694	480,963
. . .	. . .	. . .
Totals for peacekeeping	1,511,447	1,203,869
Regular budget totals	1,061,853	1,256,179
Total peacekeeping and regular budget	$2,573,300	$2,460,048
Total US peacekeeping and regular budget	$ 649,212	$ 815,778
Total Russia peacekeeping and regular budget	$ 598,954	$ 487,783

To the conscientious reader who has checked whether $298 million is 25 percent of $1,061 million I can only say I have no ready explanation for the discrepancy. But it is interesting to note that a similar discrepancy in the peacekeeping picture favors the United States more than the regular budget discrepancy harms.

The United Nations peacekeeping operations covered in this tabulation have involved Egypt, Lebanon, Iran and Iraq, Angola, Namibia, Iraq and Kuwait, the Western Sahara, El Salvador, Cambodia, Yugoslavia, Somalia, Mozambique, Cyprus, Georgia, Haiti, Liberia, Rwanda, and Cambodia.

Contributions (assessments) are due and payable as of the first of the year, but various countries have more or less valid excuses for paying at later dates. For example, it may be more convenient to pay at the beginning of the country's own fiscal year, which may not be January 1. Supplementary assessments may be made during the course of the year, which are likely to be due and payable when they are made or shortly thereafter. Thus, "the assessments through February 28" are a combination of the assessments due January 1 and some changes.

In late 1992 the Ford Foundation, in consultation with the office of the UN secretary-general, organized the Independent Advisory Group on United Nations Financing. Shijuro Ogata of Japan and Paul Volcker of the United States were the co-chairmen of the group. In February 1993 they published a report entitled *Financing an Effective United Nations*. Table 7.1, "1992 Budget for the UN and its Affiliated Programs, by Source of Financing," is a result of their labors. The totals for the regular budget and for peacekeeping look much like those already presented. The estimates of voluntary contributions represent a significant bit of additional information, as does the breakdown in terms of programs. Big numbers that emerge involve economic development ($265 million), environment and drugs ($269 million), refugees and humanitarian relief ($956 million), the UN Development Program ($241 million), and the Children's Fund ($896 million). The total for the UN and affiliates that emerges, of $5.3 billion, is significantly larger than the figures for the regular budget and peacekeeping alone of $2.5 billion.

At least up to the end of 1992, the United States continued to be an adamant opponent of providing increased funding to the UN. In each of the many agencies of the UN, as the annual budget requests were prepared, the role of the United States representative has been vigorously to argue for the principle of zero real growth. As phrased by the Department of State, "The United States does not commit itself to these arbitrary goals, nor does it support increases in international organization budget beyond zero real growth."[4]

In 1993 the United States budgeted $273 billion for the Department of Defense. It is hard to believe that it cannot find a billion or two or even ten or twenty billion to help make UN peacekeeping a credible activity.

Worth citing are the conclusions of the Ogata-Volcker (Ford Foundation) report on United Nations Financing:

> The advisory group has tried to address the problem of the U.N.'s financing in a practical and realistic way. Our recommendations are intended to provide more consistent and reliable funding of U.N. activities in the interest of the U.N.'s effectiveness, and to facilitate the work of the Secretary-General. They are also intended to make it easier for governments to meet their financial obligations to the U.N.
>
> We have been impressed in particular by the contrast between the demands placed on the United Nations and the smallness and precariousness of its financial base. Any great political institution has to develop with the times, and that development often causes growing pains. In the post–cold war era, the United Nations is being asked to develop very fast and to take on vital responsibilities of a kind, and on a scale undreamed of in its earlier years.
>
> Many of the tasks the U.N. is now undertaking are pioneering efforts in new fields. They will set precedents for vital activities in the future. It is essential that the world organization have the financial backing, as well as the administrative and operational capacity, to make these efforts successful and workable models for the difficult years to come.
>
> The United Nations remains the only existing framework for building the institutions of a global society. While practicing all the requisite managerial rigor and financial economy, it must have the resources—a pittance by comparison with our society's expenditures on arms or illicit drugs—to serve the great objectives that are set forth in its charter. Surely the world is ready for, and urgently in need of, a more effective U.N.

Possible Policies

It is important that the United Nations have a revenue source that is free of dependence on national governments, especially since, as matters stand, it lacks leverage to force the member states to make good on their legal assessments. It was the making of the United States of America when the new constitution in 1789 gave a direct source of revenue to the central government—in that case, the right to collect customs duties on imports. (The provision for direct election of members of the House of Representatives also helped to establish the independence of the national government from the whims of state

Table 7.1

1992 Budget for the UN and Its Affiliated Programs, by Source of Financing (thousands of $)

Program	Regular Budget	Peackeeping Assessment	Voluntary Contributions	Total
United Nations				
Overall policy making (includes secretary-general and General Assembly)	17,931	0	1,801	19,732
Political and Security Council affairs	11,438	0	47	11,435
Peacekeeping operations	32,797	1,327,000[a]	30,800	1,390,597
Special political questions: Palestine, disarmament, decolonization, and apartheid	21,482	0	12,671	34,153
International justice and law	24,519	83	1,494	26,096
Economic development	287,257	0	265,813	553,070
Environment and drugs	15,757	0	269,268	285,025
Human rights	12,109	0	6,200	18,309
Refugees and humanitarian relief	37,284	0	956,209	993,493
Public information	50,497	0	3,000	53,497
Administrative & capital expenses + staff assessment	670,420	6,037	18,459	694,916
Total expenditures	1,181,491	1,333,120	1,565,762	4,080,373

Affiliated Programs			
UN Development Program[b]	0	0	241,000	241,000
UN Fund for Population Activities[b]	0	0	55,305	55,305
UNICEF	0	0	896,000	896,000
Total, UN & Affiliates	1,181,491	1,333,120	2,758,067	5,272,678

Source: Shijuro Ogata and Paul Volcker, *Financing an Effective United Nations* (New York: Ford Foundation, 1993), p. 28.

[a]This figure represents the approximate amount the UN actually spent on assessed peacekeeping missions in calendar year 1992. The amount the UN assessed member states for peacekeeping in 1992 was slightly higher—about $1.54 billion.

[b]These figures represent only the core budgets of UNDP and UNFPA, which include projects executed by these agencies themselves. Most of UNDP's resources—which totaled approximately $1.5 billion in 1991—and a portion of UNFPA's are distributed to other UN programs and to the specialized agencies.

governors and legislatures.) A government, to be credible, should have both a popular base and the power to tax.

The working out of a reasonable set of taxing arrangements will, no doubt, be a continuing problem. But, provisionally, a corporate income tax applicable to corporations chartered with the UN seems a likely candidate. (This possibility is discussed in chapter 8, "The International Court of Justice.") This is especially true because of the difficulty individual countries experience in equitably taxing multinational corporations. Even as large a country as the United States finds taxing the multinationals to be difficult. Corporations that are operating internationally and using transfer pricing and tax haven techniques are adept at making their profits show up in the jurisdiction with the lowest tax rates in order to avoid taxes. Equitable taxation of corporations requires that the tax be imposed by a level of government with jurisdiction over the whole area of operation of the corporation. In the case of multinational or transnational corporations, where national government taxing efforts have generally been ineffective and frustrating, it requires a government such as the United Nations, with transnational jurisdiction, to have a chance of obtaining the information necessary for effectively and equitably taxing the corporation. The documents signed in connection with chartering the company with the UN should be strongly stated so as to insure that the UN has access to the appropriate information.

It is likely that multinational corporations would vigorously oppose an international corporate income tax—and probably effectively—unless there is more to the story. The statute of the International Court of Justice could be amended to permit appeals from decisions of national supreme courts to that court. Multinational corporations have had a continuing problem in getting what they consider to be justice at the hands of the national political and court systems of the countries where they have their investments. Such protection for firms operating internationally would be assured only by chartering with the UN, which would give that body the leverage to establish and maintain a corporate income tax on those organizations. The tendency of the corporations to cooperate could also be strengthened if the nation-level corporate tax were deductible from the UN tax up to some established percentage of the UN tax, for example 50 percent. Of course, enforcing such a corporate income tax would require that the UN have officials with police power operating within individual countries, much as the United States government has marshals with police power operating within individual states.

The cooperativeness of the governments of the debtor countries with the provision for appeals from their national courts to the International Court of Justice at The Hague could be encouraged by the realization that they were thereby gaining relief from the tendency of the British Foreign Office and the U.S. Department of State to come to the support of their corporations when they run into trouble in the debtor countries. Historically, such support has frequently involved the use of military force in addition to assorted types of economic pressures. Controlling adventures of this sort by the judicious use of a procedure for appealing cases to the international court could be an epoch-making step in sanitizing international relations.

In addition to the corporate income tax, the idea of an assessment taking the form of a percentage of the military budget of each country has some very useful implications, besides raising money at the expense of the militarily active and aggressive nations. The comparative usefulness of their military force to warlike world leaders is conditioned by their belief that their armies can win the war they are conjuring up. The provision that each nation must contribute a sum of money equal to 25 or 30 percent of its armed forces budget to the United Nations should give any warlike leader pause. That leader would be automatically looking at a United Nations force that would be intimidating.

Nations do not automatically and responsibly pay their UN assessments, and in the present system the UN lacks leverage in obtaining the funds. Until the UN is adequately financed, those who enjoy deploring the inadequacies of the UN seem blithely to disregard the reason for those inadequacies.

_____8

The International
Court of Justice

The International Court of Justice (ICJ), which is a principal
organ in the UN system, has antecedents that go back to the late
nineteenth century. An organization called the Permanent Court
of Arbitration, also called The Hague Tribunal, was established
at The Hague in the Netherlands in 1899. Its function was to
provide panels of arbitrators to handle international disputes
when the nations who were parties to the disputes decided to
make use of such machinery. The Permanent Court of Arbitration continues to exist to this day. It is not particularly busy,
but it has a role in selecting the judges on the International
Court of Justice.

At the close of World War I, in connection with the negotiation of the Treaty of Versailles and the establishment of the
League of Nations, the United States delegation headed by
Woodrow Wilson worked to set up a world court, the Permanent
Court of International Justice, also at The Hague. The court was
organized pursuant to article 14 of the covenant of the League of
Nations, its protocol having been ratified in 1921 by the requisite
number of nations. But the United States Senate refused to ratify
the protocol without reservations, and the United States failed to
join the court at the same time that it was also rejecting membership in the League of Nations itself.

Structure and Function of the
International Court of Justice

At the close of World War II it was decided to suppress the Permanent Court of International Justice and substitute for it an organization with a similar role and with its own statute, to be called the International Court of Justice. Its headquarters were also established at The Hague. Slightly modified, the statute of the Permanent Court of International Justice became the statute of the International Court of Justice and by article 92 of the charter of the United Nations was declared an integral part of that charter.

The court consists of fifteen judges who are elected by the General Assembly and the Security Council from a list of people nominated by the national groups in the Permanent Court of Arbitration. Articles 3 through 12 of the statute of the International Court of Justice are devoted to the niceties of this selection procedure. Members of the court are elected for nine years and may be re-elected. The expenses of the court are borne by the United Nations' regular budget. The membership of the court in 1994 was as follows:

Judge	Country of Nationality	End of Term
Shigeru Oda	Japan	2003
Carl-August Fleischhauer	Germany	2003
Abdul G. Koroma	Sierra Leone	2003
Robert Ago	Italy	1997
Stephen M. Schwebel, vice president	United States	1997
Mohammed Bedjaoui, president	Algeria	1997
Shi Jiuyong	China	2003
Geza Herczegh	Hungary	2003
Nikolaï K. Tarassov	Russia	1997
Gilbert Guillaume	France	2000
Mohamed Shuhabuddeen	Guyana	1997
Andrés Aguilar Mawdsley	Venezuela	2000
Christopher G. Weeramantry	Sri Lanka	2000
Raymond Ranjeva	Madagascar	2000
Sir Robert Y. Jennings	United Kingdom	2000

In a dispute court rules allow each country to add one ad hoc judge to the court's fifteen regular members.

Article 36 of the ICJ statute describes the nature of cases over which the court has jurisdiction:

    a. the interpretation of a treaty;
    b. any question of international law;
    c. the existence of any fact which, if established, would constitute a breach of an international obligation;
    d. the nature or extent of the reparation to be made for the breach of an international obligation.

The sources of the principles that the court applies in deciding cases are set out in article 38 of the statute as:

    a. international conventions, whether general or particular, establishing rules expressly recognized by the contesting states;
    b. international custom, as evidence of a general practice accepted as law;
    c. the general principles of law recognized by civilized nations;
    d. . . . judicial decisions and the teachings of the most highly qualified publicists of the various nations, as subsidiary means for the determination of rules of law.
    2. This provision shall not prejudice the power of the Court to decide a case *ex aequo et bono*, if the parties agree thereto.

This means that, with the agreement of the parties, the court may decide a case on the basis of its own good judgment.

The charter of the United Nations provides in article 93 that "All members of the United Nations are *ipso facto* parties to the Statute of the International Court of Justice." Special procedures may also grant membership to states that are not members of the United Nations.

According to article 94 of the charter: "Each Member of the United Nations undertakes to comply with the decision of the International Court of Justice in any case to which it is a party." Procedures exist by which refusal to comply may be referred to the Security Council, which may "if it deems necessary, make recommendations or decide upon measures to be taken to give effect to the judgment." There are potential teeth in the provision "decide upon measures to be taken." This has been a sticking point with the United States, which has, upon occasion, not been especially cooperative in respecting judgments made against this country. In subscribing to the charter in 1946, this country recognized the compulsory jurisdiction of the court in relation to any other state accepting the same obligation. Then it added the so-called Connally amendment, which excluded from the court's jurisdiction "disputes with regard to matters which are essentially within the jurisdiction of the United States of America as determined by the United States of America." Note that the Connally amendment was merely a rider attached to domestic legislation. It was not an amendment to the UN charter.

By article 96, either the General Assembly or the Security Council may request the International Court of Justice to give an advisory opinion on any legal question. Other organs of the United Nations and specialized agencies, if authorized by the General Assembly, may do the same. Such requests have been made, and the court's opinions have been a useful factor in resolving issues.

Member states may (article 36 of the statute of the court) "declare that they recognize as compulsory . . . the jurisdiction of the court" in the types of cases listed in article 36 and identified in an earlier paragraph. The United States has not agreed to comply with compulsory jurisdiction; Russia has. According to statute article 55, "Questions shall be decided by a majority of the judges present," and according to article 60: "The judgment is final and without appeal. In the event of dispute as to the meaning or scope of the judgment, the court shall construe it upon the request of any party."

Through 1985 the court had given forty-three judgments in contentious cases and handed down eighteen advisory opinions. One case handled by the court involved proceedings brought by the United States against Iran, November 29, 1979, for the seizure of the United States embassy and the holding of United States diplomatic and consular staff as hostages. The court found Iran at fault and set up a procedure for determining reparations. Not much has come of this, however.

A case was brought before the court by Nicaragua on April 9, 1984, involving the United States. The United States had been mining Nicaraguan harbors to prevent military supplies being brought in by the Nicaraguan government, although the United States was not in a state of war with Nicaragua. Anticipating difficulties, on April 6, 1984, "the United States Government notified the Secretary-General that a Declaration [a qualified declaration; recall the discussion of the Connally amendment] it had made in 1946, accepting the compulsory jurisdiction of the International Court of Justice, would not apply for a period of two years 'to disputes with any Central American State or arising out of or related to events in Central America.' "[1]

On November 26, 1984, the court ruled that it did have jurisdiction over the case. But on January 18, 1985, the United States refused to participate in further proceedings in connection with the case. On June 27, 1986, the court ruled anyway that the United States had breached international law and ordered it to pay reparations. The amount was not specified in the ruling, but apparently a substantial sum of money was involved, in the billions. When the government of Daniel Ortega in Nicaragua was replaced in 1990 by a government headed by Violeta Barrios de Chamorro, the International Court requested the new government to present appropriate evidence on the question of the size of reparations owed. Apparently under some pressure from the United States government, to which she feels indebted, Señora Chamorro has delayed doing this. If the government of Nicaragua never follows through with evidence on the amount of damages, the United States government may well be off the hook in this matter.

A situation involving a request by the General Assembly for an advisory opinion occurred in connection with the role of the Palestine Liberation Organization at the United Nations. On March 3, 1988, the General Assembly voted to request the court for an advisory opinion as to whether a United States effort to close down the PLO mission to the UN was a violation of the UN's 1947 headquarters agreement with the United States (which was discussed in chapter 1). The court ruled that it was a violation. The privilege of the PLO to maintain a mission has been continued. It is now called the Office of the Permanent Observer for Palestine to the United Nations.

On July 3, 1988, Iran Air Flight 655, while on an ordinary, scheduled commercial flight over the Persian Gulf, was shot down by the United States guided missile cruiser *Vincennes*. All 290 people on board were killed. On May 18, 1989, Iran filed a brief with the court asking for a ruling that the United States violated conventions regulating international air traffic. They requested a ruling that would censure the United States; order it to pay damages for the loss of the plane, its passengers, and crew; and determine the amount of damages owed. Unlike its attitude in the Nicaraguan case, on September 1, 1989, the United States agreed to accept court jurisdiction of the case and defend its position in court. The case was still pending five years later.

Other recent action by the court has involved a 1992 ruling on the location of the boundary between El Salvador and Honduras. Apparently, the parties will respect this judgment.

In a 1993 action involving genocide in Bosnia, the court ruled: "that the Government of the Federal Republic of Yugoslavia should in particular insure that any military, paramilitary or irregular armed units which may be directed or supported by it, as well as organizations and persons which may be subject to its control, direction or influence, do not commit any act of genocide, or conspiracy to commit genocide, or direct any public incitement to commit genocide or of complicity in genocide, whether directly against the Muslim population of Bosnia and Herzegovina or against any other national, ethical, racial or religious group."[2] Implementing this approach, in May 1993 the Security Council passed a resolution providing for setting up a special tribunal to prosecute war criminals in Yugoslavia. Under that resolution the tribunal will be empowered to impose prison terms but not death sentences. Membership on the tribunal is by nomination by the Security Council and election by the General Assembly.

The Nature of International Law

The principles of international law guide the ICJ in its decisions. General agreement on certain rules, such as the respectful treatment of ambassadors and heralds, has existed since ancient times. Even though these rules were sometimes violated, meaningful pressures forced most rulers to conform. A ruler had better be concerned for the welfare of his own diplomats if he abuses the diplomats of other countries. Hugo Grotius (1583–1645) attempted to codify these observed rules in the law of war and peace, *De Juri belli et pacis*, and alleged that what was involved was meaningful law. In fact, those precepts have generally been as well observed as a lot of statute law.

International law has been much disparaged. If it is conceived that, to be classified as law, a precept has to be backed up by a force (police or army) and a court capable of enforcing compliance or inflicting punishment on a transgressor, then, arguably, there may not be much international *law*. If a precept, such as one against the use of poison gas, were strongly supported by some and generally observed, but with isolated exceptions, one might within reason choose to call it a law, and countries would be under strong pressure to conform. If a precept were supported by an international convention signed by quite a few countries agreeing to condemn (or abstain from) the use of some warlike measure, it might be meaningfully considered international law, even though all countries did not sign the convention and some actively violate it. Some who violated it might have occasion to wish they had not, and they might improve their behavior. In the last two hundred years or so, the number of such conventions has increased, and perhaps, some appearances to the contrary notwithstanding, compliance with precepts of this sort has increased sufficiently to justify referring to international law as involving a substantial range of meaningful concepts.

In fact, this process has already gone far enough so that one may legitimately describe the process by which international law has grown. It is pretty much the same process as that by which the body of the common law grew in England and in the United States. The heart of the process is not the formulation of a comprehensive legal code at the beginning. There is no "beginning." One can observe that at some historical stage certain norms of behavior were expected, and those who did not respect them frequently had occasion to wish they had. Such circumstances influence ongoing change.

A possible scenario is that there exists a problem, such as slavery, one among several problems that have actually illustrated the process. By successive steps, certain official pronouncements—by Great Britain (1833), by the United States Emancipation Proclamation (January 1, 1863), and, much later, by a United Nations declaration on the subject (1956)—were made against slavery. Although no doubt vestiges of slavery still exist in the world, one can now say with some assurance that it is a principle of international law that slavery is illegal.

The meaning (and at the same time the ambiguity) of the concept of illegality may also be illustrated with the issue of torture. Third parties seeing or hearing about torture are likely to be offended, and with the passage of time they have increasingly desired to prevent such behavior. But what is or may be involved in terms of how to prevent it? On December 10, 1984, "the General Assembly of the United Nations adopted an international convention against torture and other cruel, inhuman or degrading treatment or punishment."[3] Does such a convention constitute law? If it were sufficiently persuasive to influence most, but not necessarily all, potential torturers to abstain from the practice, one might say that it is a part of international law. Also, one might speak of it as institutionalizing a behavior norm, a behavior pattern that general social acceptance constrains most people to accept.

But it does not give law enforcement officers authorization to arrest offenders. The precept may actually have the desired effect of producing observance without law enforcement officers having a role. And it may be helpful to them as they carry out their standard enforcement role. The United Nations convention as it stands does not provide enforcement machinery. What it does do is provide that "the states that are party to the Convention are obligated to take effective legislative, administrative, judicial or other measures to prevent acts of torture. . . ."[4]

The United States passed such legislation, which became United States domestic law in March 1992, the Torture Victim Protection Act (TVPA). This law gave victims of torture or summary execution the right to seek compensation from the people who injured them if the people responsible are found in the United States.[5] Such a suit has been brought in Honolulu against the estate of the former Philippine president Ferdinand Marcos and won, and the trial has moved to the stage involving the determination of the amount of compensation for damages in the cases of about ten thousand victims of torture, "disappearance," or summary execution. That process, for better or worse, will take time.

There would be a good deal more respect for the precepts of international law if more cases were brought before the International Court of Justice, if more rulings were made condemnatory of the nation practicing the objectionable behavior, and if the United Nations actually were in position to use force to enforce appropriate behavior when all else fails.

Some examples of international conventions that might be the basis for ICJ action include a 1948 convention condemning genocide, a 1949 convention banning trafficking in prostitutes and similar forms of slavery, a 1952 convention guaranteeing the political rights of women, a 1965 convention banning racism, and the 1984 convention outlawing torture, as well as restrictions on whaling, poison gas, and war as an instrument of national policy. These conventions condemn practices. They have generally been ratified by enough countries to justify the contention that they constitute international law that appropriate courts, such as the ICJ, could legitimately implement—if the courts would act and if tools for enforcement were available.

For a significant change in respect for international law to occur, it would be helpful if two or three great powers set a better example. The United States could make a contribution to establishing general respect for the rule of law in the world if, when an International Court of Justice ruling goes against this country, it would comply with the ruling. The United States' refusal to respect the court finding against it in the case involving the mining of the Nicaraguan ports in the 1980s is a case in point.

Somalia

The absence of a government in Somalia and the terrible exploitation and oppression of their own people by Somali warlords and their henchmen arguably provided a basis for international action against offending individuals, there being no government in the country at the same time that there was terrorism by the strong. The international action should not have been limited to the gentle pushing aside of the warlords and their henchmen in order to get the relief supplies through. Getting food and supplies through to starving people was important and worthwhile, but in this especially clear-cut case the action should not have been limited to those tasks.

Here was a region where there was chaos. Article 2, paragraph 7, "Nothing contained in the present Charter shall authorize the United Nations to intervene in matters which are essentially within the domestic jurisdiction of any state . . . ," was *not* applicable. There was no "state" for the UN to interfere with. There was no law, no protection for ordinary individuals against armed predators. The situation is simply not dealt with in the UN Charter. It is worth considering the proposition that under such circumstances it is desirable for the United Nations to intervene with police power, powerful police power, and run the country until the establishment of a responsible government has been worked out.

Jurisdiction and Personal Justice

As matters stand, "only states may be parties in cases before the Court" (article 34 of the statute). But also (article 65): "The Court may give an advisory opinion on any legal question at the request of whatever body may be authorized by or in accordance with the Charter of the United Nations to make such a request." Thus, there is no supranational court, no court above national supreme courts, empowered to hear appeals by private citizens of judgments of national supreme courts. But, apparently, governments might request opinions on situations involving private citizens exclusively.

Failure of local courts to provide a rough approximation of justice even to their own citizens is a state of affairs that exists. We are talking about situations where there would seem to be a general worldwide consensus that the national procedure of some particular country and its government does not necessarily provide "justice" to individuals. This might be called a world "community-accepted" value judgment, and it may be the sensitive point where it is possible to get hold of the problem of domestic injustice. Even tyrannies might, if pressured and in order to give themselves a flavor of international credibility, agree *pro forma* to permit appeals by private citizens to international courts. Then the problem becomes one of gradually making this pro forma commitment meaningful.

For the international rule of law to work, there must be satisfactory procedures for dealing with the problems of foreigners in the countries where they are operating or visiting. Some multinational corporations may have behaved improperly in the debtor or host countries and have been expropriated or confiscated or heavily taxed by that government. Rocks may have been thrown at embassies and people shot in the process. The issues wax complicated. Some in the host country may have encouraged the foreign investment in order to facilitate economic development or because they could personally profit. Arrogant and affluent foreigners may not have endeared themselves to the local population. The foreign investors may be making generous or overly generous profits, or they may be perceived in that light because of their affluent living style. The investors' property may be seized, perhaps arbitrarily. The investors may have trouble getting an impartial hearing in the local courts. The investors' home government may use pressure, even military force, to protect the interests of the creditors. The United States Marines have sometimes provided this force, especially in Central America; so have the British and French navies. This drama has been played out to an unsatisfactory conclusion innumerable times since the Napoleonic wars.

What follows is a possible pattern for dealing with such problems. It is not the only such pattern, but at least it indicates something by way of a possible acceptable solution under the rule of law. The pattern involves, on the one hand, the right of appeal from national supreme courts to an international court and, on the other hand, an international corporate income tax combined with a system of grants-in-aid to the individual countries (especially underdeveloped countries) of much of the tax proceeds from the international corporate income tax.

In the pattern being discussed here, underdeveloped countries might still apply taxes to and perhaps even expropriate or confiscate the property of foreigners, but the foreign investor who felt abused by the action of the host government would have the right to appeal from the host-country courts to an international court. The host government would be obligated to respect the ruling of the international court. Powerful countries as well as small countries would have to respect the obligation to obey the verdicts of the international courts. And creditor-country governments and their foreign offices and state departments and congresses perhaps would abstain from using force at their own discretion to protect their countries' foreign investors.

The possibility of the receipt of grants-in-aid from the United Nations as a byproduct of the international corporate income tax should be helpful in obtaining the willingness of the host-country governments to accept the abridgment of their sovereignty that might seem implied in the right of the foreign investors to appeal to international courts. A source of international economic aid that is independent of cold-war politics and the bilateral foreign-aid negotiations that have poisoned the post–World War II years should contribute to the general merit of the package from the underdeveloped-country point of view. Of course, the real test of such arrangements will occur when a great power that believes its interests will be adversely affected by so doing agrees to accept a ruling of the international court. One may hope that the changed world climate, created by the existence of a respectably strong UN-commanded international police force, would also be a healthy influence in inducing great and small powers to respect international court decisions.

If what was involved was an international corporate income tax and nothing more, the multinational corporations would undoubtedly vigorously resist the imposition of such a tax by the United Nations. But that is not all that would be involved. The multinationals, if they are capable of good judgment, have a major interest in the creation of an international system characterized by the rule of law. True, in the past they have been ingenious in taking advantage of international chaos and the weakness of small-country governments and frequently have induced their home governments to use force to protect their interests. But they have paid a price in becoming the objects of debtor-country ill will and in being a target for violence and even confiscation in the event of civil disturbance and revolution. An effectively working business community requires the existence of impartial courts and meaningful police power to enforce the sanctity of contract. If corporations can obtain the rule of law in exchange for the international corporate income tax, they will have struck a good bargain.

Enforcement

There are enforcement problems in connection with ICJ decisions against national governments and individuals. The latter problem could well become serious if the ICJ should acquire jurisdiction over cases involving individuals. As previously mentioned, it would be appropriate for the UN to have an organization of officials who could, when necessary, arrest and detain the individual transgressors wherever found.

What is involved is merely one more echelon in a hierarchy of law enforcement officers that already has more than one level in all countries. Many countries have national police or, as in the United States, federal marshals. They have, or may have, state or province level police, city or municipal police, park police, and many more varieties. Arrangements are commonly worked out that involve sharing jail facilities. Police organizations can and do cooperate. They already have an international organization. It is not necessary that all the enforcement agencies have their own jails. They may pay fees for storing their prisoners in the facilities of some other level of government.

Having a permanent and respected police force and a judicial system capable of trying individuals would be a tremendous help in regularizing and legitimizing such activities as the Nuremberg trials that followed World War II or the war crime trials that have been talked about in connection with the horrors of the Balkan/ Bosnian war. At any rate, the nature of the procedures by which ICJ judgments can be enforced is an issue needing attention. Action by the Security Council involving use of force is a possibility. Whether the prosecution of Balkan war criminals can be successful may well depend on the respect by national governments for the enforcement of judgments made by the special court now being created by the United Nations on the insistence of the United States, actually to try such people. The judges have already been appointed and are receiving evidence as a basis for such trials.

Conclusion

The people of a country such as the United States, who have prided themselves on having "a government of laws and not of men," should, in the interest of consistency, seek to generalize that state of affairs to the world. A worldwide government of law would mean that leaders would have to argue their cases before a world tribunal and accept the verdict of that procedure whether they liked it or not and whether powerful groups in their countries liked it or not. Impressing these groups with their obligation to conform is not going to be easy.

Implementation of world law requires the existence of a respected international legal system. Great powers, and even not so great powers, are prone to disrespect the jurisdiction and rulings of the International Court of Justice when they consider it in their interest to do so, and the court has no effective enforcement machinery. For international order to be meaningful, the jurisdiction of the international court must be compulsory and its rulings effectively binding.

If the United States and other countries are serious about a New World Order, orderly procedures for establishing laws and the capability for enforcing laws via courts and "police" would seem to be the serious heart of the matter. In the long run, this legal and policing function could replace the UN military force in importance at far lower cost in terms of lives and treasure.

Colonies and the Trusteeship Council

Coming out of World War I, much of the population of the world was colonial, that is to say, under the control of one or another of the great powers that had farmed out shares of the world to themselves at a conference in Berlin in 1884–85.

The League of Nations Mandates

Thinking at Versailles in 1919 divided these colonial areas into two types: (1) the colonies of the victors, and (2) the colonies of the vanquished. The control of the former was allowed to remain much as it had been, a matter pretty much left to the discretion of the great power involved. The handling of the colonies of the vanquished was different. Article 22 of the covenant of the League of Nations provided: "To those colonies and territories which as a consequence of the late war have ceased to be under the sovereignty of the States which formerly governed them and which are inhabited by peoples not yet able to stand by themselves under the strenuous conditions of the modern world, there should be applied the principle that the well-being and development of such peoples form a sacred trust of civilization and that securities for the performance of this trust should be embodied in this Covenant." This reads like a fine principle, although one might wonder why the same principle was not applied to the colonies of the victors, which it was not, for perhaps obvious reasons.

The colonies of the defeated were turned over to one or another of the victors. "Tutelage of such peoples should be entrusted to advanced nations who by reason of their resources, their experience or their geographical position can best undertake this responsibility, and who are willing to accept it and that this tutelage should be exercised by them as Mandatories on behalf of the League." So says article 22, paragraph 2.

The victors divided the colonies of the vanquished into three groups: (1) communities formerly belonging to the Turkish empire (a category including Palestine, Syria, Iraq, and much of the Arabian peninsula); (2) other peoples, especially those of Central Africa; and (3) territories, such as South West Africa and certain of the South Pacific Islands (South West Africa is now Namibia).

As to the first group, Great Britain, which had invaded Iraq during World War I, received the mandate to that area, which actually contained a hodgepodge of discordant Kurds, Sunni Moslems, and Shiite Moslems living in an area with nebulous boundaries, which the British formalized fairly arbitrarily. The British sponsored the establishment of a kingdom and a king, Faisal I, in 1921. The British obtained, from this government, oil concessions for the Iraq Petroleum Company and endorsed termination of their mandate in 1932, although retaining some military bases.

The subsequent history of Syria and Palestine was even more complicated, France having the Syrian mandate and Britain the Palestinian. Other areas asserted their own independence effectively. The disposition of the Arabian peninsula was taken care of by the army of Ibn Saud. Kuwait and an assortment of sheikdoms along the shore of the Persian Gulf also emerged from this process, somewhat by spontaneous generation.

Meanwhile, Egypt, which had been part of the Ottoman (Turkish) empire, had been made a "protectorate" by the British. This activity was independent of the mandate system. The British terminated the formal protectorate in 1937.

Libya was never a mandate, although it had been made a colony by the Italians in 1911. It passed under Anglo-French military government in 1943, and it was granted independence with Idris I as king in 1951. Muammar al-Qadaffi put an end to that kingdom in 1969.

The second group consisted largely of such Central African countries as had been under the control of the vanquished. The mandatory country was to be "responsible for the administration of the territory under conditions which will guarantee freedom of conscience and religion, subject only to the maintenance of public order and morals, the prohibition of abuses such as the slave trade, the arms traffic and the liquor traffic, and the prevention of the establishment of fortifications, or military or naval bases and of military training of the natives for other than police purposes and the defense of territory, and will also secure equal opportunities for the trade and commerce of other Members of the League." These provisions are found in paragraph 5 of article 22 of the covenant of the League of Nations. The prohibition against the use by the mandatory of the mandate for its own military purposes was a well-established principle in the League system of mandates. The overriding of this concept by the United States after World War II will be noted later. Tanganyika, later Tanzania, which was a German colony before World War I, is the chief example of a region in this second group of mandates. Its status as a mandate, administered by Great Britain, remained unchanged through World War II.

The third group of mandates involved "South West Africa and certain of the South Pacific Islands, which, owing to the sparseness of their population, or their small size, or their remoteness from the centers of civilization, or their geographical contiguity to the territory of the Mandatory, and other circumstances, can be best administered under the laws of the Mandatory as integral portions of its territory, subject to the safeguards above mentioned in the interest of the indigenous population." These provisions of paragraph 6 of article 22 applied the non-use-for-military purposes concept in this third group. Out of this third group came the South African mandate over South West Africa, or Namibia, which was to be a continuing problem down to the 1990s.

In the setting of these general principles the League negotiated with the mandatory power separate agreements corresponding to each mandate and provided for annual reports to the League.

The Trusteeship System after World War II

After World War II, the charter of the United Nations changed the mandates arrangement to a trusteeship system. For the most part, the areas that had been under the mandate of one or another of the powers passed over to a trustee arrangement with the same power. A possible exception to this generalization was South West Africa. South Africa did not recognize the shift to a trustee arrangement under the United Nations but insisted that its arrangement with South West Africa continue unchanged.

The coverage of the trusteeship system was extended to include islands in the Pacific that before the war had been controlled by Japan. The United States, Australia, and New Zealand were involved in this arrangement.

A notable change from the former League of Nations arrangement was that under the UN charter so-called non-self-governing territories, colonies of the great and not-so-great powers that had not been subject to any control under the League system, were placed under a measure of United Nations supervision.

Chapter XI of the UN charter was called "Declaration Regarding Non-Self-Governing Territories." Article 73 stated that all "Members of the United Nations which have or assume responsibilities for the administration of territories whose peoples have not yet attained a full measure of self-government recognize the principle that the interests of the inhabitants of these territories are paramount, and accept as a sacred trust the obligation to promote to the utmost . . . the well-being of the inhabitants of these territories. . . ." In particular, the member was "to this end

. . . to develop self-government . . . according to the particular circumstances of each territory and its peoples. . . ." To implement the procedure, the member was "to transmit regularly to the Secretary-General" reports "for information purposes" only "relating to economic, social, and educational conditions in the territories. . . ."

These reports, concerned with the administration of ordinary colonies by the country controlling the colony, were, it may be noted, submitted to the secretary-general and not to the Trusteeship Council. These colonies, which were those that had not belonged to the defeated powers, were not included in the trusteeship system.

The trusteeship system proper was provided for in chapters XII and XIII of the charter and applied to colonies of the defeated powers of World Wars I and II. These are called "trust territories" in the charter. The basic objectives of the trusteeship system are described in part, in article 76, as being "to promote the political, economic, social, and educational advancement of the inhabitants of the trust territories, and their progressive development towards self-government or independence. . . ."

The system was to be supervised by a Trusteeship Council working under the authority of the General Assembly, except for some so-called strategic areas (chiefly Pacific Islands that had been under the control of the Japanese and that were allotted to the United States). These strategic areas were to be administered by the trustee under the supervision of the Security Council, and the trustee was expected to avail itself of the assistance of the Trusteeship Council in dealing with ordinary "political, economic, social, and educational matters in the strategic areas." This special arrangement, running counter to the general principle that trust territories were not to be used for military purposes by the trustee, seems to have been created under United States pressure to permit using them as bases in support of United States military strategy in the Far East.

The Trusteeship Council members are the nations administering trust territories plus such of the permanent members of the

Security Council as are not administering trust territories plus "as many other Members elected for three-year terms by the General Assembly as may be necessary to ensure that the total number of members of the Trusteeship Council is equally divided between those Members of the United Nations which administer trust territories and those which do not" (article 86 of the charter). The total membership of the council is thus variable. In fact, by 1991 it consisted of only the five permanent members of the Security Council. This was possible because the United States was the only remaining custodian of a trust territory.

In 1946 eight countries administering either trust territories or other non-self-governing territories (Australia, Belgium, Denmark, France, the Netherlands, New Zealand, the United Kingdom, and the United States) committed themselves to filing the appropriate reports with the United Nations. Later Spain and Portugal joined the group, but South Africa was never cooperative.

Following 1945 there occurred incidents involving the termination of trusteeships and the setting up of new independent states. Early dramatic episodes of this sort, in the late 1940s, involved Palestine and are discussed in chapter 4.

The Liquidation of Colonialism

At the end of World War II, almost a third of the population of the world, some 750 million people, were living in non-self-governing territories or trusteeships, dependent on a colonial power or trustee. By the end of the 1980s, fewer than three million lived in that setting, and more than eighty independent nations had been formed from former colonies and trusteeships. They had made their contribution to raising the membership of the United Nations from an initial 51 to some 184 by 1993. In 1991 one of the last major non-self-governing territories, Namibia, obtained its status as a nation independent of South Africa. South Africa had not given up easily.

The process by which the trust territories and former colonies obtained their independence had its difficulties. By 1960 the

General Assembly was not satisfied with the progress being made in decolonization. In that year a Declaration on the Granting of Independence to Colonial Countries and Peoples (the Declaration on Decolonization) was adopted, proclaiming that colonialism should be brought to a speedy and unconditional end. In 1962 the General Assembly took note that repressive measures, including armed action, continued to be taken against dependent peoples. Then during the 1960s and 1970s there was a massive wave of newly independent or largely self-governing former colonies or trusteeships, many of which became UN members.

It seems worthwhile, in an effort to emphasize the sheer magnitude of what has happened, to list many of the lands involved in these changes.[1] The country losing the colony or trust territory or at least implementing some "change of status" is listed first, followed by the territories whose status changed, and the date of the change. Any name changes that occurred are given in parentheses.

- Australia
      Cocos (Keeling) Islands, 1984
      *Papua (Papua New Guinea), 1975
      Nauru, 1968
      *New Guinea (Papua New Guinea), 1975
- Belgium
      *Belgian Congo (Zaire), 1960
      Ruanda-Urundi (*Rwanda and *Burundi), 1962
- Denmark
      Greenland, 1954
- France
      French Equatorial Africa:
      *Chad, 1960
      *Gabon, 1960
      *Middle Congo (Congo), 1960

---

*Member of the United Nations.

*Ubangi Shari (Central African Republic), 1960
French establishments in India, 1947
French establishments in Oceania, 1947
*French Guiana, 1947, Guyana
*French Somaliland (Djibouti), 1977
French West Africa:
   *Dahomey (now Benin), 1960
   *French Guinea (Guinea), 1958
   *French Sudan (Mali), 1960
   *Ivory Coast (Côte d'Ivoire), 1960
   *Mauritania, 1961
   *Niger Colony (Niger), 1960
   *Senegal, 1960
*Upper Volta (now Burkina Faso), 1960
Guadeloupe and dependencies, 1947
Indo-China, comprising *Cambodia, *Laos, and *Vietnam, 1947
*Madagascar, 1960, and dependencies, especially Comoro Archipelago (*Comoros), 1975
Martinique, 1947
*Morocco, 1956
New Caledonia and dependencies, 1947
New Hebrides under Anglo-French Condominium (*Vanuatu), 1979
Réunion, 1947
St. Pierre and Miquelon, 1947
*Tunisia, 1956
Cameroons (*Cameroon), 1960
*Togoland (the eastern part became Togo), 1960

- Italy
Somaliland (joined with British Somaliland to form *Somalia), 1960
- Netherlands
Netherlands Indies (*Indonesia), 1949
Netherlands New Guinea (Irian Jaya), 1963
Netherlands Antilles (Curaçao), 1951

Surinam (now *Suriname), 1951, 1975
- New Zealand
  Cook Islands, 1965
  Niue Islands, 1974
  Western Samoa (now *Samoa), 1962
- Portugal
  *Angola, including the enclave of Cabinda (Angola), 1975
  *Cape Verde Archipelago (Cape Verde), 1975
  Goa and dependencies, 1962
  Guinea, called Portuguese Guinea (*Guinea-Bissau), 1974
  Macao and dependencies, 1972
  *Mozambique, 1975
  São João Batista de Ajuda, 1961
  *São Tomé and Príncipe, 1975
- South Africa
  South West Africa (now *Namibia, under UN administration), 1966; independent, 1990
- Spain
  Fernando Póo and Río Muni (*Equatorial Guinea), 1968
  Ifni, 1969
- United Kingdom
  Aden (Southern *Yemen), 1967
  *Bahamas, 1973
  *Barbados, 1966
  Basutoland (*Lesotho), 1966
  Bechuanaland (*Botswana), 1966
  British Guiana (*Guyana), 1966
  British Honduras (*Belize), 1981
  British Somaliland (joined with Italian Somaliland to form Somalia), 1960
  Brunei (now *Brunei Darussalam), 1983
  *Cyprus, 1960
  *Fiji, 1970
  *Gambia, 1956

Gilbert and Ellice Islands (Kiribati and Tuvalu), 1979
and 1978, respectively
Gold Coast (*Ghana), 1957
Hong Kong, 1972
*India, 1947
*Jamaica, 1962
*Kenya, 1963
Leeward Islands:
   Antigua (*Antigua and Barbuda), 1981
   St. Kitts-Nevis-Anguilla (separated from Anguilla to
   form *St. Kitts and Nevis), 1983
Malaya, Union of (Federation of *Malaysia), 1957
*Malta, 1974
*Mauritius, 1968
*Nigeria, 1960
North Borneo, 1963
Northern Rhodesia (*Zambia), 1964
Nyasaland (*Malawi), 1964
Sarawak, 1963
*Seychelles, 1976
*Sierra Leone, 1961
*Singapore, 1963, 1965
*Solomon Islands, 1978
Southern Rhodesia (*Zimbabwe), 1980
*Swaziland, 1968
*Trinidad and Tobago, 1962
*Uganda, 1962
Windward Islands:
  *Dominica, 1978
  *Grenada, 1974
  *St. Lucia, 1979
  *St. Vincent and the Grenadines, 1979
Zanzibar, 1963
British Cameroons (northern British Cameroons joined
Nigeria and southern British Cameroons joined *Cam-
eroon), 1961

Togoland (the western part united with Gold Coast to
form *Ghana), 1956
Tanganyika, 1961
• United States
Alaska, 1959
Hawaii, 1959
Panama Canal Zone, 1947
Puerto Rico, 1952 (which has a unique "commonwealth"
status)

Further changes occurred between 1985 and 1992, but not
many. By 1993 the only remaining trusteeship was that of the
United States—which had prided itself on not being a major
colonial power—over Palau. In addition, it was a trusteeship justified on military grounds. Also, there remained a few ordinary
colonies. The British still had the Falkland Islands (Malvinas),
Gibraltar, Hong Kong, and a few others. The United States still
had Guam, American Samoa, and, perhaps one could say, Puerto
Rico. Portugal still had Macao. There is the possibility of future
trouble in all of these places; the situation is not simple in any of
them.

Nevertheless, between 1945 and 1992 a massive liquidation of
the colonial system had occurred. This does not mean there was
general satisfaction with the resulting situation. But change there
was.

The Nature of the Liquidation Process

The western powers had acquired colonies because they wanted
them, and they initially resisted the idea of giving them up. But
once the liquidation process was under way, two regrettable
attitudes came to dominate what was going on. The colonial
powers wanted to wash their hands of the transition problems as
quickly as possible, and the leaders of the independence movements in the colonies were eager to take over forthwith.

Little serious effort was devoted before independence was given to establishing the conditions for workable self-government. This was in spite of the admonishment in the United Nations charter relative to the non-self-governing territories (article 73, paragraph b): "to develop self-government, to take due account of the political aspirations of the people, and to assist them in the progressive development of their free political institutions, according to the particular circumstances of each territory and its people and their varying stages of advancement. . . ." A similar admonition in connection with the trusteeships (article 75, paragraph b) reads: "to promote the political, economic, social, and educational advancement of the inhabitants of the trust territories, and their progressive development towards self-government or independence as may be appropriate to the particular circumstances of each territory. . . ."

Perhaps it was almost inevitable that as pressure mounted, pointing in the direction of self-governing independence, a sort of fatalistic precipitation would come to dominate the situation. The first and powerful example of this process was the manner in which the British gave up their mandate/trusteeship in Palestine in 1947 in a setting of erupting conflict between Arabs and Jews.

The colonial powers, no doubt, had done some things in support of education and development in their colonies and mandates, some much more effectively than others. And many revolutionary leaders and followers had visions of peaceful and prosperous independent countries. But there needed to be provision for a government structure and for circumstances that would permit an enlightened electorate to make intelligent choices quickly. In retrospect it is easy to see and say that it was an illusion to believe that under the circumstances such conditions could exist.

For worse, not better, the following script was played out in many situations, in French, Belgian, and English colonies in Africa, the Middle East, and elsewhere, and in the colonies of other countries as well: The colonial power had originally acquired the colony by the exercise of its power, and it may not subsequently have profited quite as much from the colony as it thought was going to be the case. That aspect of the story was developed years ago by Sir Norman Angell in *The Great Illusion*. The colonial system had not worked out satisfactorily from the viewpoint of either the powers greedy for colonies or the populations supposedly benefiting from "the white man's [handling of his] burden." Thus in many territories after World War II colonial powers soured on their roles. Governing colonies involved a lot of headaches and not much gain, although individual citizens of the colonial power may have profited mightily, while enjoying a lifestyle in the colonies, replete with servants and luxury such as even the most wealthy could scarcely have enjoyed at home.

Into this setting came the UN, pressuring the colonial power to grant independence to the colony, plus another element: disgruntled local people who were indignant about the lifestyle of their conquerors and the abysmal poverty prevailing in the colony. So, there existed for years, in many of these lands, independence movements. As time passed, those independence movements, frustrated by the lack of response on the part of the colonial powers and their representatives in the colonies, resorted increasingly to violence—terrorism, if you will. The movements acquired tough leaders with blood on their hands, and they offended the sensibilities of the foreigners in their midst.

There then existed in the post–World War II period a situation in which the colonial power was willing, even anxious, to divest itself of the colony or trusteeship. But little constructively was done to foster self-government, to take due account of the political aspirations of the peoples, and to assist them in the development of their free political institutions.

The situation was frequently complicated by the presence of more than one independence movement in a given territory. Perhaps there were two distinct and assertive religions in the territory, or two or three different races that had cultivated animosity toward each other over the years or centuries. Brotherly (or sisterly) love may be an aspect of the religious doctrine of various religions, but it does not follow that it is commonly practiced by the membership of one religion toward the adherents of others.

The retiring colonial power had the problem of working out, with particular individuals or groups, arrangements for ceding political power to such group, or groups. It is easy and even glib to say: "Let democracy prevail"—in other words, "Have a democratic election." There seems to be some feeling in the United States to the effect that that is all that need be said, or done: elections in six months, and all is well. Unfortunately, it may take longer than that to unseat some institutionalized behavior norms that have been in place for aeons. Behold Ireland.

Naturally, the colonial power, of a mind to get out, wants to get out as painlessly as possible. But how to do it? The form of a democratic election, accompanied by the hasty departure of the officials and armed forces of the colonial power, has been a common procedure, especially in Africa and Asia, and one that is followed by a situation in which the new, inexperienced, "democratically elected" government simply lacks the organization to govern effectively and with an even hand. The new rulers may not even be particularly interested in meting out evenhanded justice, but rather in perks, luxury, and power.

In a not uncommon situation, the colonial power, toward the end, might recognize the presence of more than one contending revolutionary group in the territory (as in Palestine and Ireland) and opt for creating two or more countries out of the one (witness the number of countries carved out of the French colonies of Africa). The thought was that civil wars would thus be avoided. However, it proved quite impossible to fix satisfactory boundaries under such circumstances (the border between Iraq and Kuwait is an example).

In the face of these conditions, what often happened immediately after independence was that a terrorism-tested leader took over a country, perhaps legitimately winning the first post-independence election, but his skills did not run to administration and the conciliation by peaceful means of differences within his government. Proceeding to lose or think he was going to lose the second post-independence election, he suppressed the election or its results by force and established a dictatorship that lasted until he was overthrown violently (witness numberless examples) or died.

So one aspect of the resulting situation was the difficulty in getting rid of a ruthless, entrenched dictator even after it became evident to the world at large that there was trouble and terrorism rampant in the helpless country. The exploitative ruler is protected in his position by the concept of national sovereignty, which can be something of a fetish in small countries as a symbol of their right to reject the influence of the great powers. As a result, the country must live with a tyrant who is accountable to no higher authority.

It is time that the United Nations freed itself of the constraint represented by article 2, paragraph 7: "Nothing contained in the present charter shall authorize the United Nations to intervene in matters which are essentially within the domestic jurisdiction of any state." This self-denying principle should be deleted from the charter, and the implications of the concept of national sovereignty should be reviewed. This issue is further discussed in chapters 13 and 14.

Unsatisfactory Finis

Colonies and trusteeships are no longer a significant condition on the world scene. They have been transformed into small independent sovereign states and are an important factor and problem on the world scene, in their own right. Small countries in a world of trade barriers frequently do not have domestic markets large enough to justify building manufacturing plants of the size necessary for productive efficiency.

It is not much help for us to preach to them that they can solve their problems by becoming democracies, holding elections, and practicing the market system. Among much of the population of the former colonial territories, the market system, the giant corporations and military interventions of the western democracies, has not left entirely pleasant memories. As for the Trusteeship Council, it would now seem to be pretty much functionless, but, as institutions generally do under such circumstances, it is looking around for a way to justify its continued existence. It is handling supervision of the remaining United States trust territory of Palau for the Security Council, for example.

Also, there remain quite a few small territories or colonies that have never been trust territories but have been, all along, under control of one or another of the World War II victors, or that for one reason or another still have an ambiguous status: American Samoa, Anguilla, Bermuda, British Virgin Islands, Cayman Islands, Guam, Montserrat, Turks and Caicos Islands, United States Virgin Islands, Gibraltar, the Falkland Islands (Malvinas), Pitcairn, St. Helena, Tokelau, Western Sahara, East Timor, and, not to forget, Puerto Rico, Hong Kong, and Macao.

Regional Arrangements

Article 52 of chapter VIII of the UN charter states: "Nothing in the present charter precludes the existence of regional arrangements or agencies for dealing with such matters relating to the maintenance of international peace and security as are appropriate for regional action. . . ." But the charter goes well beyond not precluding: "The Members . . . entering into such arrangements . . . shall make every effort to achieve pacific settlement of local disputes through such regional arrangements . . . before referring them to the Security Council." And beyond that: "The Security Council shall encourage the development of pacific settlement of local disputes through such regional arrangements. . . ."

The UN might have operated as though it was in competition with the existing regional organizations of countries such as the Organization of American States for Latin America and the Caribbean, the Organization of African Unity for much of Africa, the European Community for much of Europe (or the Helsinki Accord group, the Conference on Security and Cooperation in Europe, for even more of Europe), the League of Arab States, the Organization of the Islamic Conference, and the Association of South-East Asian Nations (ASEAN), as well as the very important North Atlantic Treaty Organization (NATO). We are not talking about those organizations that are part of the UN structure, such as the Economic Commission for Latin America and the Caribbean, or the Economic Commission for Europe.

However, instead of looking on these regional organizations as though they were competitors, the UN elected to cooperate with them and even to encourage their establishment and strengthening. The result was chapter VIII of the charter, "Regional Organizations."

In some peacekeeping operations the clashing countries might react more favorably to the intervention of organizations of neighboring countries with much the same culture, while in other circumstances they might react more cooperatively to intervention by the more distant UN, which they might conceive of, therefore, as being more impartial. Therefore, it has seemed desirable for the UN and the regional organizations to operate one crisis at a time, discussing the best way to proceed. But the UN charter, especially in article 53, provided that, in general, final authority would rest with the UN.

Also many social and economic problems are primarily regional in nature, and, despite an international aspect to the problem, they may have relatively little significance for most of the world. Such problems may well be more knowledgeably and effectively resolved at the regional level. Thus, for example, it may work better for Argentina, Brazil, Paraguay, and Uruguay to cooperate in dealing with the problems and possibilities created by the presence of the River Plate drainage system than for the full United Nations to try to deal with the problem in detail. If those countries were to have difficulty in cooperating and become bellicose, however, conciliation by the full Organization of American States might successfully deal with the problem. If that effort does not succeed, intervention by the full UN might be a resort.

Liberia

An example of the regional handling of disputes has been in Liberia. In December 1989 Charles Taylor led a revolt against the military dictatorship of Samuel K. Doe. The latter was killed in September 1990, but the civil war went on and involved numerous atrocities and massacres. None of the involved parties had demonstrably clean hands. Certainly Charles Taylor did not.

International agencies that sponsored settlement of the dispute included both the Economic Community of West African States and, later, the Organization of African Unity. The Economic Community of West African States was attempting to mediate the dispute as early as 1990. It "sponsored" the presence in Liberia of troops from Nigeria, Ghana, Sierra Leone, Guinea, and Gambia, which were in Liberia from August 1990 on, attempting to "impose" a truce. They did set up an interim government, led by Amos Sawyer. So, the contending parties during the next three years were the Charles Taylor rebels (the National Patriotic Liberation Front), the Amos Sawyer "government," the followers of Samuel Doe (called the United Liberation Movement), plus the "peace-enforcement" forces of the other West African nations.

Negotiations took place in Geneva, involving these groups, the Organization of African Unity, and the United Nations central organization, and an arrangement was worked out in late July 1993. According to this arrangement, the contending factions would be disarmed by a peacekeeping force that would include troops from Egypt, Zimbabwe, and Tanzania. The whole operation, including elections in February 1994, would be monitored by two hundred or three hundred UN people.

To some extent it may have been pure exhaustion that made the arrangement possible. Kenneth B. Noble of the *New York Times* reported that Charles Taylor told his troops to go home and said: "Some of you were shoeshine boys, carpenters and farmers. We ask you to return to your towns and villages and begin to rebuild your lives. The war is over." It had cost perhaps 150,000 lives. But it was not over. In 1994 a new faction called Liberian New Horizons, headed by a General Charles Julue, became active and sporadic fighting was continuing among the various factions.

Haiti

The situation in Haiti in the early 1990s is another example of coordination between a regional organization and the UN. Father Jean-Bertrand Aristide, a liberal Catholic priest, was elected president of Haiti by an impressive majority in December 1990, Haiti being a country with a long tradition of rule by tyrants who made free use of force and violence to support their power. Aristide was overthrown by the army in September 1991 and went into exile. General Raoul Cedras became the country's ruler, and large numbers of Haitians began desperate efforts to flee the country, especially trying to cross in unseaworthy boats to Florida.

The Organization of American States (OAS) and the UN, the United States also being involved, cooperated in an effort to negotiate with General Cedras and obtain the return of Father Aristide to the presidency. For present purposes it is relevant that the OAS and the UN cooperated in selecting a former Argentine foreign minister, Dante Caputo, as the chief negotiator in the effort to return Aristide to power.

Caputo worked out an agreement involving Cedras and Aristide at Governors Island in New York harbor in early July 1993. It provided for Aristide's immediate nomination of a prime minister and his approval by Parliament, amnesty for the military who effected the coup against Aristide, resignation of the military high command including Cedras, and return of Aristide to the presidency on October 30, 1993. About the only item on this agenda that happened was the appointment and approval of Robert Malval as prime minister. Meanwhile, the Clinton administration continued to implement the Bush policy of forceful return of Haitian refugees to Haiti. A limited trade embargo, particularly on oil, was applied to Haiti, then a more inclusive embargo.

It is argued in this book that it is not appropriate for one nation to interfere with force in the affairs of another nation. But it may well be appropriate for the UN or regional organizations to do so. The author argues that the use by the UN of a substantial peacemaking force operating under the UN flag and consisting of Latin American regional troops could, early on, have occasioned the speedy flight of Cedras and his group from Haiti, resulted in the reinstallation of Aristide as president of Haiti, and redounded to the great credit of the UN and the United States. Something similar to this did finally happen in September 1994, three years later. A commitment, endorsed by Father Aristide, to hold credible elections at the constitutionally provided time and then turn over the office of president to the duly elected candidate in February 1996 in a process supervised by the UN, not the U.S. gives a hopeful ring to the process. Will it work? Time will tell.

Other Situations Involving Regional Aspects

Regional groups and organizations played a significant role in dealing with the Central American difficulties of the 1980s and early 1990s. Both the UN and the United States have been involved. In working out an arrangement in Nicaragua that resulted in the election of Violeta Barrios de Chamorro to the presidency of that country to replace Daniel Ortega, an important group involved Central American leaders headed by the president of Costa Rica, Oscar Arias Sanchez, who won a Nobel Prize for this effort.

In the difficult Somalia situation in 1993, the Organization of African Unity has played very little role, although surely a regional African organization could have been useful in dealing with the intractable tragedy.

The European countries have failed to cooperate in dealing with the mayhem in what was Yugoslavia since 1991. But surely with a major commitment of force, and the force was available in the NATO army, peacemaking could have worked in Yugoslavia. Surely a major European force of several hundred thousand troops would have been welcomed by most of the population of Yugoslavia, including many Serbs, at least early in the process. And Europe could have regained much of the self-respect it seems to have lost. Functionless NATO would have found something useful to do, or at least a swan song of which it could be proud.

Peacemaking

A permanent, volunteer UN military force, such as was recommended in chapters 4 and 5, is an example of an institution that should be in position to make use of regional arrangements. The UN force might take the form of a decentralized organization, highly trained but with varying emphases in its training depending on the geographical region where it operated. The type of loyalty emphasized could well be oriented to responsibility for fostering a pleasant, diversified world where considerate people could live pleasantly and free of fear of autocratic governments or rampant crime and violence.

The permanent force might have a series of regional headquarters in various areas such as those now corresponding to the established regional organizations. Certainly, if an emergency called for it, units could be called from one area of the world to serve in another. Some regional problems could best be dealt with by such locally oriented units, others not. A squabble over frontiers between El Salvador and Honduras might best be handled in Latin America. An argument over the Falkland Islands, between Argentina and Britain, might best be dealt with by the central UN authorities. Even a border dispute between Portuguese-speaking Brazil and one or another of Brazil's Spanish-speaking neighbors might less acrimoniously be dealt with by the central authorities, rather than by a group of all Spanish-speaking, ostensibly noninvolved Latin American countries.

Although when matters come to a head, it should be clear that the central UN organization makes the controlling decision, the United Nations surely could work more effectively in controlling the meanness of the world's trouble spots if the knowledge and cooperation of the people of different regions were utilized as a major aspect of the UN operation. The force would want to be oriented to diversity and cooperation rather than to centralization of power.

Secretary-General Boutros-Ghali made such considerations a major aspect of his 1992 Agenda for Peace:

> Under the Charter, the Security Council has and will continue to have primary responsibility for maintaining international peace and security, but regional action as a matter of decentralization, delegation and cooperation with United Nations efforts could not only lighten the burden of the Council but also contribute to a deeper sense of participation, consensus and democratization in international affairs.

The now functionless NATO army might be integrated into the new scheme of things as the military organization of the European Community, if the United States withdrew as a participant in NATO. And the European Community itself could function as a regional organization integrated into the UN framework. An additional attractive possibility might involve transferring much of the military equipment of a dissolving NATO over to the permanent, volunteer force of the UN. The redundant troops might find enlistment in the UN permanent military force as well. And the UN force could become a professional and well-equipped army with fair rapidity.

Nonmilitary Role of Regional Arrangements

Regional arrangements have a useful role quite apart from peace-making and peacekeeping considerations. The Organization of American States, for example, is active in the matters described in chapter 6, "The Economic and Social Council and the Subsidiary Organs." A recent example of a major nonmilitary regional activity is the creation of a North American Free Trade Association (NAFTA) involving Mexico, the United States, and Canada. Many other Latin American countries would like to join. Of course, Europe has a similar organization in the European Economic Community (EEC) and its umbrella organization of the

European Union. An increasing number and variety of such activities, some of which will work well, some not, surely involves a healthy process and can contribute to a world that will be an increasingly pleasant place in which to live.

Regional organizations certainly have a constructive role to play in cooperation with the UN, but the relationship must be one in which it is understood that, in case of disagreement, the position of the UN must prevail.

Part II

The Ingredients in the Pattern

The Pattern and
the Role of Technology

The first ten chapters of this work represent an effort to describe how the United Nations works as an institution. These later chapters represent an effort to place the United Nations in the stream of general social process. Then, chapter 15 sets forth suggestions for change in the UN structure and functions such as, we may judge, would help to produce a more pleasant and livable world at the beginning of the twenty-first century.

Ingredients in Social Process

For present purposes the ingredients in social process are: technology, institutions, environment, and people, four in all. (The reader familiar with orthodox economics will realize that this classification is significantly different from the factor of production terminology: land, labor, capital, and enterprise.) Technology is the application of knowledge that enables us to do certain things. Institutions involve groupings of people with a set of common or similar behavior patterns. Environment is the whole physical and energy content of the universe around us. The people are the individuals who are, at least from their own point of view, the prime actors in the scheme of things. Institutions, environment, and people are discussed more fully in chapters 12, 13, and 14.

The Role of Technology

A reason for being especially concerned about technology in a book on the UN is that certain technological advances can create conditions that cry out for a worldwide organization capable of controlling those advances. The use of atomic power and the control of the disposition of nuclear residue, regulation of the use of dangerous chemicals like poison gas and identification and the facilitation of the use of benign chemicals, and developments in communication and transportation desperately need international regulation, for example in connection with the identification of users of different wave lengths in communication services. The UN did not call forth such technological developments, but their existence has made an institution like the UN highly desirable or even necessary to monitor how such developments are used.

The accumulation of knowledge—of technical knowledge, scientific knowledge, technology, call the process what you will—is a dynamic process in the sense that it contains its own internal drive. An outside influence, such as the profit motive or congressional appropriations, may direct energy in particular directions and make it somewhat more likely that an increased amount of knowledge will be obtained in one area rather than another, but people have minds that would be active with or without the profit motive. The obtaining of knowledge is a cumulative process that depends on the prior accumulation of relevant background knowledge.

How does this knowledge accumulation process work? The invention of the wheel was a major breakthrough in the development of transportation. Knowledge as to how to smelt "low melting point" minerals, such as copper, was an important preliminary to acquiring the ability to do the same thing to "higher melting point" iron ore. Knowledge of calculus was necessary as one of the preliminaries to sending someone to the moon. Knowledge of reading and writing is an absolute prerequisite to the serious accumulation of knowledge in general.

Perhaps a thought or a speculation is in your mind. Or you are puzzling with a homework problem in algebra. You are stumped. You try different possibilities. You look out the window. You think about something else. Then suddenly the idea that will solve the problem comes to you. *An impulse jumps a synapse in the nervous system in the brain and you are aware of a relationship you had been unaware of the moment before.* "To some extent we control what we are thinking about and the results of our thoughts. But also we have to be aware that frequently we are thinking about certain things without any conscious decision or desire to do so. We are caught up in an ongoing process over which we have some control, but also which in some sense controls us. And occasionally, if we pause to think about it, we are quite surprised at the turn our thinking and conclusions have taken. But this does not keep us from continuing to participate in ongoing mental processes, idle and not so idle speculations (idle and not so idle curiosity), daydreaming, reverie, analysis."[1] (*Idle curiosity* is Thorstein Veblen's term.)

The explanation as to what guides or motivates the accumulation of knowledge should be looked for especially in the physiology of the brain.

Two advances in knowledge that stand out among the many technical (scientific) advances that have occurred in recent decades and that have reference to the United Nations are the nuclear and the communications revolutions.

In a world of nation states obsessed with the prerequisites of sovereignty, it is important for one's own country to take the lead in assimilating and using new knowledge in such areas. United States world leadership depends on its success in this activity, and in making the institutional changes necessary to foster and permit successful and rapid adoption of the new technology. It helps to be the country where the discovery of the new technology occurs, but adapters of imported technology, witness Japan, can also be quite successful if they are ingenious in making such changes in behavior norms.

The Nuclear Revolution

United States leadership in the nuclear field assured the final victory in World War II. Then the Soviet Union successfully made the necessary institutional adjustments to copy and use the atom bomb capability and rival the U.S. for world leadership for forty years. The Soviet Union then failed to adjust its institutions sufficiently, specifically the nature of its governmental operation and socialist planning, and it collapsed in the bipolar struggle for power in the world during the 1980s.

A facet of the United States reaction to the growth in the relative nuclear power of other countries in recent years has been its attempt to limit the availability of nuclear weapon technology in the world and to keep countries without such knowledge from acquiring it. It occurred to leaders in the United States that a useful measure in protecting United States leadership was to block the development in other countries of nuclear weapon industries. Consequently the U.S. and the Soviet Union, which had a similar type of interest, pressed for the approval of a multilateral agreement called the Treaty on the Non-Proliferation of Nuclear Weapons (1970) that has over 130 signatories. Responsibility for checking on compliance with the treaty was given to the International Atomic Energy Agency of the United Nations, which had been created in 1957 to deal with the peaceful uses of atomic energy.

Some of the influences that made it possible for the UN General Assembly to approve a nuclear weapons treaty were: (1) the attitude of many concerned scientists who viewed the nuclear industry as being a potentially serious threat to humanity; (2) many other people feeling this way; (3) the Baruch plan of the early postwar period for an international agency to control atomic power and weapons—the proliferation of nuclear weapons production by the 1950s; (4) ongoing international negotiations in efforts to work out a policy for dealing with nuclear proliferation; (5) a proposal by the Soviet Union to ban nuclear weapons, a proposal that did not call for inspection; (6) an agreement in 1968 between the Soviet Union and the United States to propose to the UN a nonproliferation treaty. This proposal then became the Treaty on the Non-Proliferation of Nuclear Weapons.

The core of the treaty was that the countries that already had nuclear weapon capability could retain that capability. However, countries which did not, at that time, have a nuclear weapon capability could not develop one in the future.

The role of the UN's International Atomic Energy Agency became crucial in monitoring for noncompliance with the treaty. The imprimatur of an international agency such as the IAEA has been essential to give credibility to the United States concern in connection with the suspected existence of programs to build atomic bombs in such places as Iraq and North Korea. The IAEA has been active and frustrated in its efforts to check for the existence of nuclear weapons programs in those and other countries.

It is worth worrying about policy in connection with the nuclear weapons situation. If this situation remains as is, a small group of countries will have nuclear weapon capability, but most will not. To heighten the matter for the non-nuclear countries, they will be subject to intrusive investigation on the part of the IAEA while the countries fortunate enough to have had a nuclear capability before the non-proliferation treaty will not be subject to such an annoyance. Increasingly the non-nuclear weapon countries will wonder as to the basis for this distinction. What is the particular merit of the nuclear weapon powers that entitles them to this favorable position? And it will be increasingly difficult for the nuclear weapon powers, beginning with the United States, to justify their favored position.

To deal with this situation the following possibility is suggested: The United States should volunteer to turn all aspects of its nuclear military capability over to the United Nations on the condition that other nuclear weapon powers do the same. The IAEA would then have the power to inspect all countries to make sure that they have no nuclear war capability. Such policy would give credibility to inspections in countries with rulers attempting to develop nuclear weapon programs and justifying their behavior on the grounds that they see no special reason why the nuclear weapon nations should enjoy the special power role that they have come to possess. All governments in non-nuclear power countries would surely be entitled to the same concern.

It is of interest that General Charles A. Horner of the U.S. Air Force has taken a position which is quite similar to the one being advocated here. On July 16, 1994, *The Houston Post* reported:

> The United States should eliminate all its nuclear weapons, a top Air Force general said Friday in a sharp break from Pentagon orthodoxy.
>
> Gen. Charles A. Horner, head of the U.S. Space Command, said the nation would secure "the high moral ground" worldwide while losing little militarily by eliminating its nuclear arsenal.
>
> The nuclear weapon is obsolete, Horner said at a breakfast meeting with defense reporters. "I want to get rid of them all."
>
> Horner made clear he was "talking long term" and said nuclear disarmament should only take place if other nuclear powers, especially Russia, go along.
>
> . . .
>
> "I want to go to zero and I'll tell you why: if we and the Russians can go to zero nuclear weapons, then think what that does for us in our efforts to counter the new [next?] war," Horner said.
>
> The new military threat, unlike the superpower tensions of the past, comes from smaller, less stable countries that obtain weapons of mass destruction, Horner said.[2]

The nuclear powers should consider these suggestions very, very seriously.

Technology-Institutions Interaction

New technology, to be used, must be assimilated by institutions. It must be put to use by institutions that, up to the moment, have been using organizational and productive methods that will have to be changed to accommodate the peculiarities of the new technology if that knowledge is to be effectively used.

The Communication Revolution
and the UN

Not too long ago it took months to get messages from one end of the world to another. Information about a typhoon, or a volcanic eruption, or an earthquake in Indonesia would scarcely arrive in western Europe in time for disaster relief supplies to be of any use. Effective reaction on a worldwide basis was not a viable arrangement because of the information problem, the communication problem, and the transportation problem.

The communication and transportation revolution of the past hundred years has changed all that. We hear, almost instantaneously, about problems around the world. We sometimes voluntarily provide generous aid quickly to faraway places in all sorts of uncoordinated ways. Also, on the basis of such speedy information we frequently meddle and even use force in trying to resolve difficulties in other countries or between other countries, difficulties we would not have known about or particularly concerned ourselves with in another era.

Sometimes the solutions we offer or impose are not welcomed by the ostensible beneficiaries or approved by third countries. Generous assistance in some situations and the enforcement of solutions to problems in other situations, by individuals and by assorted sovereign states, are activities that are going on all the time and frequently in a very disorganized and inefficient manner. We can see this. The information is in front of our noses. However, very useful action on the basis of information provided by the communication revolution calls for the nations to coordinate their activities through agencies such as the International Civil Aviation Organization, the International Telecommunication Union, and other such UN organizations.

Conclusion

New technical capabilities are calling for new institutions and new behavior norms so that the fantastic array of new technological and scientific capabilities can be dealt with in a manner that controls the introduction and use of the new knowledge to general satisfaction. This assumes we do not want to self-destruct or permit irresponsible scientists to exploit the peculiar capabilities of the new knowledge. These are matters that call for a consensus of humanity, not just the accident of the results which follow when each sovereign state arrogantly pursues its "national interest."

It is worth meditating on the very real possibility that in a world characterized by the sanctity of national sovereignty and national behavior oriented to implementing only perceived national interest, an Adolf Hitler would win World War III and establish a Reich that would last a thousand years, aided and abetted by mastery of nuclear arms and the tools of the communications revolution adroitly used by a Joseph Goebbels.

12

Institutions

An institution involves a group of people with a set of common or similar behavior patterns. Institutions should not be conceived of as buildings, or even as groups of people without regard to the influences that link them. The essence of the institution is the behavior pattern (of institutionalized behavior norms) that is observed by the group and that may be the product of long years or even centuries of evolution. New features of the institution's behavior patterns probably came into use at some earlier time because of influences then prevailing, and those then new behavior patterns were probably more or less appropriate responses to those influences. The limited liability of stockholders in corporations and group solidarity in labor unions are examples of institutionalized behavior norms appropriate to the conditions at the time they came into being.[1]

The UN As an Institution

It seems legitimate to surmise that the United Nations, viewed as an institution, was in major degree a response to the needs created by technological developments in transportation and communication. At the same time, particular prevailing behavior norms have frustrated the UN as it has tried to do its job since 1945.

The veto in the Security Council is an example of a behavior norm prevailing in that institution. It is a norm that came into being in response to the relative power positions of the United States and the Soviet Union, both of whom desired the veto. Their power positions were largely a result of the strength of their armies, which to a considerable degree reflected their industrial strength, which in turn reflected their degree of technological advancement.

Compulsion exerted by great powers and not-so-great powers results in behaviors that are clear violations of articles in the charter of the United Nations. For example, article 100 says: "In the performance of their duties the Secretary-General and the staff shall not seek or receive instructions from any government or from any other authority external to the Organization." Failure to follow this mandate by successive secretaries-general, beginning with Trygve Lie, is documented by Shirley Hazzard in *Defeat of an Ideal*.[2] Examples, some discussed in chapter 5, included the hiring of particular employees on the insistent recommendation of member countries. From this practice there has resulted a group of employees generally devoted to serving the interests of their home governments more than the interests of the United Nations. This deference to the wishes of individual member nations has become an established *institutionalized behavior norm* in the UN and one that has not contributed to the effectiveness of the UN.

The U.S. and the UN

Despite its role as a major proponent of the UN at the end of World War II, the United States has succeeded in establishing several counterproductive behavior norms, which the UN has succumbed to because of the power and persistence of this country.

The United States has asserted the power to exclude people coming from abroad to participate in UN activities. The physical location of the UN in New York City has made this type of behavior possible. Another example is the failure of the United States to keep reasonably current in paying its financial obligations to the UN. This practice has been justified over and over, especially since 1980, on the grounds that the UN is inefficiently run, or engaged in improper expenditures, or engaged in some peacekeeping operation of which the United States does not approve. The insistent repetition of United States representatives that UN expenses for this or that purpose should be restrained, or should, on principle, not exceed the expenditures of last year has become virtually a broken record at committee meetings. As matters stand, this insistence on curtailing UN activities has become a prevailing United States institutionalized behavior norm on a level with "no new taxes." How the United States expects the United Nations to finance the innumerable new peacekeeping operations, that it undertakes as a result of decisions made in the Security Council by the vote of the national government members, is a mystery.

Another, rather human, behavior norm of the United States and its citizenry is a propensity for passing (unfavorable) value judgments on the behavior of other nations and people at the same time that we strenuously reject outside judgments on our own behavior. This latter attitude has been reflected in the United States' occasional refusal to abide by decisions of the International Court of Justice.

The Concept of National Sovereignty

National sovereignty is an institutionalized behavior norm (value judgment) much prized in many quarters. It has been said to imply an absolute, uncontrolled state. Philip Jessup has argued with regard to this concept as follows:

> There must be basic recognition of the interest which the whole international society has in the observance of its law. . . . Sovereignty, in its meaning of an absolute, uncontrolled state . . . is the quicksand upon which the foundations of traditional international law are built. Until the world achieves some form of international government in which a collective will takes precedence over the

individual will of the sovereign state, the ultimate function of law, which is the elimination of force [war] for the solution of human conflicts, will not be fulfilled. There must be organs empowered to lay down rules (a legislature); there must be judicial organs to interpret and apply those rules (a judiciary); and there must be organs with power to compel compliance with the rules (a police force). These organizational developments must take place. . . .[3]

The view that the nation state is uncontrolled in relation to its handling of matters within its domestic jurisdiction is endorsed in article 2, paragraph 7, of the UN charter: "Nothing contained in the present Charter shall authorize the United Nations to intervene in matters which are essentially within the domestic jurisdiction of any state." Where did this concept as to the sacredness of national sovereignty come from? In terms of the great sweep of history, it seems to be of fairly recent origin, dating back only to the rise of the nation state as a form of government in the sixteenth and seventeenth centuries.

Following independence for the United States and the adoption of the Constitution in 1789, the states insisted on their individual sovereignty in relation to the federal government. But, as the years passed, the implications of this sovereignty became minimized as the federal government effectively asserted its power, in many matters, relative to the states.

More recently the concept of national sovereignty has been strongly asserted both by large countries such as the United States and the Soviet Union (in its day) and by small and newly independent governments. Not only the former colonies, which have obtained their independence since World War II, but also the Latin American countries, which have mostly been independent since the early nineteenth century, demand vigorously that other countries respect their national sovereignty. The rulers of the small and underdeveloped (and developed also) countries relish the freedom of action that they personally gain when operating under the national sovereignty umbrella. In fact, taken seriatim, each country large and small, developed and underdeveloped, is enthusiastic for the concept, especially as pertaining to itself. Many a ruthless dictator has plied his trade under the umbrella of the concept.

A relevant situation has involved the worldwide reaction to the Chinese government's massacre of those seeking greater democracy in that country that occurred at Tiananmen Square in Beijing in 1989. On January 31, 1992, Li Peng, the Chinese premier, took the occasion at a meeting of the Security Council of the United Nations to stress that it is a violation of China's national sovereignty for other nations to generate hue and cry and partial embargoes against China to pressure that country to be more lenient toward those who participated in the 1989 demonstrations. A usefulness of the Chinese example is that in that case it is fairly clear that calling the principle of national sovereignty to witness is in the interest of the ruler but hardly in the interest of the demonstrators and, one may fairly reasonably surmise, not in conformity with the desires of the great mass of Chinese people.

Yet, by and large, in the twentieth century and going into the twenty-first, the generality of the populations of the nation states is mesmerized by the concept of national sovereignty. It is "us against them." And "us" has a meaningful interest in not having its actions questioned by world society. United States citizens are likely to be outspoken in this regard, as also is the citizenry of most other countries. Yet the rank and file of humanity is quite likely to get a better "break" from world society than from its own national leadership. That institutionalized behavior norm, the reverence for national sovereignty, is one that does not serve well the citizenry in general.

Over the course of history the world has seen a lot of tyrannical rulers oppressing their own people. And the rash of newly independent states since World War II has carried with it, as a byproduct, a new order of tyrants, fortified behind the concept of national sovereignty. Also, there are pleasure-loving rulers, who are not necessarily tyrants, reveling to the discomfort of their people. They may merely be pleasure lovers who, indifferently, translate their pleasure-loving needs into results that sacrifice the standard of living of their people in general. Ferdinand Marcos of the Philippines could be an example. In one or another of these categories one can find most of the independent countries of the world for extended periods of years since World War II. The heroes who won independence for their countries find it difficult to surrender power, and they find they must use violence if they are to retain power in the face of increasing popular discontent.

Surely it is not too outlandish to suggest that it would be helpful if there were a world government empowered to pass judgment on national rulers and even to force more or less free elections on reluctant presidents-for-life. But interventions, to be entitled to respect, should be by world government, not by national governments that have appointed themselves to be the judge in such matters. It is pure arrogance for the United States to appropriate to itself the role of judge as to domestic regimes in other countries and to effectively sabotage efforts to create conditions permitting the UN to play this role.

The more powerful countries have not always respected the principle of nonintervention in their dealings with weaker countries. The number of interventions by the United States, with military force, in Latin American countries in the last hundred and fifty years is evidence (Nicaragua, Haiti, the Dominican Republic, Panama, Grenada, Cuba, and so on). But also, in recent years, the increasing willingness of some countries to permit foreign observers to come in and check whether their ostensibly democratic elections are being fairly conducted is a beneficent example to the contrary.

The practice of intervention has been sufficiently common, in situations where the affected state has not desired the external assertiveness, so that groups of Latin American countries over the past hundred years have argued vigorously to the effect that there does exist a nonintervention principle in international law. The question came to a head at a Pan American Conference in Montevideo in 1933. At that time, the American nations, including the United States, which was acting in accord with the recently enunciated Good Neighbor Policy, agreed that "no state has the right to intervene in the internal or external affairs of another" (article 8 of the Convention on Rights and Duties of States).[4]

Even more to the point is a statement by Under Secretary of State James Edwin Webb in 1949:

> I should like to state for the record as forcefully as I can that whatever may have been our mistakes in the past, it is the policy of this Government not to intervene in the domestic affairs of foreign countries. . . . The particular form of government in any country and the particular persons who constitute that government are a matter of domestic concern to the peoples of that country. The fact that there may be American investments abroad in no way alters the fact that this Government will not intervene in the affairs of other nations. The treaty between the United States of America and other American Republics relative to nonintervention, signed at Buenos Aires on December 23, 1936, and ratified by the President of the United States on July 15, 1937, provides in Article I that "The high contracting parties declare inadmissible the intervention of any one of them, directly or indirectly, and for whatever reason, in the internal or external affairs of any other of the parties." This treaty is the law of the land.[5]

That was many years ago. Later American governments have frequently acted as though they had no awareness of this aspect of the American tradition.

Dictators have a strong stake in defending and fostering the concept of national sovereignty. Their power position is at stake. There would seem to be considerable doubt that the interests of the general population of underdeveloped countries are well served by the national sovereignty behavior norm. It provides a setting in which the average citizen has little protection against tyranny, arbitrary arrest, torture, and exploitation by rulers and their sycophants.

It would be helpful to populations at large if the UN were to assert the power to pass judgments on whether regimes are practicing some at least roughly defensible, humane procedures and are not engaging in massive violations of individual human rights.

It is worth defending the proposition that, far from endorsing national sovereignty and the principle of nonintervention, the United Nations should assert itself regularly to pass judgments on the respectability of each of the world's governments, disregarding the rulers' assertion of the national-sovereignty-given right to rule as they choose. The UN should have established procedures for forcing compliance on the part of recalcitrant governments who oppress their own people. (Leslie H. Gelb, writing in the *New York Times*, had a wonderful article along this line in the issue of September 25, 1991.)

This is not the same thing as saying that it is appropriate for the United States or any other government or nation to pass a judgment on its neighbor and use force and coercion and even invasion to unseat one government and facilitate the assumption of power by some other government. The principle of nonintervention should vigorously apply to the relationship between two sovereign nations. One government should not presume directly to try to enforce its standards of morality on other countries, although it would be appropriate for it to argue the case for its brand of morality in the councils of the UN, and for all and each to do the same. In recent times there has been an encouraging amount of endorsement of this concept—that intervention is appropriate when it is done by the appropriate people.

The secretary-general seems concerned by this issue. In his "Agenda for Peace" of June 1992, Boutros-Ghali wrote in paragraph 17 a qualification after his ostensible endorsement of the concept of national sovereignty: "The time of absolute and exclusive sovereignty, however, has passed; its theory was never matched by reality. It is the task of leaders of States today to understand this and to find a balance between the needs of good internal governance and the requirements of an ever more interdependent world. . . . The United Nations has not closed its door." And passages in paragraphs 18 and 19 hint further at erosion of the strong implications of the national sovereignty concept.

The United Nations should be empowered to identify domestic

tyrants as well as international aggressors and should have the duty and the power to do something about both. This amounts to claiming that the international community has a duty to protect the citizenry of countries ruled by tyrants. To this end there does exist the Universal Declaration of Human Rights of 1948 in which the right of every human being to life, liberty, and the security of person was affirmed, but the United Nations has lacked the power to make this declaration meaningful.

The process by which the UN may execute effective judgments on the performance of national governments is serious business. The United Nations should have readily available and under its direct control a substantial well-financed, well-equipped force, and the United Nations charter should be amended to delete paragraph 7 of article 2, which says: "Nothing contained in the present Charter shall authorize the United Nations to intervene in matters which are essentially within the domestic jurisdiction of any state. . . ."

Too Many Too Small Countries

As was pointed out in chapter 2, the populationwise smallest half of the UN members, a possible voting majority, represent only about 4.5 percent of the world population. This might not be a matter of great concern in a free trade world where representation in elected bodies is proportioned to population rather than to national units. But in the UN, as presently constituted, there is a tendency for each delegation to be entitled to and to utilize equal time at the podium. Of course, put that way, it is an overstatement, but there is a significant problem here, especially when the language used is frequently demanding or denunciatory. The offended great-power delegates are more and more inclined to listen with closed ears or to absent themselves from the chamber.

Also, in a world of trade barriers, many of the small countries do not have large enough markets to permit the establishment of industries or companies or plants large enough to take advantage of reasonably low production costs, since their only market is the small local market.

Secretary-General Boutros-Ghali is worried by this problem. He remarks in paragraph 17 of "Agenda for Peace": "Yet if every ethnic, religious or linguistic group claimed statehood, there would be no limit to fragmentation, and peace, security and economic well-being for all would become ever more difficult to achieve."

Borders and Self-Determination

Shortly after the United States entered World War I in 1917, President Woodrow Wilson made a statement on war aims. The statement, Wilson's Fourteen Points, became a major influence in the formulation of the Treaty of Versailles. A concept in this pronouncement was the right to self-determination of peoples. Another concern was what principles were to be followed in the drawing of new national boundaries. In fact, eight of the fourteen points had to do with borders. The borders singled out were those of Russia, Belgium, France (Alsace-Lorraine), Italy, Austria-Hungary, the Balkans, Turkey, and Poland. The principles to be applied in locating borders were to be respect for historically established allegiances and respect for nationality. In the effort to implement those principles, the look of the map of Europe was revolutionized, and many a nation and numerous boundaries were established that endured less than twenty-five years.

What went wrong with the implementation of these well-meant intentions? Or was the trouble merely with an unkind fate, plus some uncooperative Europeans such as Georges Clemenceau, David Lloyd George, Vittorio Orlando, Benito Mussolini, and Adolf Hitler and the secret deals that had been made among several of them during the years of the war?

No doubt the lack of statesmanship on the part of world leaders was unhelpful. But the implementation of self-determination and the identification of a coherent pattern of historically established allegiances turns out not to be feasible. In 1919 this principle seemed to justify uniting all of the South Slavs into Yugoslavia, but in the 1990s South Slav Slovenians, Croats,

Serbs, Macedonians, and Bosnians expressed the opinion that they were entitled to existence as separate nations.

How is the group of people that is to exercise the right of self-determination to be identified? Nationalities are not conveniently located in coherent geographical areas. Pockets of varying nationalities are scattered hither and yon. There are pockets of Serbs in Croatia, Germans in Danzig/Gdansk, Great Russians in Ukraine, and Mexicans in the United States. People with German-sounding names may turn out to have French loyalties, and people of Spanish background in the United States may not recognize affinity with mestizo Mexicans. Do Scots want independence from England, or are they proud of having taken over England by providing a Scottish king, James I? Or neither?

A conscientious respecter of the rights of nationalities and of the establishing of boundaries according to long-standing historical allegiances could labor till judgment day relocating borders and encounter only a rising crescendo of indignation as to the merits of the results of such labors.

As to identification of a satisfactory alternative, there is no satisfactory alternative. But there is some pious advice that can be given. Pray that homo sapiens, the knowledgeable person, will come to realize that practicing a bit of live and let live and common courtesy is in order. This is no mandate that one should love one's neighbor as one's self. That is asking a bit much. But recognize that, on the whole, people, regardless of race, can live in association with each other and get along pleasantly. Combative instincts can find expression on athletic teams, where hopefully, behavior will be reasonably sportsmanlike, or at least limited to the stadium.

This is a way of saying that the problem of locating borders should be recognized as a non-problem. Leave the boundaries where they are. And the people had better get along, dammit. If some consideration (I have difficulty imagining what it would be) makes it reasonable to change a border, one principle that might be applied is that it is better to run borders along mountain ridges than along rivers. But that and similar principles are not going to carry us very far.

Robert Cullen has written an interesting article along this line, "Human Rights Quandary."[6] He makes a distinction between "individual rights" and "collective rights." Individual rights inhere in individuals, and examples are freedom of speech, freedom of religion, the separation of church and state, freedom to travel, and freedom from discrimination on the basis of race, creed, or sex. Collective rights inhere in institutions composed of peoples of different creeds or races and deal with questions such as whether they have a right to split off and establish a nation of people of their own creed or race. Collective rights come close to what is being called institutionalized behavior norms in this book.

Cullen argues that the defense of individual rights is important, the defense of collective rights is not. At least the defense of the right of each creed or race to constitute a separate nation unto itself is not worth the strong support of anybody. For one thing, it is not practically feasible to do this, for reasons that have been argued above.

I disagree with Cullen in terms of one aspect of his argument. He seems to say that it is appropriate for the United States to intervene with force in other countries to defend individual rights but not to defend collective rights. I would argue that it is not appropriate for the United States to intervene in other countries to protect individual rights, either. As already discussed, what would be appropriate would be for the United States to argue in the United Nations for intervention by the UN to protect individual rights.

Leave the borders where they are, as I said, and hope that a more effectively working democracy will, as the years pass, provide improving procedures for dealing with problems. Meanwhile, effectively working democracy has swept the self-determination problem under the rug. And the criterion for identifying improvement is the judgment of society at the time as to whether a change constitutes improvement. The job of the would-be reformer is to convince a society that is set in its ways that such and such a change is desirable.

Loyalty of Armies

In the situations involving the use of force by the UN, in particular in Korea in 1950, and the Persian Gulf in 1991, the armies involved have retained their national identities as United States or British or French armies, and their effective commander has been a United States general. In the Korean case, Douglas MacArthur was an American general, pro forma identifiable as the UN commander. In the case of the Persian Gulf, President Bush insisted that there be no subterfuge. The United States troops involved remained United States troops, not UN troops. The commanding general was a United States general (co-commander with a Saudi who left operational control to the American general). Fortunately, the other troops involved were not quite so sensitive and were willing to fight under an American general.

Articles 42 through 51 of chapter VII of the United Nations charter have never been made operative. They describe a procedure for organizing a UN force of previously agreed upon units of national armies. These units would have extensive training, which should prepare them for the special nature of their assignments. When called on, the army would be commanded by generals borrowed from national armies, presumably with some experience and training in their role as servants of the UN. If these procedures were in place, which they are not, the UN itself would be dealing with the military aspects of operations such as those in Somalia in the 1990s and acquiring experience as to how to use a multinational force on such special assignments. In Somalia it has worked out that such experience is being wasted on troops and generals whose primary loyalty is to the nations whose service they have never left.

Merely implementing the charter provisions dealing with these matters should improve the UN's ability to handle the increasing number of disputes. Such a force would probably still have mixed loyalties to home nations and to the UN, but it would be at least somewhat more committed to meet the UN's needs than has been the case in the Persian Gulf and Somalia. Also, difficulties such as the dispute between the United States and the UN with regard to whether the Somali warlords and their adherents should be disarmed could have been avoided. (It is argued in chapter 15 that the charter should be revised to permit the UN directly to recruit forces, but here some comments will be made about the behavior and loyalties of armies.)

It is almost trivial to say that the loyalty of an army is, or should be, to the nation that creates it. Other armies and nations are viewed as actual or potential enemies. It seems questionable whether troops can be expected to have meaningful loyalties both to their home countries and to the UN. Realistically, in most problem situations it may be possible for the UN not to use the troops of a given nation under circumstances that would put too much strain on their two loyalties. But occasionally such situations could get nasty. That is a reason the UN should recruit its own forces directly, troops that, as soldiers, will swear to only one loyalty. A French Foreign Legion or Swiss Guard sort of force augmented by large numbers of young international (brotherhood of people) idealists could make a most interesting army. Also, it could well turn out that quite a few countries have generations of youths who might prefer a career with such a force to a life of poverty in the home country.

Assembling adequate numbers of soldiers for a UN force should not be a major problem, and they would come a lot cheaper than do soldiers in the United States army. Molding this motley array into an army should be a challenging activity, but the effort could have a major positive payoff.

Procedures for calling up units from national armies probably should remain in place. But in any given peacekeeping or peacemaking operation the core of the force would be units of the UN's own army, supported if need be by units from national armies.

If the UN establishes its own army and recruits directly, it would become necessary for the UN itself to establish an officer training academy, such as most national governments possess. At the United Nations military academy the students would be screened, especially in terms of a commitment that, as long as they remained in the UN force, their primary loyalty must be to the UN and to the UN force. Of course, there would also be basic training camps for the regular UN troops, with an understanding of basic loyalty to the UN.

The ordinary UN Secretariat would need to pay attention to the training of the core of civilian personnel serving as the channel of communication between the troops in the field and UN headquarters. The civilian guidance of the troops in the field should, emphatically, not follow the model of Somalia, where guidance was provided by a United States State Department employee, Ambassador Robert Oakley, and a staff of United States government officials who were committed to the proposition that confiscating the weaponry of the Somalis and dominating or arresting the assorted warlords and thugs was not part of the assignment of the intervening troops. This was the view of the American decision makers in Somalia and of President Bush at the same time that it was the view of the UN secretary-general that confiscating the weaponry and arresting the warlords were high-priority items. The quick in-and-out scenario of President Bush, which was implemented cooperatively by President Clinton, did not work. The United States remained highly involved.

Institutions: Their Role

Institutions and the behavior norms they impose on people are one of the most important concepts, if not the most important concept, to understand in studying society. Note that the concepts of national sovereignty, geographical borders, armed forces, loyalties, and self-determination, which have been discussed in this chapter, are examples of institutions and their behavior norms. Discussion of change in behavior norms and how it happens and why is at stake.

_____ **13**

The Environment

If it chooses, world society may control the manner in which people exploit the environment. That it now permits individual nations to abuse the environment in deference to a concept such as national sovereignty, represents a self-imposed limitation, not some sort of natural law that sanctifies exploitation. Whether or when world society chooses to override national sovereignty in establishing norms to control the use by people of the environment, it may do so.

Erich Zimmermann, Neutral Stuff, and Resources

Erich Zimmermann has called the (what should one call it?) physical presence that is the universe: neutral stuff.[1] That terminology does not deny that the neutral stuff may be continually undergoing change in its physical structure as a result of the workings of nature. The relevance of the term is that it points out that, by and large, the stuff making up the universe has no market value, that is to say value on which a price is placed in the economic markets of planet earth.

Zimmermann's point is that it is usefulness in production or consumption that leads people to make the value judgment that such and such a rock, for example, is valuable. If it has the attribute of usefulness, Zimmermann then calls it a "valuable" resource. It is a "resource," a part of the environment that has value. "Resources *are* not, they *become* . . . ," says Zimmermann. They "become" as the result of the evolution of technical knowledge. New resources are identified as a byproduct of the technology accumulation process. The type of clay called bauxite had no particular value until it was discovered that it could be used to make aluminum. Thereafter, it was valued, and the quantity available became a matter of economic concern. Bauxite became a resource.

The accumulation of new technical knowledge is a result primarily of the way the mind works, new ideas being an automatic result of the ongoing process. And, as a part of this process, the use of the new technical knowledge makes profitable the exploitation of neutral stuff that had previously been of no market value. Classical economics (c. 1800) identified the recipients of this type of gain as landlords and called their gain rent instead of profit. Rent seekers and rent takers, thus, one might say almost by definition, become the recipients of something for nothing (getting a free lunch, you might say). (Landlords, in the sense we ordinarily use the term, are something quite different.) Any landlady of a boarding house who collects rent from not always affluent tenants, and who, herself, is not awash in monetary gain, will readily testify to this. Most of the "rent" she receives is, according to the professional economics definition, wages for labor—or interest for providing capital.

At any rate, the process by which neutral stuff turns into valuable resource, and landowners become thereby the recipients of gains for which they have not worked, is one of the important aspects of the capitalist system, an aspect that is likely to be disregarded or brushed aside when the virtues of the market system are extolled. However, such was the happy fate of many a Texas landowner as the oil industry developed in that state in the first half of the twentieth century. Enterprising businessmen, some as a result of their geological or engineering skills, some as a result of their promotional skills, also profited, but "the big and easy" money went to the landowners, the King Ranch and the XIT people.

But who pays for the infrastructure in the form of highways and bridges and garbage collection that supports the gains of the rent and profit takers and makers? What is the social cost of environmental changes such as the loss of agricultural land and natural habitat? Who pays for the byproduct pollution of land, water, and air? How is the ordinary citizen compensated for the loss of "global commons"—to use a fancy term much used in academic circles?

The Forests and Photosynthesis

The production process that is a money maker in one country may only cause damage elsewhere in the world. For example, the cutting of vast areas of tropical hardwood trees in the Amazon valley in Brazil may reduce the ability of the earth to transform carbon dioxide back to oxygen. But it makes money for the lumber companies. Under those circumstances, what could motivate Brazil to slow down deforestation and regulate its forest industry for the benefit of the whole world?

In recent decades Brazil has developed a program to open the Amazon area to development. An infrastructure program of road building was begun, involving trans-Amazon highways that would reach all the way to Peru and Bolivia, and perhaps even Colombia and Venezuela. As a byproduct of this road building, internal migration was encouraged, and land was cleared for agriculture and cattle raising. Logging the tropical hardwoods has been engaged in on a massive scale by lumber companies, domestic and foreign. Hostilities have broken out between the lumbermen and cattlemen on the one hand and workers, such as those gathering rubber latex, on the other hand. The native Indian people have found their way of life suddenly devastated by this overpowering of immigration from outside Amazonia. Also, landing strips have been built in the jungle as part of a transportation network for moving cocaine from Bolivia to the United States, compounding the problem.

Some of this activity is the sort of thing that has traditionally been considered protected under the doctrine of national sovereignty and free-private-enterprise profit making. Does world society have a stake here that overrides the implications of national sovereignty? The answer would seem to be "Yes, but. . . ." The rest of the world should be willing to shoulder much of the cost involved, since the world as a whole is the gainer from the policy.

But also the very nature of the international rights and duties situation needs to be clarified. Would it not be better for such changes to take place in a more orderly and less violent way under laws and rules laid down by a United Nations? Brazil would perhaps be more likely to make the appropriate changes by its own action in response to hearing the problem discussed in some United Nations assembly that was legally entitled to express its concern. Surely, the situation would be less likely to come to a crisis in a world possessing a strong and respected United Nations than in a world with a weak United Nations or none at all, where powerful nation states might resort, on their own initiative, to strong measures to work out the problem to their own satisfaction, for example, by putting pressure on Brazil.

Global Warming and the Hothouse Effect

The depletion of the forests is an aspect of a more general problem involving the possibility of global warming, a long-run tendency for the world to get hotter, the polar ice caps to melt, and the level of the oceans to rise and flood cities located close to sea level.

An example of the global warming argument runs to the effect that there is a rise in the carbon dioxide level in the air relative to the level of oxygen, perhaps because of the forest depletion, but also as a result of the burning of fossil fuels by manufacturing industries in the industrialized countries. There is a tendency for those excessive quantities of carbon dioxide to form a protective belt at fairly high altitudes around the earth. Sun rays come in through this carbon dioxide belt and warm the earth as they have done for thousands of years, but in the past, as the heat became excessive, it could escape into outer space. Now, however, this expanding carbon dioxide belt inhibits the escape of the heat accumulating close to the earth's surface, with the result that the earth's atmosphere inside the carbon dioxide belt tends to warm up. This has been called the hothouse effect, leading to global warming.

Whether the earth is actually warming up would seem to be observable by collecting the relevant data on temperatures over a long period of years. However, a considerable amount of such data has been compiled, and the results appear inconclusive. There may or may not be a serious problem here, but it is surely a sufficiently serious question to call for worldwide cooperation in continuing efforts to ascertain the facts. That should happen in a setting where there is an international agency available to take appropriate action, and where control is not abdicated to self-serving interests.

The Ozone Hole

The "hole" is a hole in the ozone layer that surrounds the earth some distance from the surface. The function of the ozone layer is to ward off much of the sun's rays, rays capable of giving sun worshipers more of a suntan than they want, plus, eventually, skin cancer. In fact, enough destruction of the ozone layer—and we have no way to be sure how much is too much—could make the earth quite uninhabitable by homo sapiens in our present form.

Enlargement of this ozone hole has been detected in the Antarctic, and also recently in the Northern Hemisphere close to the North Pole. Cause for this enlargement has been fairly authoritatively attributed to the diffusion in the atmosphere of certain chemicals, in particular chlorofluorocarbons (CFCs), which have been used in aerial sprays, refrigerants, etc. The United States, after some delay, since the nature of the problem was known at least in the early 1970s, has moved to regulate the use of CFCs.

Surely, there is no question but that an international government should have the authority to regulate or even to prohibit as
appropriate in such matters as this. Treaty agreements should not
be necessary before the UN could take action against offenders.
The problem is to reorganize the UN so that it will be capable of
such regulation.

The Oceans: Whales and Fishing

The oceans occupy some three-quarters of the earth's surface. In
the past it has not been feasible, as a matter of organization, for
individual nations to assimilate and administer control over most
of this area—there was just too much water—nor has the concept of national sovereignty been sufficient to control the exploitation of this or that part of the oceans. The "freedom of the
seas" then was a handy defense to use against governments
tempted arbitrarily to interfere with commerce, and that has been
the accepted means of controlling the rights of different nations
in the open ocean.

True, nations have attempted to exert some degree of administrative control for short distances out into the ocean, and
various principles have been asserted to define the territory
involved: the distance a cannon could shoot from the shore, or
three miles, nine miles, ten miles, two hundred miles. Rights of
passage through narrow straits and territorial waters have been
conditioned by the right (or power) of a nation's warships to
stop and search, and even seize or confiscate, commercial ves-
sels and their cargoes (of tuna or salmon, or drugs, or arms, or
. . .). Some of the early United States international adventuring
involved trying to protect American shipping from "the Bar-
bary pirates" off the coast of Africa along about 1800. More
recently, there have been similar but different problems resulting from Ecuador's ordering tuna fishing boats from Califor-
nia, operating within two hundred miles of that country's
coast, into Ecuadorian ports and confiscating or threatening to
confiscate the cargo. The shoe has been on the other foot in

connection with Russian fishing boats operating off the coast of New England.

Sometimes the concern has centered on the type of fish being caught or the methods being used. Drift nets, possibly as long as thirty miles, have been used in fishing for, perhaps, squid. But they catch and kill everything in their path: sharks, sea birds, marine mammals, sea turtles. The United Nations in 1989 adopted a conditional ban on drift-net fishing to take effect June 30, 1992. The United States took the lead in insisting that Japan, South Korea, and Taiwan comply, threatening retaliatory tariffs in case of noncompliance.

Japan resisted the enforcement of the ban on drift-net fishing, arguing that it would mean the loss of jobs by about ten thousand fishermen and the crippling of a fish-processing industry of some fifty thousand others. In the United States the same argument is used to oppose limiting tree cutting in the Pacific Northwest. It is tempting to add a comment on the logic of that argument. It savors of one advanced years ago by John Maynard Keynes in favor of pyramid building to solve the unemployment problem. But there is this difference that argues for pyramid building: at least the jobs are created without destroying something worthwhile.

Surely it would contribute to a healthier international atmosphere if there existed adequate machinery permitting the United Nations to enforce its own regulations, as for example the restrictions on drift-net fishing. The practice of a domineering world power such as the United States (using its leverage to induce Japan, say, to behave) gains little long-run goodwill in the world for the "enforcer" or respect for the process.

There have been international conventions regulating or trying to regulate whaling well back into the nineteenth century, but that did not prevent whaling from being an issue in 1991, when Norway planned to kill 382 minke whales over the following three years, violating a moratorium ostensibly in effect. Norway argued that killing whales is justified if it is for "research" purposes. Perhaps the nature of the research requires elucidation.

The Oceans: Law of the Sea

In the past it may not have been feasible, as a matter of organization, for individual nations to assimilate and administer control over most of the oceans. But the rapid accumulation of technical knowledge, especially in the fields of transportation and communication, means that administering such control has become more feasible, whether or not that is the desirable course to take. Increasing knowledge as to the wealth to be found in the oceans and on the ocean floors prompts nations to establish workable rules governing sovereignty over the areas of open ocean.

After World War II, for reasons that included jockeying for position in ocean fishing, countries with coastlines were claiming various degrees of control of coastal waters up to the aforementioned two hundred miles at sea. In response to the desire to use new technologies for mining the deep ocean floor, legal rights that had never been clarified needed to be worked out. In consequence, the United Nations sponsored two conferences on the law of the sea, in 1958 and 1960. Those conferences failed to work out satisfactory new rules, so a Third UN Conference on the Law of the Sea (UNCLOS III) was held, beginning in 1973 and involving sessions in New York, Geneva, Montego Bay, and Caracas; it finally resulted in a draft convention in 1982.[2]

With regard to territorial waters, the convention recognized twelve miles as the maximum breadth of the territorial sea and provided for "transit passage" (freedom of navigation and overflight) for ships and aircraft through and over "narrow straights." With regard to fishing rights, coastal states were permitted to establish "exclusive economic zones" (EEZs) in an area up to two hundred miles from their coast. Within this area they would have "sovereign rights" to the living resources, but with the proviso that they undertake conservation measures to ensure that the fish were not overexploited. Complicated rules were set out with regard to fishing by foreigners in the EEZs.

A trailblazing section of the treaty dealt with mineral resources on the floor of the open ocean. Various minerals were involved, but considered especially important at the time were manganese modules. These mineral resources were declared to be "a common heritage of mankind." In 1970 the UN General Assembly had adopted a declaration of principle to the effect that the seabed, ocean floor, and subsoil thereof were not subject to appropriation by individual nations. No state was entitled to claim or exercise sovereign rights thereto. The convention on the law of the sea, then, contained a provision for regulating the production of minerals in the deep ocean by means of an International Seabed Authority and granting mining rights to interested private or not-so-private enterprises, groups of companies, or consortia. Royalty and/or tax payments were to be made to the Authority, and so the world community would gain from the exploitation of this common heritage of mankind. There was also provision for sharing the technical knowledge available for ocean mining. United States mining companies, which were the chief possessors of that technical knowledge, may not have been happy about the possibility of having to share that knowledge.

The convention was endorsed in 1982 by the Third UN Conference on the Law of the Sea and was ready for submission to the treaty ratification processes of the various governments. Since there had been quite general consensus among the delegates of the participating governments, it seemed probable that the treaty would be quickly endorsed. One of the compromises (involving sharing of seabed sites) that made the final agreement possible had been suggested by Henry Kissinger, the United States secretary of state at the time, in 1976, and the head of the United States delegation at the conference had been Elliot L. Richardson; thus, the treaty seemed to have strong Republican endorsement. However, the Reagan administration decided not even to submit the treaty to the Senate for ratification.

Apparently, the U.S. attitude was, in large part, in response to strong lobbying against the treaty by United States mining companies that wanted a freer hand to exploit the minerals on the ocean floor than they would have had under the treaty. They felt that there was some sort of natural law (institutionalized behavior norm) to the effect that mining companies should be permitted to operate everywhere the way things were done in the United States in the nineteenth century, including such practices as staking claims by whoever got there first. We wanted to apply the principles of the Old West to the world. Also, it seems, the Reagan administration was ill-disposed, in general, to working through the United Nations to solve problems. Nevertheless enough countries have signed to place the treaty in effect and some implementation has gone on. But as of the time of writing (July 1994) much remains uncertain, especially in connection with the International Seabed Authority.

Biodiversity: Endangered Species

A United States law of 1973 called the Endangered Species Act provides that in the event a species of plant or animal is threatened with extinction there shall be implemented a strategy to increase its population and protect individual species members from harm. The law is not as drastic as it might appear because of the possibility of administrative delays in declaring a species to be endangered. But once a species has been declared endangered, it receives thenceforth some powerful protection, as witness the northern spotted owl in the Pacific Northwest. More than 520 species of plants and animals native to the United States have been protected.[3] The law has helped to save from extinction "the bald eagle, the American alligator, the timber wolf, the brown pelican, and the grizzly bear." But some thirty-four species have become extinct while waiting to be put on the endangered list.

As to how much is at stake in protecting species, it is difficult to synthesize. It has been said that there exist between 5 million and 100 million species on planet earth, and that some 150 species are being lost every day. If true, one might wonder why all the fuss over the spotted owl. Yet the protection of the spotted owl provided the leverage for trying to prevent the destruction of the unique rain forest in the Pacific Northwest.

The UN is concerned with biodiversity problems. It has in

existence an Environment Program (UNEP), and in 1990, under the wing of UNEP, it established a Global Environmental Facility to handle a $1.3 billion, three-year pilot program to provide grants, concessional loans, and technical aid to various countries to preserve biological diversity (as well as natural habitats).

Other Environmental Problems

The preceding examples scarcely begin to list the environmental problems of the world. How to dispose of the garbage? Plastics with long life expectancies float in the rivers. Wetlands are being drained. Rivers and lakes are contaminated. Soil is eroding. Acid rain is formed when sulfur dioxide and nitrogen oxide from burning coal combine with moisture in the atmosphere; the acid rain then blows over Canada, coming from United States industries in the Northeast and the Midwest, and this disturbs U.S.–Canadian relations. Then there are desertification, falling water tables, salination of the soil, artificial lakes that fill with silt, rivers running dry because of upstream use of the water, and disposal of the waste from the use of atomic power and atomic explosions. Poison gas. Chemical warfare. Unexploded land mines. The possible self-destruction of the world as a byproduct of atomic war. The UN is in the process of establishing an Organization for the Prohibition of Chemical Weapons to deal with some of these problems. But, to be trite, much remains to be done.

The Rio Conference

In 1987, a World Commission on Environment and Development, which had been set up by the UN, issued a report called *Our Common Future*. The chair of the commission was Gro Harlem Brundtland, at that time the prime minister of Norway. The report called for an approach to environment and development problems labeled sustainable development. "Sustainable development is development that meets the needs of the present without compromising the ability of future generations to meet their own needs" (p. 43 of the report). Economic development that did not deplete the environment was the concept. And it was the concept that underlay the planning for the June 1992 United Nations Conference on Environment and Development (UNCED) in Rio de Janeiro.

In preliminary meetings the conference leaders had made plans to strengthen the biodiversity program to protect endangered species by sharing technical knowledge and greatly increasing the financing available to support this work such as the UNEP program. The biodiversity treaty, containing provisions for doing this, had the general support of the participating governments, but President Bush refused to sign, apparently on the grounds that sharing technical knowledge would violate the patent rights of American inventors and that the proposed financing arrangements would be a burden on this country. The United States held out until June 4, 1993, when Ambassador to the UN Madeleine Albright signed the treaty in the name of the Clinton administration.

The other proposed treaty was designed to control climate change and originally was formulated to contain a series of deadlines by which the member countries would actually have implemented the procedures provided in the treaty for reducing carbon dioxide emissions by fixed percentages. President Bush objected to the United States being bound to observe such internationally imposed deadlines, so the other countries agreed to remove the deadlines as the price necessary to get an American signature and President Bush's presence in Rio.

A United Nations Commission on Sustainable Development has been established as a watchdog over the implementation of the effort to maintain the existence of the environmental resources necessary to maintain and even increase the productivity of the world. Also, in 1990 the World Bank and the UN jointly established a Global Environmental Facility to channel money from rich countries to poor ones for environmental projects.

The Gore Agenda

The views of Al Gore on the environment took on special importance as a result of his becoming vice president of the United

States.[4] He endorses a comprehensive program for protecting and improving the environment, which he calls a Global Marshall Plan. The strategic goals that he endorses are: (1) the stabilizing of world population, (2) the rapid creation, development, and sharing of environmentally appropriate technologies, (3) a comprehensive and ubiquitous change in the economic "rules of the road" by which we measure the impact of our decisions on the environment (a new global economics), (4) the negotiation and approval of a new generation of international agreements, and (5) the establishment of a cooperative plan for educating the world's citizens about our global environment (a new global environmental consensus).

Details are extensively and carefully developed in connection with each strategic goal. There seems to this writer to be merit in virtually all of the proposals. Gore says with regard to the feasibility of adoption of the program:

> Yet while public acceptance of the magnitude of the threat is indeed curving upward—and will eventually rise almost vertically as awareness of the awful truth suddenly makes the search for remedies an all-consuming passion—it is just as important to recognize that . . . ironically, at this stage, the maximum that is politically feasible still falls short of the minimum that is truly effective. . . . It seems to make sense, therefore, to put in place a policy framework that will be ready to accommodate the worldwide demands for action when the magnitude of the threat becomes clear.[5]

What this means in terms of procedures, that should be initiated is "the successful negotiation and resolution of an entirely new generation of international treaties and agreements aimed at protecting the environment. Just as democracy and market economies are important . . . so is a further extension of the rule of law. . . . The prototype of this kind of agreement was the Montreal Protocol [1987] which was global in scope and called for a worldwide phasing out of the chemicals (like CFCs) that are destroying the ozone layer and featured a cost-sharing arrangement between the industrial and the impoverished nations."[6]

The role that Gore envisages for the United Nations is addressed as follows: "The world's most important supranational organization—the United Nations—does have a role to play, though I am skeptical about its ability to do very much. Specifically, to help monitor the evolution of a global agreement, the United Nations might consider the idea of establishing a Stewardship Council to deal with matters relating to the global environment—just as the Security Council now deals with matters of war and peace."[7]

Gore is realistic about the difficulties, however. On the preceding page (p. 301), he says:

> The mere mention of any plan that contemplates worldwide cooperation creates instant concern on the part of many—especially conservatives—who have long equated such language with the advocacy of some supernational authority, like a world government. . . . But this notion is both politically impossible and practically unworkable. . . . The fear that our rights might be jeopardized by the delegation of even partial sovereignty to some global authority ensures that it's simply not going to happen. . . . What conceivable system of world governance would be able to compel individual nations to adapt environmentally sound policies. . . . As Dorothy Parker once said about a book she didn't like, the idea of a world government "should not be tossed aside lightly; it should be thrown with great force."

After his comment about the Stewardship Council, he writes: "Similarly, it would be wise to establish a tradition of annual environmental summit meetings, similar to the annual economic summits of today, which only rarely find time to consider the environment."[8] The economic summits, it may be recalled, are an activity unconnected with the UN. The Montreal Protocol of 1987, which Gore cites as the prototype for his international agreements, and the International Convention on the Law of the Sea (generated by the UN Conference on the Law of the Sea), which would make an even better prototype, are both agreements worked out under the sponsorship of the

United Nations. The Rio de Janeiro conference was also under the aegis of the United Nations.

So What?

Many environmental problems, such as loud music in the next apartment, are best dealt with at the local level; but the great environmental problems that affect the ability of the human race to survive on planet earth are entitled to handling by an institution that is answerable to the whole race.

People

The interests of people are the central concern of people if people think so. Some "higher power" may not necessarily be particularly concerned with the interests and desires of people. But in considering their problems people are going to do so from the perspective of people. Judgments about right and wrong, or whether one type of technology works better than another for a particular purpose in a particular setting, are people judgments. Knowledge accumulates in the minds of people as they think about and rethink what they consider to be problems and what will be, from their perspective, solutions to problems. And it is people who make the judgments as to which technique serves best in the interests of people—not necessarily in the interests of coyotes.

The Valuation Process

Out of a clear sky to say that a rose is worth a dollar is a statement without meaning. Value does not inhere in any quantifiable sense as a permanent characteristic in a bit of technical knowledge or a certain amount of work or dirt or a mansion. Rather than speaking of the quantity of value inherent in the technology or the machine or the land, it is more meaningful to speak of the valuation being made by people at a given time, having in mind a given purpose, and relative to alternatives. Such a valuation may be favorable or unfavorable, or more favorable or less favorable by comparison with something else.

The relation of people to institutions is twofold. It is people who are indoctrinated by institutions with behavior norms or opinions about values. On the other hand, it is people who are capable of changing the behavior norms that institutions are fostering. They may do so as a result of new knowledge as to the capabilities of new or old technologies in relation to changing problems, or because the nature of the available resources changes as new varieties of neutral stuff become resources. People are at the hub of an ongoing mixed-up process. Their views reflect the views of the institutions under whose influence they were brought up, and their institutionalized behavior norms reflect their own changing perceptions.

Are the people we speak of taken as individuals, one at a time, or as some sort of a collective whole? The answer is both or either. The considerations at stake will be ruminated over in the individual minds of those who choose to ruminate. Others may be more concerned with the CD release of the week or with nothing in particular. The group consensus, or lack of consensus, is arrived at by whatever decision-making processes are operative at the time: free market demand and supply, not-so-free market demand and supply, democratic processes, dictatorial processes, the ability of the ideas of individuals or small groups to penetrate and influence the attitudes of other people. These attitudes and influences are institutionalized behavior norms; they are value judgments. Whatever views prevail generally are the outgrowth of these influences interacting in an ongoing process over time.

Certain individuals, at any given time, may disapprove of the consensus, or lack of consensus. They may continue to try to change it, using the procedures available at the given stage in the historical process. Any individual may feel and allege that she or he possesses knowledge of the truth of the matter and may mount some pulpit and say so. But somebody else may mount another pulpit and allege a different truth. Philosophy may offer no logic by which it is possible to stand apart and say with certainty what one pulpiteer is alleging is the ultimate truth and that what the other is alleging is therefore not, or which is more valuable and by how much. To one alleging the contrary, another may say: But how do you prove the correctness of your vision of the truth? Definitive proof may be hard come by.

Despite this difficulty, society, using different decision-making processes, does make decisions and gets things done in ways that people later may consider satisfactory, well done, too well done, or not cooked enough. Judgments are made as to valuations and prices are set. The market, perfect or imperfect, rational or irrational, is important and influential. And the process, involving grouping and regrouping, goes on.

Valuations that people make as to how well things work, or how desirable they may be, are made in minds whose attitudes have been conditioned by their upbringing. And these conceptions (as to appropriate behavior) that are projected by institutions onto people are a product of the prior history of the institution. A particular behavior norm (shaking hands, driving on the right, or left, side of the road) came into being at an earlier time in response to the prevailing circumstances. It follows that a given behavior norm was probably more appropriate to that earlier time when it came into existence than it is to present circumstances. It may still be a useful norm. On the other hand, blind continuing adherence to inherited practices may well hinder the adoption of new behavior norms that some or most people may conceive to be better.

Thus, a behavior norm, such as exaggerated respect for the principle of national sovereignty, may inhibit world society (the United Nations) from providing what would generally be considered to be, once adopted, a desirable solution to some problem, such as the defense of the tropical rain forests or the protection of the world against global warming. Or United States government resistance to birth control and the government's success in suppressing birth control measures, even in other countries, may contribute to undesirably large increases in world population— undesirable in terms of the opinion of some or many people concerning appropriate balance between population density and the ability of the world, in the current state of the arts and sciences, to provide for the material needs of people into the future.

So, value judgments are made by people. Perhaps one of them has to do with the identification of the best technique for solving a particular problem. The technique is used. A judgment is made as to whether it worked well or some other technique might have worked better. Then, the same technique or an alternative may be used next time.

This process for making value judgments, evaluating them, and changing them has been called a self-correcting value judgment process. It might, equally well or better, be called an experience-dependent value judgment process.

A hodgepodge of United Nations agencies and conferences has dealt with people and their problems. One group in this hodgepodge is the United Nations Population Fund.

Population Size Problems

In a report issued in April 1992, the United Nations Population Fund (UNPF) estimated that the population of the world would rise from 5.48 billion in mid-1992 to 10 billion in 2050. It stated that these figures were too large and rising fast and should be reduced to lessen poverty and hunger and to protect the earth's natural resources. The fund expressed the opinion that 97 percent of the increase would occur in the underdeveloped countries, with 34 percent of that increase occurring in Africa.

The executive director of UNPF, Dr. Nafis Sadik, a Pakistani physician, commented in releasing the report: "This crisis heightens the risk of future economic and ecological catastrophes."[1] In the effort to deal with the problem the fund has been seeking to encourage family planning and campaigning in favor of smaller families. Its program would include better education and health care for women in the developing world, and its effort to raise the status of women would advocate giving women property rights and improved access to labor markets.

To encourage the developed countries to be financially supportive of its program, the fund pointed out that, unless the rate of population increase is held down, more and more poor people will seek to migrate to the richer countries in search of a better life. This will happen at a time when the active working population of the industrialized countries will be static or declining, although the number of retired people will be increasing.

The activities of the fund have largely been supported by the voluntary contributions of member governments rather than out of the regular UN budget. The United States used to provide 27 percent of the voluntary contributions, but in 1976 it suspended all funding as a protest against the role of the fund in encouraging programs supportive of abortions. The current annual budget of the fund is about $225 million a year, which has been without United States support until Clinton became president.

The world has not heard the last of this issue nor the last of the question as to whether individual countries should be able to pressure poor countries into terminating or restricting their efforts to contain the rate of population growth.

Voluntary Migration

Sovereign states generally control migration (immigration and emigration) with national laws that are enacted without clearing through international agencies or diplomatic negotiation. Massive immigration to the United States during the period 1900 to 1910 led to a series of national laws to limit the amount and to favor immigrants from one region by comparison with those from another. In the 1920s the favored ones were those from northern and western Europe by comparison with southern and eastern Europe and the Orient. Over the years the identity of favored groups has changed. But immigrants come in illegally despite such laws.

What should immigration policy be? Is it appropriate that people be able to live anywhere in the world they choose? Perhaps they will tend to go to the region that has the most generous social welfare system, and their arrival will bankrupt the system. What are the pros and cons when people who are lucky enough to live in a region richly endowed with resources that are useful in the exploitation of the latest technological developments decide to keep immigrants out? Maybe the inhabitants of poverty-stricken regions would like to have a world order capable of saying they have a right to migrate to lands or cities that offer greater opportunities, even if they are somewhat crude and uncivilized, or perhaps a different color.

Would it be better to have a United Nations capable of effectively dealing with such issues? Is it better to have sovereign states capable, at least for the moment, of protecting their favorable position from interlopers? Does advocacy of free markets and free trade include advocacy of free movement of people? Is the "rule of law" desirable and appropriate to the situation if the law is made by an organization with worldwide coverage as a byproduct of the self-correcting or experience-dependent value judgment process?

An example may bring the issue down to earth. During the years of the bipolar world of the Cold War, the United States frequently condemned the Soviet Union for not allowing the emigration of all who wished to leave. At the same time, the United States was energetically trying to develop techniques for keeping out immigrants. If all nations effectively implemented both United States policies, there could result a situation involving emigrants with no place to immigrate. Can people have a meaningful right to emigrate without a corresponding right to immigrate?

Refugees and Forced Migration

During the twentieth century homeless and destitute (and not so destitute) refugees have always been a problem with the human race: uprooted Palestinians, dispossessed by Israelis and not welcome in other Arab countries; Cambodians in Thailand; Jews trying to get out of Russia and preferring the United States to Israel; Mexicans slipping across the border to work in the United

States; Korean refugees; Vietnamese refugees; Sudanese refugees; Kurdish refugees; Afghan refugees; refugees from assorted Latin American dictatorships coming and going; East Germans going (or trying to go) to West Germany before the Berlin wall came down, Hutus and Tutsis in Rwanda killing and fleeing.

There are those fleeing from destitution of their own volition, as the Haitians. There are those being forced to leave against their will, as the Palestinian four hundred expelled by Israel and rejected by Lebanon in the winter of 1992–93. There have been the escapes from terror and the forced ejections in former Yugoslavia, also in 1992 and 1993. It has been estimated that in 1992 there were in the world seventeen million refugees outside their own countries and another twenty million uprooted within their home countries by war, natural disaster, or poverty. Is it possible there have been seven *million* Afghan refugees?[2] Some refugees may be in the process of being assimilated in countries to which they have succeeded in migrating. Others may be existing under terrible conditions in refugee camps, even for decades.

This is not a happy situation. And it is especially unhappy in a world that has seen the threat of nuclear war between the Soviet Union and the United States dissipate, and that has heard the promise of a New World Order. Do we want a New World Order capable of saying that these millions of people shall be forced to live in limbo year after year, decade after decade?

In terms of Israel and Palestine this issue has been a maker of trouble continually since World War II. During the late 1940s, and as an aspect of the fighting that brought the state of Israel into existence, large numbers of Palestinians fled from their homes, their abandoned lands in many cases apparently being occupied by Israelis. The issue of their right to return to the area that is now the state of Israel, and to repossess their lands, or be compensated therefore, continues to fester. The United Nations passed a resolution in 1948 setting out the Palestinian "right to return." In May of 1992 the issue came up at a conference in Ottawa involving the effort to resolve the Middle East difficulties that followed the Persian Gulf war. The chief Palestinian delegate, Elias Sanbar, asserted: "Without the solemn recognition of the Right to Return, the life of the Palestinian people as well as the affairs of the region cannot be normalized." And Israeli Prime Minister Yitzhak Shamir is reported to have said: "It will never happen in any way, shape or form. There is only a Jewish right of return to the land of Israel."[3]

Between 1945 and 1950 terrible things went on in Palestine. And a minority of the population managed by 1950 to establish there the independent state of Israel. When it was over, large numbers of uprooted Palestinians were in refugee camps, living under undesirable conditions for the next forty years in the Gaza Strip, Jordan, Lebanon, and parts of what remained of Palestine, much of which was gradually taken over by the Israelis.

Great Britain and the United States were guilty of a major "cop out" in the late 1940s when they should have insisted on the establishment of a democratic government in Palestine that would guarantee equal rights to all its citizens, Arabs and Jews. It is easy to say, but this situation could have been worked out with a reasonable amount of compassion and understanding by reasonable people at that time. And hopefully now it has been.

The United Nations is the appropriate agency to endow with the power and prestige to ensure that tolerant voices are heard over the screams of the intolerant. The UN will not have the appropriate power and prestige until the great powers, including now especially the United States, prove willing to take a back seat, cooperate, and pay their dues.

Article 49 of the 1949 Fourth Geneva Convention states: "Individual or mass forcible transfers, as well as deportations of protected persons from occupied territory to the territory of the Occupying Power or to that of any other country, occupied or not, are prohibited, regardless of their motive." Unlawful deportation is defined as a "grave breach" of the convention.[4]

Another refugee issue, that involving Haitians attempting to get to the United States in the late 1980s and early 1990s, involves the international law principle that has been called *non-refoulement*: "This principle has become well established in international law. According to the convention of 1951 and the Protocol Relating to the Status of Refugees of 1967 and other related instruments, refugees shall not be returned against their will to the land of origin where they are in danger of persecution on political, racial, religious, or other grounds."[5]

It had become the policy of the United States by 1992 to intercept the Haitian boats on the high seas and forcibly return the people to Haiti. With regard to this practice, the *New York Times* reported that the United Nations high commissioner for refugees, Mrs. Sadako Ogata of Japan "sharply criticized the Bush Administration today for returning Haitian refugees to Haiti without giving them the chance to appeal for protection and asylum." The *Times* continued, "United Nations officials said they believe that the United States is in violation of international agreements prohibiting the forced return of refugees rescued on the high seas."[6] (These comments should be updated and yet the update would soon be outdated.)

The demoralizing problems of refugees need a more meaningful hearing on the part of world society than these problems have received. Ad hoc decisions by individual governments do not represent appropriate resolutions.

Terrorism

Since World War II, the disaffected of the world (disaffected for good or not so good reasons), unable to find a channel through which they may work to obtain a reasonable hearing, or unwilling to believe that anything is reasonable, have found an attention-getting tool at their disposal: terrorism. Maybe the terrorists are sponsored or organized by some government. Maybe they are on their own or motivated by considerations of religion or race or. . . . However, retaliation by bombing Tripoli when the terrorists may have been organized from Syria or Iran (and killing a lot of civilians in the process) is not the most civilized way to deal with the problem.

The United Nations should have an organized police empowered to investigate such crimes and make arrests anywhere in the world. And the crime should be tried in an international court. Governments that refused to permit such investigations and arrests within their territory should find themselves deprived of their country's vote in the UN assembly or council, or suffer even stronger sanctions.

Oppression

Many rulers oppress their own people. The reports of Amnesty International are a grim reminder. The daily newspaper is a perpetual reminder. Rulers, the longer they stay in office, gather to themselves wealth, power, and privilege. And they do it with the help of a substantial clique of hangers-on. The hangers-on, at least many of them, have the will to do the rulers' dirty work, even with relish.

In recent times, if an organization such as the UN protests, it has become customary for the ruler to remind the world of the sacred principle of national sovereignty, as discussed in chapter 12, and the world community has chosen to act as though it was helpless.[7] Here, without further justification, I allege that it is desirable that the world community arrogate to itself the power to dispossess the rulers of the world whom it finds to be oppressors of their own people.

But this is an appropriate place to say something emphatic about the follow-up to dispossessing the oppressive ruler. The situation is that UN forces are in control in a country without organized governmental machinery. The UN is assuming that the people of the country wanted the ruler removed but were helpless to do this by themselves. At this point it is easy for the UN authorities to make a major mistake, a mistake that the United States has chronically made after an intervention that has resulted in the dispossessing of some Latin American president. The leaders of the intervening forces identify someone whom they judge to be well intentioned and who promises to hold democratic elections shortly. And the problem is solved.

What actually happens is that the judgment of the leaders of the intervening forces is frequently flawed. And the temporary president uses the leverage of his position to win the job of permanent president in a rigged election. Or some ruler from earlier times may merely be reinstated as was done in Kuwait after the Persian Gulf War in 1991. The Emir who was reinstated may well have reimposed a regime that is not particularly disposed toward democracy.

But what is the alternative? For one thing, the alternative is neither "in and out fast" nor "stick around forever." It involves a difficult balancing act. The intervening forces must be UN forces and not a military force under the command of any national government, and they must limit their role to maintaining law and order for an indefinite period of time while the domestic population is allowed spontaneously to generate its own new order, without the intervening forces pulling strings in the background. The intervening forces must get completely out when the new political order is judged by the UN to be capable of governing credibly. This is not an easy agenda.

If the intervention is by forces which are genuinely UN forces, rather than by forces that are effectively the forces of an individual nation, and the purpose is to reinstate a democratically elected and still popular legal president, surely the intervening forces need not have to stay long if the situation is well handled by the interveners and by the popular legal president.

Ethnic and Religious Hatred and Feuds

People are not always the innocent victims of situations beyond their control. Ancient, perhaps long-dormant feuds, that are suddenly revived for trivial reasons or accidentally because of circumstances, may quickly generate conditions not easy to control. Why did ethnic, or is it religious, hatreds suddenly create bitter warfare among Croats, and Slovenes, and Serbs, and Bosnian Muslims in Yugoslavia in the early 1990s? These sources of difficulty seemed pretty much dormant during the Tito years from the 1940s to the 1990s. Was the inciting factor the vision of Estonia, Latvia, and Lithuania gaining independence? Was it a case of leaders who chose to excite the people to emotional reactions that could well have continued dormant otherwise?

José María Mendiluce of Spain was the special envoy of the United Nations Commissioner for Refugees in the Balkans during the 1991–93 period. In May 1993, on the occasion of his transfer, he commented:

> People can be transformed into hating and killing machines without too much difficulty.
>
> There is an attitude in the West that war is raging three hours from Venice only because Balkan people are fundamentally different from other Europeans. That is a very dangerous mistake, because it is leading Europeans to become immobilized and to think only about their new cars and their beach holidays.
>
> When I look at far-right groups emerging in various European countries, including some that have had electoral successes, I realize that Yugoslavia-type conflicts could easily break out there. All it takes is an economic crisis and a few cynical politicians who blame it on immigrants or poor people or people who are somehow different.
>
> Here you see how easy it is for cynical leaders to stir up hatred by spreading lies in the media and fomenting provocations on the ground. The rest of Europe is not immune to this kind of manipulation. It could happen in Britain or France or Germany or Spain. . . .
>
> Even those who have signed peace agreements don't change their behavior. I don't expect them to become prophets of peace and love, but at least to stop hating and killing. This has not happened.
>
> Maybe our greatest success here has been that for the first time we have established the principle that the world community has the right to humanitarian intervention in a country during wartime. We are using all the tools we have to penalize those who use force against others. We aren't doing enough, but we have established a very important new direction.[8]

The problems created by ethnic and religious hatreds and feuds become serious when a human tendency to combativeness, frequently associated with ethnic, religious, and historical excuses, is added to the picture. It is the control of this tendency that establishes the distinction between being civilized and being a barbarian.

As they tried to civilize cruel, vicious, and warlike people, early societies discovered the great usefulness of religion, and especially the aspect of religion that emphasizes the fear of hellfire and damnation after death. The priesthood of many religions found very early in the process that impressing troublemakers with their likely destination in a land of perpetual, extreme discomfort could have a useful humbling and restraining influence. In more modern times, psychologists may also usefully deal with hatred and feuds, especially by emphasizing that identifying a feud as long standing is not carte blanche for resigning oneself to its continuing inevitability.

Vienna 1993

The United Nations has already done much in the area of defending individual rights. There is the historic Universal Declaration of Human Rights of 1948, which catalogues some twenty-nine rights. As it stood, this declaration was a statement of principle that simply urged governments and people to implement its precepts. There was no enforcement mechanism. But, as has been mentioned in chapter 8, there has since been enough endorsement of the Universal Declaration in high places to give some credibility to the claim that it does represent law, compliance with which has been implemented in many cases by the range of powerful social and other pressures that institutions are capable of generating.

In addition, over the years since 1948 there have been many occasions, such as UN conferences, where formal endorsement of the existence of assorted human rights has also occurred. As the latest development in this sequence of events, a World Conference on Human Rights met in Vienna in June 1993. At this conference there developed a cleavage between what might be called western countries headed by the United States and various non-western countries. This cleavage was described by Alan Riding in a *New York Times* article of June 26, 1993:

The West's main concern was that a bloc of mainly Asian nations, led by China, Iran and Syria, might succeed in their attempt to challenge the universality of human rights by arguing that they existed as a function of a country's history, level of development, cultural tradition and religion.

While the conference's final declaration does take note of these variables, it commits states to promote and protect all human rights "regardless of their political, economic, and cultural systems." And it adds, "The universal nature of these rights and freedoms is beyond question."

This issue is worth pursuing. Consensus in a country as to what human rights shall prevail there does exist as a product of that country's history. But so does the consensus of world society exist as a product of the history, level of development, cultural tradition, and assorted religions that have prevailed in the world. Enthusiasts on the subject of human rights are making a mistake when they allege that there is some natural law identifying an appropriate catalogue of such rights. No philosopher has by logic identified such a list. Nor does there exist, as the American Declaration of Independence affirms, an endowment by the "Creator" of "certain unalienable Rights." Nor is it within the competence of any legislative body to identify any such list that it can compel future society to honor.

But at any stage in history, the people of that time may, by the choice processes available to them, identify a list of rights that particular nations, groups, and individuals may disrespect at their peril. Such a list may bind society currently, and, as the Chinese should have realized after Tiananmen Square, may be meaningful in the here and now, at least.

Conclusion

Perhaps a brief conclusion is best: People are the victims of the system. They are also responsible for the system. It is not merely pious platitude to say that the creation of a more pleasantly livable world depends on the willingness of people, individual people, and low levels of government, to cooperate in protecting individuals from each other and from oppressive government. The individuals need to check on their own behavior norms and rise above many of them. This is all glib and at the same time it is near to being that truth that we will probably "never" entirely understand how to implement. We need an effective, free-standing United Nations to monitor the process. The UN needs to have the tools to intervene and do something about scandalous situations, and the checks and balances in the system need to be such that UN officials are not "in our hair" all the time. Various levels of government can operate side by side with rough understanding as to what is the reasonable domain of action of the various levels of government. Are people and their leaders capable of meeting the challenge?

In 1994 the United Nations created a new position, United Nations High Commissioner for Human Rights, and José Ayala Lasso of Ecuador was nominated by the secretary-general for the post.

At all events, in the end (which will never come) we will see, and yet we will almost for certain never see for sure.

Reform of the United Nations

The United Nations charter, in article 109, provided for "a General Conference of the Members of the United Nations for the purpose of reviewing the present charter." As mentioned in the Introduction to this book, paragraph 3 of that article says: "If such a conference has not been held before the tenth annual session of the General Assembly . . . the proposal to call such a conference shall be placed on the agenda of that session of the General Assembly." Such a conference is now overdue by well over thirty years. Even the founders anticipated the probable need for improving the charter. The procedures are there. They should be used.

At the time of the Persian Gulf War in 1990–91, President George Bush spoke of glowing prospects for a New World Order. The central ingredient in a world order is the manner in which world society in general and individual nations in particular interact in dealing with world problems. A forum where this can happen has been provided. The long delayed general conference of the members of the United Nations should be called to review the manner in which world society wants to operate the world. This should be done, and let us see what happens.

Reorganization Plans

Preliminary plans as to how the United Nations restructuring and world society decision making should be handled will be torn apart early in such a conference. Nevertheless, it will be helpful to have an assortment of such proposals in hand as a basis for discussion; in fact, many already exist.

The United Nations Association–USA has formulated such a plan, which is set forth in Peter J. Fromuth's *A Successor Vision: The United Nations of Tomorrow*. Elliot L. Richardson of the United States was the chair of the group that prepared the report proper called "UN Management and Decision-Making Project," which constitutes the first eighty pages of the book. The suggested reforms were fairly modest and chiefly in the economic and social fields; better structural organization and more efficiency were goals suggested. But the factual material in the report represents a devastating critique by knowledgeable people of the functioning of the United Nations organization.

On p. xviii appears the following synthesis:

> The panel has given considerable attention to the deficiencies of the present U.N. structure in the economic and social area, these include: a generally low level of representation; overlap between the General Assembly, the Economic and Social Council, and UNCTAD; a lack of intellectual authority; the absence of a system for identifying emerging global issues; and the weakness of coordination and joint planning in the U.N. system. While institutional changes are clearly needed, a balance has to be struck between what may be desirable ultimately, and the kinds of constructive practical steps which member states could undertake immediately.

The World Federalist Association in Washington, D.C., has been an imaginative group advocating the formation of a federal union of the nations of the world with limited but positive governmental powers. Clarence K. Streit was for many years the leader in this group. One among many of his publications is Streit, Roberts, and Schmidt, *The New Federalist*; another is *Union Now*.

Among many more recent publications in World Federalism, Ronald J. Glossop has recently written *World Federation? A Critical Analysis of Federal World Government*. This work is a well-done plea for a federal type of government for the world. There would still be independent nations, but: "One of the main tasks of a world government would be the preservation of law and order for the whole world. Such a government would need some kind of legislature to make laws for the whole world. . . . In a federal system certain powers or areas of authority will belong to the national governments, and the world government will be restricted to making laws only in those areas where it has been given jurisdiction by the world constitution."

A major study of the United Nations was that of the Palme Commission (Independent Commission on Disarmament and Security Issues), entitled *Common Security: A Blueprint for Survival.* Olaf Palme was twice prime minister of Sweden and was assassinated in 1986. This report was especially concerned with disarmament and arranging that peace*making* be more effectively handled. Several of the study's recommendations follow:

"A doctrine of common security must replace the present expedient of deterrence through armaments. International peace must rest on a commitment to joint survival rather than a threat of mutual destruction."

"The Commission strongly supports the goal of general and complete disarmament."

"The Commission considers the notion of political linkage an unsound principle which should be abandoned."

"We conclude that it is impossible to win a nuclear war and dangerous for states to pursue policies or strategies based on the fallacious assumption that a nuclear war might be won."

"The idea of fighting a limited nuclear war is dangerous."

Published in 1982, the Palme report was addressed chiefly to the relationship of the United States and the Soviet Union. It scarcely addressed itself to the organizational changes in the United Nations structure that might contribute to making the UN an effective international peacekeeper. Also, it was not concerned with the social and economic work of the UN or with the question of how to make the views of world society on those matters enforceable.

In the 1950s there was a proposal by the Commission to Study the Organization of Peace (Arthur N. Holcombe, chairman) entitled *Strengthening the United Nations*. Clyde Eagleton was on the drafting committee of this group. The group recommended that in the case of conflict between contending factors the right of a particular government to represent a member state in the UN should be decided by a two-thirds vote in the General Assembly. It also advocated very substantial reduction in the veto power of the permanent members in the Security Council. Further recommendations included that the UN should have its own permanent military force consisting of volunteers plus contingents from national armies in genuine readiness to be placed under the authority of the UN. And the United States should modify the reservation attached to its ratification of the optional clause in the statute of the International Court of Justice, the so-called Connally amendment discussed in chapter 8. In the event of breaches of the peace, situations involving aggression should be dealt with by the UN, not by nations or collective defense arrangements acting independently.

Then there is *A Study of Future Worlds*, an imaginative work by Richard A. Falk, who recommends a United Nations with sufficient authority to override national sovereignties.

Grenville Clark and Louis B. Sohn, in *World Peace Through World Law*, recommend the same thing.

A United Nations mandated study, prepared by a commission of which Robert Jackson of Australia was chair, called the Jackson Report and entitled *A Study of the Capacity of the United Nations Development System*, consisted largely of a major critique of mismanagement and failure to manage in the United Nations administration. It recommended reinforcement of the central authority of the United Nations, effective leadership, and meaningful implementation of the high principles expressed in the charter. It was chiefly addressed to the problem of poor administration.

There is also a report of the United Nations Joint Inspection Unit on Personnel Problems in the United Nations, submitted by

Maurice Bertrand, called *Some Reflections on Reform of the United Nations*. I have not seen this report, but I understand its recommendations are similar to those of the Jackson report.

A comprehensive proposal by Harlan Cleveland entitled *Birth of a New World: An Open Moment for International Leadership* was published in early 1993. It is worth reading because of its thoughtful coverage of the whole range of problems involved in making the world a better place in which to live.

On January 30, 1992, the Security Council, with John Major, the British prime minister serving as chair and principal promoter, requested that the new secretary-general prepare by July 1, 1992, an "analysis and recommendations on ways of strengthening and making more efficient within the framework and provisions of the charter the capacity of the United Nations for preventive diplomacy, for peacemaking and for peace-keeping." Given the wording of the charge to Boutros-Ghali, it seems that the calling of a major charter-rewriting conference was not contemplated. Boutros-Ghali produced the requested report on June 17, 1992. It was entitled "An Agenda for Peace: Preventive Diplomacy, Peacemaking and Peace-Keeping."

The endorsement of national sovereignty is one of the suspect concepts in the charter as it stands. Perhaps the passage in article 2, paragraph 7, "Nothing contained in the present charter shall authorize the United Nations to intervene in matters which are essentially within the domestic jurisdiction of any state . . . , " can be reinterpreted.

The secretary-general says in his 1992 report, paragraph 17: "The foundation-stone of this work is and must remain the State. Respect for its fundamental sovereignty and integrity are crucial to any common international progress. The time of absolute and exclusive sovereignty, however, has passed; its theory was never matched by reality." The last sentence hints that the secretary-general really favors weakening of the implications of the national sovereignty concept.

This report ostensibly is limited to the procedures involved in dealing with war, aggression, and warlike situations, and yet much of it is devoted to preventive diplomacy and post-conflict peacebuilding. It calls for the activation of unused aspects of the peace-making machinery actually provided for in the charter. Under article 42 the Security Council "may take such action by air, sea or land forces as may be necessary to maintain or restore international peace and security." The truth of the matter, however, is that the UN has no forces automatically available to it for use in such situations. It may request to borrow troops from member states, but this is done on an ad hoc basis in connection with each crisis. As matters stand, no country is under any obligation to provide such troops.

Article 43 states: "All Members of the United Nations . . . undertake to make available to the Security Council, on its call and in accordance with a special agreement or agreements, armed forces, assistance and facilities . . . necessary for the purpose of maintaining international peace and security." The trouble is that no such special agreements have been worked out with any member nation since 1945.

At present, when the Security Council enacts a resolution calling for the use of force in a particular situation, the secretary-general considers which nations he will request to provide how many troops in that situation. If details can be worked out, the nation provides the contingent of troops agreed on at that time. If the secretary-general, following the resolution providing for the use of force, can find no country willing to provide troops, the Security Council might as well have saved its breath to cool its porridge. Of course, some, or at least one, of the Security Council members voting for the use of force has probably done so under circumstances making it willing to provide the troops. This was the case with the United States in the Korean War, Persian Gulf War, and Somalia situation. But the resulting situation is then very much one in which the country providing the troops "calls the tune." The United Nations is not in effective charge of the operation, as it never was in Korea, Kuwait, or Somalia.

Boutros-Ghali has made a serious effort to arrange to establish a permanent standing UN military force that would be acting under UN orders. He says in paragraph 43 of the "Agenda for Peace":

> This will require bringing into being, through negotiations, the special agreements foreseen in Article 43 of the Charter whereby Member States undertake to make armed forces, assistance and facilities available to the Security Council for the purposes stated in Article 42, not only on an ad hoc basis but on a permanent basis.

The press reported in early January of 1993 how almost idolizing of President George Bush were the Somalis, but on the occasion of the visit of Boutros-Ghali, they staged a massive demonstration against him and denounced the UN for its ineffectual assistance.[1] The situation was saved, but in a manner humiliating to Boutros-Ghali and the UN. One can only imagine how different the situation would have been if the U.S. Marines had been wearing UN uniforms, as they should have been if the American president had really been interested in building up the prestige of the UN.

In the *New York Times*, Leslie Gelb said with regard to this effort: "Mr. Boutros-Ghali then makes a sad admission. He has suspended efforts to establish standing U.N. military force. The opposition of the U.S. and other major powers, he says, remains too strong."[2] Gelb went on. "Instead he wants member nations to 'earmark certain forces' for UN use. He hopes that 'at a minimum' the U.S. will provide logistical support under UN command." This would not seem to be much to ask, since such action is provided for in the charter, if the nations would just get around to negotiating the agreements called for in article 43, paragraph 1, which will provide for the armed forces a given country must make available to the UN in an emergency.

Several other positions taken by the secretary-general in the "Agenda for Peace" are worth noting. With regard to financing the UN, he says (paragraphs 69, 72): "A chasm has developed between the tasks entrusted to this Organization and the financial means provided to it. The truth of the matter is that our vision cannot really extend to the prospect opening before us as long as our financing remains myopic. . . . Member States must pay their assessed contributions in full and on time. Failure to do so puts them in breach of their obligations under the Charter." He then fails to recommend the major changes in financing that are necessary and appropriate. But he does say he is setting up a committee.

He shows awareness of the problem created by the dominance of the Security Council by the cabal of great powers with their veto (paragraph 78): "And it follows that agreement among the permanent members must have the deeper support of the other members of the Council, and the membership more widely, if the Council's decisions are to be effective and endure." But, again, where is the strong medicine that is called for?

With regard to "democracy" in UN governance (paragraph 82): "Democracy within the family of nations means the application of its principles within the world Organization itself. . . . Democracy at all levels is essential to attain peace for a new era of prosperity and justice." But too much deference to the sovereign state as the basic unit (one nation, one vote in the General Assembly) is not conducive to a UN representing people.

In making his recommendations, the secretary-general was inhibited by the charge under which he was working, and possibly also by the realization that he was very new at his job. The charge he was given included the provision that his recommendations should be "within the framework and provisions of the Charter. . . ." Perhaps, for this reason, he does not recommend revision of the charter.

Possible Changes in Structure

Consideration of complete reorganization of the United Nations by a general conference is called for. Once assembled, and after much discussion, the conference may decide to recommend certain specific changes but to leave the overall structure much as it stands. In earlier chapters many suggestions have been made as to specific changes that might well be appropriate under such circumstances. On the other hand, it may be decided that restructuring from the ground up is called for. The following highly general framework is offered for consideration in case the latter is the course taken. The three basic areas for consideration for changes in structure are the legislative, the administrative (executive), and the judiciary branches. Then there are changes in function.

The Legislative Branch

It is suggested that in the legislative branch there would be two houses: an assembly and a council. The general assembly representatives would be elected by direct, popular vote in single-member districts of roughly equal population. The council would be elected by national legislative bodies, larger countries having as many as three councillors, quite small countries being grouped to elect one councillor. Genuinely prestigious people, such as former presidents and former prime ministers, might find their way to the council under this procedure.

The terms of office of general assembly representatives would be four years, half of the number being elected every two years. There would be a four-term limit on service. The councillors would have six-year terms, a third elected every two years, and with a three-term limit. But there is probably no point at this stage in spending a lot of time arguing the "length of terms" issue. It is a bit early in the process for that. It is important that representatives and councillors not be selected by the executive or administrative branches of the national governments. The legislative body should not be the mere creature of existing governments.

Election of the assembly by direct popular vote is an intriguing possibility. In areas of the world where several nations are entitled to only one representative among them, transnational popular elections would be an interesting phenomenon. Or perhaps the election might occur only in the country whose turn has come, in some sort of agreement on rotation of seats. The elections might well be fairly honestly conducted, as the nations would watch each other's voting with more than disinterested attention.

Apart from the innate appeal of popular election, there is another tempting argument for this procedure. It would tend to undermine the position of the goodly number of worthless rulers spread around the world. Especially if the United Nations exercised its authority to disqualify representatives not selected in reasonably free elections, the United Nations being the judge on this score, this would be a significant sanction that would be automatically and effectively applied. The shoe would then be on the other foot. Lack of representation in the General Assembly, on the grounds of fraudulent elections, could be significant in undermining the position of unsavory rulers.

However, powerful influences will resist democratizing the assembly. The people of the affluent countries (large and small) are afraid of having their influence swamped by the votes of the poor of the world. For their part, the poor countries, and especially their leaders, are jealous of the prerogatives they possess as a result of the possession of national sovereignty. So vested interests in large and small countries will continue to defend national sovereignty and its perquisites against a system capable of representing a step toward genuine worldwide democracy. Democracy in the selection of national representatives should represent a major step in giving credibility to the United Nations.

Laws would become valid on passage by both houses. The chief of the administrative branch would have a veto power, but only a 55 percent majority would be required to override the veto. It is important that the chief administrator not become overly powerful.

Administrative or Executive Branch

The chief of the administrative or executive branch would be selected by the legislative branch. Popular election of a world-level chief administrator or executive sounds infeasible; it is difficult to imagine a campaign in which candidates would make worldwide swings, trying to communicate with people who speak many different languages.

A likely procedure would be that the future chief would have to be approved by majority vote in both houses, voting separately. If there occurred a series of failures (perhaps three or four) to elect anyone, the margin for election might be dropped to 45 percent in both houses, then 40 percent, and so on, or the power to make the choice might be turned over to one house, say the council.

The three highest-ranking assistants to the chief would be: one in charge of peacemaking and the handling of difficulties involving tyrannical leadership in a member country, a second in charge of activities in the economic and social areas, and a third in charge of the UN personnel and planning organizational structure. These three assistants, after recommendation by the chief, would be subject to confirmation by a majority vote in the two houses, or, if that proved difficult, confirmation might be left to just one of the houses.

Revenue and Expenditure

To begin with, the United Nations should have at least two major sources of revenue: a percentage, perhaps 25 or 30 percent, of each country's military budget, however large or small that budget might be (see chapters 4 and 6); and a corporate (or business) income tax (see chapters 6 and 8).

It is important that a significant part of the revenue of the UN be collected directly from corporations active internationally in the form of a corporate income tax and that the UN have the police power to make such collections effective. Access to an independent source of revenue, it may be remembered, was essential to making the federal government of the United States viable in 1789. It is not enough merely to pound the table and say governments ought to be good and pay their assessments.

On the expenditure side, to mention only one matter in particular, there should be a system of grants-in-aid to the poorer developing countries. It is especially important that a system of United

Nations grants-in-aid substitute for most of the foreign aid arrangements that have prevailed since World War II. The system of bilateral development aid by governments, in circumstances where political strategies have been a major consideration, has been thoroughly unsatisfactory as a means of fostering economic development, or now we might say, "sustainable" development.

The Judiciary

Procedure for selecting the justices on the International Court of Justice might remain much as it has been. Those procedures seem to have produced a court that is reasonably independent of the influence of the great powers. Such independence is a necessity.

The area of jurisdiction of the court, however, should be substantially expanded. It should include disputes among national governments, and advisory opinions, when asked for, by the legislative or administrative branches. Also, it should be empowered to hear appeals, at its discretion, by individuals or corporations of the decisions of national supreme courts. This possibility should be used sparingly, at least at first, to give the nations of the world time to get used to the idea.

In one area, the International Court of Justice should be at the center of the stage, as it should have been when it was first established at the close of World War II. That area has to do with the trial of war criminals and tyrants and warlords who have been accused of behavior that violates what society considers a reasonable or civilized standard.

Matters to be decided might be whether the ICJ itself should conduct the trials or whether it should play a supervisory role over the establishment of the court that does, the latter being the manner in which the situation in the Balkans is being handled. It is important that the United Nations and the International Court not overreach themselves in the beginning. What is desirable, of course, is an arrangement in which there is a balance between central control and decentralization.

The Secretariat/Personnel/Organizational Structure of the Administrative or Executive Branch

To return to the problems of the assistant to the chief in charge of personnel and planning, the provisions in the United Nations charter having to do with the Secretariat envisage a personnel with a basic loyalty to the United Nations and independence from the influence of national governments in the selection of that personnel. This process has been a travesty.[3] But the personnel problem is one that should be solvable by changed administrative procedures in the hands of people who care to make the United Nations a free-standing organization that is not subservient to the influence of particular nations or interests.

The administrative structure of the United Nations is an incoherent, uncoordinated mess. The assistant chief in charge of personnel and planning has his work cut out for him.

Possible Changes in Function

Area of Jurisdiction

The assembly and the council should legislate primarily in areas of international concern, there being also a presumption that responsibility for action should be left to the lowest possible level of government whenever action by a higher level is not called for to obtain necessary coordination. The way things are in most countries, including the United States, different levels of government actually do legislate on different types of problems. The United Nations would become merely one more level in this hierarchy, albeit the top one. Areas in which it would concentrate its legislating will be tentatively identified at the start of the process and subject to revision as the process goes on. This is the experience-dependent or self-correcting value judgment process. The pattern will be worked out and continually revised as an ongoing process, in the give and take of history. It involves learning by experience, followed by correcting one's judgment, with the passage of time, as to where the legislative borderlines should be drawn between different levels of government. It should not be unthinkable that, in appropriate areas, the United Nations legislative bodies might legislate for the world.

It is not true that society disapproves of government regulation. To put it a bit brutally, it depends on whose ox is being gored. If society thinks some matter ought to be regulated, society will have a go at formally regulating the matter. If society believes automobile drivers should drive to the right, or the left, for good and sufficient reasons, it can issue a fiat to that effect and punish nonconformists. If society believes the army of country X should stay home instead of venturing into a neighboring country and raping a lot of women, killing a lot of children, and mutilating a lot of other people, then world society can (who is to say it can't?) take measures to force the army of country X to go home. If local warlords are stealing the relief supplies going to the starving in the warlords' country and there is no responsible government in that country, world society can take measures calculated to force the warlords to behave better if it chooses to do so.

The UN exists because world society decided that an organization calculated to regulate or control or influence the behavior of people all over the world is desirable. The suggestions for reform of the United Nations are calculated to create an organization or structure capable of doing this job better. This discussion of function has to do with determining the manner in which the UN will operate to implement the behavior that world society believes proper.

The pressures that world society, working through the UN, may choose to use when it believes "social pressure" alone is not accomplishing the desired results include the use of laws accompanied by some use of force to see to it that the laws, or regulations, or orders are obeyed or observed.

Legislation or Conferences/ Treaties/Ratifications

As a practical matter, rules with the force of laws may come into being as a result of international conferences at which multilateral treaties are developed for endorsement by each country's government, or a legislative body may be authorized to establish laws directly. The process of making laws will be infinitely more satisfactory and expeditious if a legislative process is used in preference to the conferences/treaties/ratification ordeal.

At an international conference involving delegates from 184 or so countries much time must be expended establishing convention rules before complicated discussions can even begin. And after agreement is reached at the conference there remains the difficult problem of getting the draft treaty approved by the governments. Maybe the government of the country that is most crucial for making the plan work balks at ratifying. Unsatisfactory as legislatures may sometimes seem, they are models of expedition and efficacy, and probably fairness, by comparison with the conference and treaty-making procedure.

A case in point involves the effort to agree on "the law of the sea." Reasonably clear rules as to "who controls what" in the open ocean have become a matter requiring clarification. Who and under what circumstances has the right to mine the ocean floor? Who has the right to fish where? What rules may be applied to police the drug trade? In the case of the effort to establish the law of the sea by international conference and treaty ratification the tale is one of long-drawn-out frustration.

Levels of Government

Americans are socially conditioned to see red at the thought of an international body passing laws that affect our behavior. A soft answer may or may not mitigate this wrath, but it is worth a try. We have been over this ground in the states' rights controversy in the United States. Individual "sovereign" states periodically wax indignant about federal laws increasingly regulating matters like interstate commerce, welfare, and smoking.

Surely the defensible position on this matter is that regulation for its own sake is undesirable. The more freedom of action the better up to the point that one person's freedom of action creates problems for other people. Regulation begins to be called for, but how much and by whom? In the interest of as little total regulation as possible, the concept to guide decision making might well be that decisions regulating a situation should be made by the lowest level of government capable of doing the job satisfactorily: town (city, school district), county, state, nation, international agency. Some problems, like the law of the sea, require international action to be handled satisfactorily. Maybe health care can be handled best at the national level. Police departments to deal with most crimes—robbery, disturbing the peace, arson, etc.—can appropriately be managed at the level of towns and cities.

We feel our way as to which level of government can best handle which problems. With the passage of time, it may work out that some problem can be better handled at another level. With much huffing and puffing a change may occur.

Tentatively, the UN might be validated to deal with a range of international problems. But that list is not chipped in concrete. Some problem areas might be moved to lower areas, or the UN might take on new chores. What are some of the chores to which the UN might well address itself initially?

Social and Economic Problems

A brief, perhaps controversial list of social and economic problems that might be regulated by the UN includes fostering the international dissemination of technical and scientific knowledge; controlling small-country dictators who have gotten control of atom bombs; handling international aid to regions victimized by catastrophes; fostering the economic development of poor countries; controlling the international spread of disease; perpetuating the virgin and not-so-virgin forests, both tropical and temperate zone; controlling the policies of individual nations that contribute to contaminating the world; influencing what happens in Antarctica and the Arctic, especially relevant to the ozone hole, mining, and contamination; regulating the practices of ships at sea and airplanes on international routes; dealing with international trade restrictions; collecting and disseminating weather information to be then further collected and disseminated by other levels of government; handling international mail; regulating atomic energy in some national aspects as well as international aspects; possible regulation of production of exhaustible resources; playing an appropriate role in dealing with international migration and the refugee problem; collecting revenues independently of the cooperation of national governments, and so on and on. In fact, of course, the UN is already doing a lot of these things. Time and experience will influence which activities should be removed from such a list and which might be added. There will still be plenty of work for governments at every other level.

Peacemaking

Under the charter as it stands the UN is authorized under chapter VII and especially articles 41 and 42 to do far more and with more authority than it has done, and articles 43 and 47 provide for implementation procedures that have not been used. Whether these are particularly desirable or effective procedures is an open question. The United Nations should have the *power* to impose peace. It is to be hoped that it would also have the judgment to take action in a manner conducive to the existence of civilized society as a consequence of its action. Initially, however, the United Nations (not the United States or Russia or China) must possess a dominating military power. After the nations "get the idea" the UN will surely need to maintain far less military force on a permanent basis.

As a first step in this process a rewriting of chapter VII of the charter ("Action with Respect to Threats to the Peace, Breaches of the Peace, and Acts of Regression") should be in order. Article 47 calls for "a Military Staff Committee to advise and assist the Security Council on all questions relating to . . . the employment and command of forces. . . ." It further says that the Military Staff Committee shall consist of the Chiefs of Staff of the permanent members of the Security Council or their representatives. And: "The Military Staff Committee shall be responsible under the Security Council for the strategic direction of any armed forces placed at the disposal of the Security Council. Questions relating to the command of such forces shall be worked out subsequently."

It is a bit much to expect that the other members of the United Nations community will be satisfied to have the five great powers, and particularly the United States, thus dominate the control and guidance of the UN force. The solution to this problem may be to permit a new and revised UN decision-making machinery to control the command structure of the UN force.

The United Nations should have a core permanent, voluntary force directly recruited by the UN. It might be argued that this could be accomplished under the present charter, but that is not clearly evident. It would be desirable to have a charter amendment providing for such a force. The initial number should be in the 100,000 to 200,000 range.

A cadre of officers and enlisted men, trained to address the types of problems with which the UN is confronted, would be desirable. In fact, it is amazing that such a force does not exist. Are the nations so afraid of the potential power of the UN that they insist on its being incompetent to do its job?

Internationalists, people with an interest in other races and cultures, should be intrigued by the opportunities presented by participation in such a force. For young people a five-year or so tour of duty in such a force should provide excellent credentials for a wide variety of jobs in later life. And it would provide idealists with the opportunity to do a job they can be proud of.

Concern as to the possibility of too much power at the headquarters of a permanent, volunteer UN force would be tempered by deconcentrating the actual forces. Deconcentration is desirable, anyway, in order to have troops handy near as many problem places as possible. Such deconcentration could be implemented through organizations ready to hand such as the Organization of American States, the Association of Southeast Asian Nations, and the Commission on Security and Cooperation in Europe.

The troops must be UN troops, however, taking an oath of loyalty to the UN. It is worth noting that a person may be loyal to more than one institution—most people are—but oaths must be worded appropriately. Individuals will, no doubt, occasionally be put in positions that result in crises of conscience. So be it.

It is desirable to say something about NATO, the North Atlantic Treaty Organization and its governing body the North Atlantic Council. The arrangement among some of the Allies of World War II was created in 1949 to consolidate the opposition to the Soviet Union during the Cold War. A major aspect of its work involved the presence in Western Europe of powerful United States forces integrated with some forces drawn from various western European countries, under command of an American general and headquartered in Belgium.

With the collapse of Soviet power, NATO became largely functionless, its lack of role made evident during most of the period of the Yugoslav struggle. But NATO was and still is a powerful force with powerful equipment and high technology capability. It would be a service to humanity for NATO to cease to exist in a process that would involve turning much NATO equipment and installations over to the United Nations; this procedure would also provide employment possibilities for much of NATO's personnel, which might be interested in shifting over to service with the new UN permanent force. Such behavior would be mutually beneficial and would permit the UN permanent force to come into being with a core of competent and well-equipped personnel. Much delay in building from the ground up would be avoided, especially since naval and air forces should be involved in addition to the land-based army.

Incidentally, the United States could use the situation to its own financial benefit. It might be able to arrange to eliminate its arrears in the assessments it owes the UN in the form of payment for some of the NATO/U.S. equipment.

Meanwhile, and perhaps also as permanent procedure, much of the peacemaking forces could still be raised under the terms of article 43, a procedure that has not yet been followed. Under this article it seems that once the agreements were in place the providing of troops on UN call would be automatic and not subject to the discretion of the troop-providing state. Equally important, the particular troops in the national armies given these UN assignments can be given special training as to how to play their role. And the assignment of troops from the UN permanent force, to help in orienting them to their special role, should be helpful all around.

As stated earlier, the financing of this UN force could take the form of an assessment determined as a percentage of the military defense budget of each nation. In chapter 4 the figure of 25 or 30 percent of the nation's armed forces budget was mentioned to indicate roughly the magnitude of what would be involved. This approach should dampen the enthusiasm of power-hungry rulers for arms buildups if, at the same time they are building up their own armed forces, they are also building up the strength of the forces that will hold their aggression in check. This tendency could be strengthened if the assessment was increased to 50 percent of any *increase* in a country's military budget.

It is not inappropriate, while one is dreaming in these terms, to remind ourselves of another possibility. A nation reducing the size of its military budget might be rewarded with some sort of a bonus. A formula might be worked out to involve reducing the 25 or 30 percent figure somewhat as a country cut its military budget. This procedure would have the additional advantage of decreasing the size of the UN military establishment as the need for its services decreased. It is not especially desirable for the UN to have permanently on its hands a powerful Praetorian Guard with nothing to do.

Then there are the non-military procedures for peacemaking that are set out in article 41. Such measures may include "complete or partial interruption of economic relations and of rail, sea, air, postal, telegraphic, radio and other means of communication, and the severance of diplomatic relations." To the extent that these measures are judged to be effective they are to be preferred to military action.

An opinion is here offered on the merit of the trade embargo in particular. Trade embargoes are not a satisfactory tool in peacemaking. Apparently the philosophy underlying their use is that if a suffering population suffers more, it will rise up and remove the tyrant. But this, frequently futile, approach is a procedure that victimizes victims, and also it does not necessarily work, as witness the futile use of the embargo on Iraq following the Persian Gulf War and in Haiti in 1993.

Evaluation

With the passage of time there will be occasions when most of the people of the world will be of one opinion on a matter of policy and there will be a few determined nonconformists. One may guess and hope that, in such situations, the will of the majority will prevail, and peacefully. But surely, if there is a clear-cut majority will, it should prevail. And that is about all we can say as to the source of the value judgments that will and should prevail in the world.

Perhaps with the passage of time, society will decide that other criteria are needed. So be it. The world and world society are not going to stand still. The future is waiting to ambush us with new and different problems, which we will perforce deal with as the spirit moves us.

The life process goes on. It is interesting and will remain so. One may hope it will also be generally pleasant for most people. At least, may the general run of people somehow have the wit to control the aggressive and cruel, the power hungry and the selfish. The world hereafter will be as civilized as people make it. What better way to conclude a book on the reform of the United Nations than with a quotation from Senator William Fulbright: "We do not think the United Nations is a failure. We think it has never been tried."

If humanity wants to survive civilized in the face of the now known proliferating technological and scientific capabilities, it had better organize itself in a way that permits it to control itself, with representatives selected by the people rather than delegates appointed by and voting at the behest of the rulers.

Appendix

CHARTER OF THE UNITED NATIONS
PREAMBLE

WE THE PEOPLES
OF THE UNITED NATIONS
DETERMINED

to save succeeding generations from the scourge of war, which twice in our lifetime has brought untold sorrow to mankind, and

to reaffirm faith in fundamental human rights, in the dignity and worth of the human person, in the equal rights of men and women and of nations large and small, and

to establish conditions under which justice and respect for the obligations arising from treaties and other sources of international law can be maintained, and

to promote social progress and better standards of life in larger freedom,

AND FOR THESE ENDS

to practice tolerance and live together in peace with one another as good neighbors, and

to unite our strength to maintain international peace and security, and to ensure by the acceptance of principles and the institution of methods, that armed force shall not be used, save in the common interest, and to employ international machinery for the promotion of the economic and social advancement of all peoples,

HAVE RESOLVED TO
COMBINE OUR EFFORTS TO
ACCOMPLISH THESE AIMS

Accordingly, our respective Governments, through representatives assembled in the city of San Francisco, who have exhibited their full powers found to be in good and due form, have agreed to the present Charter of the United Nations and do hereby establish an international organization to be known as the United Nations.

CHAPTER I

PURPOSES AND PRINCIPLES

Article 1

The Purposes of the United Nations are:

1. To maintain international peace and security, and to that end: to take effective collective measures for the prevention and removal of threats to the peace, and for the suppression of acts of aggression or other breaches of the peace, and to bring about by peaceful means, and in conformity with the principles of justice and international law, adjustment or settlement of international disputes or situations which might lead to a breach of the peace;
2. To develop friendly relations among nations based on respect for the principle of equal rights and self-determination of peoples, and to take other appropriate measures to strengthen universal peace;
3. To achieve international co-operation in solving international problems of an economic, social, cultural or humanitarian character, and in promoting and encouraging respect

for human rights and for fundamental freedoms for all without distinction as to race, sex, language or religion; and

4. To be a centre for harmonizing the actions of nations in the attainment of these common ends.

Article 2

The Organization and its Members, in pursuit of the Purposes stated in Article 1, shall act in accordance with the following Principles:

1. The Organization is based on the principle of the sovereign equality of all its Members.
2. All Members, in order to ensure to all of them the rights and benefits resulting from membership, shall fulfill in good faith the obligations assumed by them in accordance with the present Charter.
3. All Members shall settle their international disputes by peaceful means in such a manner that international peace and security, and justice, are not endangered.
4. All Members shall refrain in their international relations from the threat or use of force against the territorial integrity or political independence of any state, or in any other manner inconsistent with the Purposes of the United Nations.
5. All Members shall give the United Nations every assistance in any action it takes in accordance with the present Charter, and shall refrain from giving assistance to any state against which the United Nations is taking preventive or enforcement action.
6. The Organization shall ensure that states which are not Members of the United Nations act in accordance with these Principles so far as may be necessary for the maintenance of international peace and security.
7. Nothing contained in the present Charter shall authorize the United Nations to intervene in matters which are essentially within the domestic jurisdiction of any state or shall require the Members to submit such matters to settlement under the

present Charter; but this principle shall not prejudice the application of enforcement measures under Chapter VII.

CHAPTER II

MEMBERSHIP

Article 3

The original Members of the United Nations shall be the states which, having participated in the United Nations Conference on International Organization at San Francisco or having previously signed the Declaration by United Nations of 1 January 1942, sign the present Charter and ratify it in accordance with Article 110.

Article 4

1. Membership in the United Nations is open to all other peace-loving states which accept the obligations contained in the present Charter and, in the judgment of the Organization, are able and willing to carry out these obligations.
2. The admission of any such state to membership in the United Nations will be effected by a decision of the General Assembly upon the recommendation of the Security Council.

Article 5

A Member of the United Nations against which preventive or enforcement action has been taken by the Security Council may be suspendeKd from the exercise of the rights and privileges of membership by the General Assembly upon the recommendation of the Security Council. The exercise of these rights and privileges may be restored by the Security Council.

Article 6

A Member of the United Nations which has persistently violated the Principles contained in the present Charter may be expelled from the Organization by the General Assembly upon the recommendation of the Security Council.

CHAPTER III

ORGANS

Article 7

1. There are established as the principal organs of the United Nations: a General Assembly, a Security Council, an Economic and Social Council, a Trusteeship Council, an International Court of Justice and a Secretariat.
2. Such subsidiary organs as may be found necessary may be established in accordance with the present Charter.

Article 8

The United Nations shall place no restrictions on the eligibility of men and women to participate in any capacity and under conditions of equality in its principal and subsidiary organs.

CHAPTER IV

THE GENERAL ASSEMBLY

Composition

Article 9

1. The General Assembly shall consist of all the Members of the United Nations.
2. Each member shall have not more than five representatives in the General Assembly.

Functions and Powers

Article 10

The General Assembly may discuss any questions or any matters within the scope of the present Charter or relating to the powers and functions of any organs provided for in the present Charter, and, except as provided in Article 12, may make recommendations to the Members of the United Nations or to the Security Council or to both on any such questions or matters.

Article 11

1. The General Assembly may consider the general principles of co-operation in the maintenance of international peace and security, including the principles governing disarmament and the regulation of armaments, and may make recommendations with regard to such principles to the Members or to the Security Council or to both.
2. The General Assembly may discuss any questions relating to the maintenance of international peace and security brought before it by any Member of the United Nations, or by the Security Council, or by a state which is not a Member of the United Nations in accordance with Article 35, paragraph 2, and, except as provided in Article 12, may make recommendations with regard to any such questions to the state or states concerned or to the Security Council or to both. Any such question on which action is necessary shall be referred to the Security Council by the General Assembly either before or after discussion.
3. The General Assembly may call the attention of the Security Council to situations which are likely to endanger international peace and security.
4. The powers of the General Assembly set forth in this Article shall not limit the general scope of Article 10.

Article 12

1. While the Security Council is exercising in respect of any dispute or situation the functions assigned to it in the present Charter, the General Assembly shall not make any recommendation with regard to that dispute or situation unless the Security Council so requests.
2. The Secretary-General, with the consent of the Security Council, shall notify the General Assembly at each session of any matters relative to the maintenance of international peace and security which are being dealt with by the Security Council and shall similarly notify the General Assem-

bly, or the Members of the United Nations if the General Assembly is not in session, immediately the Security Council ceases to deal with such matters.

Article 13

1. The General Assembly shall initiate studies and make recommendations for the purpose of:
   a. promoting international co-operation in the political field and encouraging the progressive development of international law and its codification;
   b. promoting international co-operation in the economic, social, cultural, educational and health fields, and assisting in the realization of human rights and fundamental freedoms for all without distinction as to race, sex, language or religion.
2. The further responsibilities, functions and powers of the General Assembly with respect to matters mentioned in paragraph 1 (b) above are set forth in Chapters IX and X.

Article 14

Subject to the provisions of Article 12, the General Assembly may recommend measures for the peaceful adjustment of any situation, regardless of origin, which it deems likely to impair the general welfare or friendly relations among nations, including situations resulting from a violation of the provisions of the present Charter setting forth the Purposes and Principles of the United Nations.

Article 15

1. The General Assembly shall receive and consider annual and special reports from the Security Council; these reports shall include an account of the measures that the Security Council has decided upon or taken to maintain international peace and security.
2. The General Assembly shall receive and consider reports from the other organs of the United Nations.

Article 16

The General Assembly shall perform such functions with respect to the international trusteeship system as are assigned to it under Chapters XII and XIII, including the approval of the trusteeship agreements for areas not designated as strategic.

Article 17

1. The General Assembly shall consider and approve the budget of the Organization.
2. The expenses of the Organization shall be borne by the Members as apportioned by the General Assembly.
3. The General Assembly shall consider and approve any financial and budgetary arrangements with specialized agencies referred to in Article 57 and shall examine the administrative budgets of such specialized agencies with a view to making recommendations to the agencies concerned.

Voting

Article 18

1. Each member of the General Assembly shall have one vote.
2. Decisions of the General Assembly on important questions shall be made by a two-thirds majority of the members present and voting. These questions shall include: recommendations with respect to the maintenance of international peace and security, the election of the non-permanent members of the Security Council, the election of the members of the Economic and Social Council, the election of members of the Trusteeship Council in accordance with paragraph I (c) of Article 86, the admission of new Members to the United Nations, the suspension of the rights and privileges of membership, the expulsion of Members, questions relating to the operation of the trusteeship system, and budgetary questions.
3. Decisions on other questions, including the determination of

additional categories of questions to be decided by a two-thirds majority, shall be made by a majority of the members present and voting.

Article 19

A Member of the United Nations which is in arrears in the payment of its financial contributions to the Organization shall have no vote in the General Assembly if the amount of its arrears equals or exceeds the amount of the contributions due from it for the preceding two full years. The General Assembly may, nevertheless, permit such a Member to vote if it is satisfied that the failure to pay is due to conditions beyond the control of the Member.

Procedure

Article 20

The General Assembly shall meet in regular annual sessions and in such special sessions as occasion may require. Special sessions shall be convoked by the Secretary-General at the request of the Security Council or of a majority of the Members of the United Nations.

Article 21

The General Assembly shall adopt its own rules of procedure. It shall elect its President for each session.

Article 22

The General Assembly may establish such subsidiary organs as it deems necessary for the performance of its functions.

CHAPTER V

THE SECURITY COUNCIL

Composition

Article 23

1. The Security Council shall consist of fifteen Members of the United Nations. The Republic of China, France, the Union

of Soviet Socialist Republics, the United Kingdom of Great Britain and Northern Ireland and the United States of America shall be permanent members of the Security Council. The General Assembly shall elect ten other Members of the United Nations to be non-permanent members of the Security Council, due regard being specially paid, in the first instance to the contribution of Members of the United Nations to the maintenance of international peace and security and to the other purposes of the Organization, and also to equitable geographical distribution.

2. The non-permanent members of the Security Council shall be elected for a term of two years. In the first election of the non-permanent members after the increase of the membership of the Security Council from eleven to fifteen, two of the four additional members shall be chosen for a term of one year. A retiring member shall not be eligible for immediate re-election.

3. Each member of the Security Council shall have one representative.

Function and Powers

Article 24

1. In order to ensure prompt and effective action by the United Nations, its Members confer on the Security Council primary responsibility for the maintenance of international peace and security, and agree that in carrying out its duties under this responsibility the Security Council acts on their behalf.

2. In discharging these duties the Security Council shall act in accordance with the Purposes and Principles of the United Nations. The specific powers granted to the Security Council for the discharge of these duties are laid down in Chapters VI, VII, VIII and XII.

3. The Security Council shall submit annual and, when necessary, special reports to the General Assembly for its consideration.

Article 25

The Members of the United Nations agree to accept and carry out the decisions of the Security Council in accordance with the present Charter.

Article 26

In order to promote the establishment and maintenance of international peace and security with the least diversion for armaments of the world's human and economic resources, the Security Council shall be responsible for formulating, with the assistance of the Military Staff Committee referred to in Article 47, plans to be submitted to the Members of the United Nations for the establishment of a system for the regulation of armaments.

Voting

Article 27

1. Each member of the Security Council shall have one vote.
2. Decisions of the Security Council on procedural matters shall be made by an affirmative vote of nine members.
3. Decisions of the Security Council on all other matters shall be made by an affirmative vote of nine members including the concurring votes of the permanent members; provided that, in decisions under Chapter VI, and under paragraph 3 of Article 52, a party to a dispute shall abstain from voting.

Procedure

Article 28

1. The Security Council shall be so organized as to be able to function continuously. Each member of the Security Council shall for this purpose be represented at all times at the seat of the Organization.
2. The Security Council shall hold periodic meetings at which each of its members may, if it so desires, be represented by

a member of the government or by some other specially designated representative.

3. The Security Council may hold meetings at such places other than the seat of the Organization as in its judgment will best facilitate its work.

Article 29

The Security Council may establish such subsidiary organs as it deems necessary for the performance of its functions.

Article 30

The Security Council shall adopt its own rules of procedure, including the method of selecting its President.

Article 31

Any Member of the United Nations which is not a member of the Security Council may participate, without vote, in the discussion of any question brought before the Security Council whenever the latter considers that the interests of that Member are specially affected.

Article 32

Any Member of the United Nations which is not a member of the Security Council or any state which is not a Member of the United Nations, if it is a party to a dispute under consideration by the Security Council, shall be invited to participate, without vote, in the discussion relating to the dispute. The Security Council shall lay down such conditions as it deems just for the participation of a state which is not a Member of the United Nations.

CHAPTER VI

PACIFIC SETTLEMENT OF DISPUTES

Article 33

1. The parties to any dispute, the continuance of which is likely to endanger the maintenance of international peace

and security, shall, first of all, seek a solution by negotiation, enquiry, mediation, conciliation, arbitration, judicial settlement, resort to regional agencies or arrangements, or other peaceful means of their own choice.

2. The Security Council shall, when it deems necessary, call upon the parties to settle their dispute by such means.

Article 34

The Security Council may investigate any dispute, or any situation which might lead to international friction or give rise to a dispute, in order to determine whether the continuance of the dispute or situation is likely to endanger the maintenance of international peace and security.

Article 35

1. Any Member of the United Nations may bring any dispute, or any situation of the nature referred to in Article 34, to the attention of the Security Council or of the General Assembly.
2. A state which is not a Member of the United Nations may bring to the attention of the Security Council or of the General Assembly any dispute to which it is a party if it accepts in advance, for the purposes of the dispute, the obligations of pacific settlement provided in the present Charter.
3. The proceedings of the General Assembly in respect of matters brought to its attention under this Article will be subject to the provisions of Articles 11 and 12.

Article 36

1. The Security Council may, at any stage of a dispute of the nature referred to in Article 33 or of a situation of like nature, recommend appropriate procedures or methods of adjustment.
2. The Security Council should take into consideration any procedures for the settlement of the dispute which have already been adopted by the parties.

3. In making recommendations under this Article the Security Council should also take into consideration that legal disputes should as a general rule be referred by the parties to the International Court of Justice in accordance with the provisions of the Statute of the Court.

Article 37

1. Should the parties to a dispute of the nature referred to in Article 33 fail to settle it by the means indicated in that Article, they shall refer it to the Security Council.
2. If the Security Council deems that the continuance of the dispute is in fact likely to endanger the maintenance of international peace and security, it shall decide whether to take action under Article 36 or to recommend such terms of settlement as it may consider appropriate.

Article 38

Without prejudice to the provisions of Articles 33 to 37, the Security Council may, if all the parties to any dispute so request, make recommendations to the parties with a view to a pacific settlement of the dispute.

CHAPTER VII

ACTION WITH RESPECT TO THREATS TO THE PEACE, BREACHES OF THE PEACE, AND ACTS OF AGGRESSION

Article 39

The Security Council shall determine the existence of any threat to the peace, breach of the peace, or act of aggression and shall make recommendations, or decide what measures shall be taken in accordance with Articles 41 and 42, to maintain or restore international peace and security.

Article 40

In order to prevent an aggravation of the situation, the Security Council may, before making the recommendations or deciding upon the measures provided for in Article 39, call upon the parties concerned to comply with such provisional measures as it deems necessary or desirable. Such provisional measures shall be without prejudice to the rights, claims or position of the parties concerned. The Security Council shall duly take account of failure to comply with such provisional measures.

Article 41

The Security Council may decide what measures not involving the use of armed force are to be employed to give effect to its decisions, and it may call upon the Members of the United Nations to apply such measures. These may include complete or partial interruption of economic relations and of rail, sea, air, postal, telegraphic, radio and other means of communication, and the severance of diplomatic relations.

Article 42

Should the Security Council consider that measures provided for in Article 41 would be inadequate or have proved to be inadequate, it may take such action by air, sea or land forces as may be necessary to maintain or restore international peace and security. Such action may include demonstrations, blockade, and other operations by air, sea, or land forces of Members of the United Nations.

Article 43

1. All Members of the United Nations, in order to contribute to the maintenance of international peace and security, undertake to make available to the Security Council, on its call and in accordance with a special agreement or agreements, armed forces, assistance and facilities, including rights of passage, necessary for the purpose of maintaining international peace and security.
2. Such agreement or agreements shall govern the numbers and types of forces, their degree of readiness and general location, and the nature of the facilities and assistance to be provided.

3. The agreement or agreements shall be negotiated as soon as possible on the initiative of the Security Council. They shall be concluded between the Security Council and Members or between the Security Council and groups of Members and shall be subject to ratification by the signatory states in accordance with their respective constitutional processes.

Article 44

When the Security Council has decided to use force it shall, before calling upon a Member not represented on it to provide armed forces in fulfillment of the obligations assumed under Article 43, invite that Member, if the Member so desires, to participate in the decisions of the Security Council concerning the employment of contingents of that Member's armed forces.

Article 45

In order to enable the United Nations to take urgent military measures, Members shall hold immediately available national air-force contingents for combined international enforcement action. The strength and degree of readiness of these contingents and plans for their combined action shall be determined, within the limits laid down in the special agreement or agreements referred to in Article 43, by the Security Council with the assistance of the Military Staff Committee.

Article 46

Plans for the application of armed force shall be made by the Security Council with the assistance of the Military Staff Committee.

Article 47

1. There shall be established a Military Staff Committee to advise and assist the Security Council on all questions relating to the Security Council's military requirements for the maintenance of international peace and security, the em-

ployment and command of forces placed at its disposal, the regulation of armaments, and possible disarmament.

2. The Military Staff Committee shall consist of the Chiefs of Staff of the permanent members of the Security Council or their representatives. Any Member of the United Nations not permanently represented on the Committee shall be invited by the Committee to be associated with it when the efficient discharge of the Committee's responsibilities requires the participation of that Member in its work.

3. The Military Staff Committee shall be responsible under the Security Council for the strategic direction of any armed forces placed at the disposal of the Security Council. Questions relating to the command of such forces shall be worked out subsequently.

4. The Military Staff Committee, with the authorization of the Security Council and after consultation with appropriate regional agencies, may establish regional sub-committees.

Article 48

1. The action required to carry out the decisions of the Security Council for the maintenance of international peace and security shall be taken by all the Members of the United Nations or by some of them, as the Security Council may determine.

2. Such decisions shall be carried out by the Members of the United Nations directly and through their action in the appropriate international agencies of which they are members.

Article 49

The Members of the United Nations shall join in affording mutual assistance in carrying out the measures decided upon by the Security Council.

Article 50

If preventive or enforcement measures against any state are taken by the Security Council, any other state, whether a Member of the United Nations or not, which finds itself confronted with special economic problems arising from the carrying out of those measures shall have the right to consult the Security Council with regard to a solution of those problems.

Article 51

Nothing in the present Charter shall impair the inherent right of individual or collective self-defence if an armed attack occurs against a Member of the United Nations, until the Security Council has taken measures necessary to maintain international peace and security. Measures taken by Members in the exercise of this right of self-defence shall be immediately reported to the Security Council and shall not in any way affect the authority and responsibility of the Security Council under the present Charter to take at any time such action as it deems necessary in order to maintain or restore international peace and security.

CHAPTER VIII

REGIONAL ARRANGEMENTS

Article 52

1. Nothing in the present Charter precludes the existence of regional arrangements or agencies for dealing with such matters relating to the maintenance of international peace and security as are appropriate for regional action, provided that such arrangements or agencies and their activities are consistent with the Purposes and Principles of the United Nations.
2. The Members of the United Nations entering into such arrangements or constituting such agencies shall make every effort to achieve pacific settlement of local disputes through such regional arrangements or by such regional agencies before referring them to the Security Council.
3. The Security Council shall encourage the development of pacific settlement of local disputes through such regional ar-

rangements or by such regional agencies either on the initiative of the states concerned or by reference from the Security Council.

4. This Article in no way impairs the application of Articles 34 and 35.

Article 53

1. The Security Council shall, where appropriate, utilize such regional arrangements or agencies for enforcement action under its authority. But no enforcement action shall be taken under regional arrangements without the authorization of the Security Council, with the exception of measures against any enemy state, as defined in paragraph 2 of this Article, provided for pursuant to Article 107 or in regional arrangements directed against renewal of aggressive policy on the part of any such state, until such time as the Organization may, on request of the Governments concerned, be charged with the responsibility for preventing further aggression by such a state.

2. The term enemy state as used in paragraph 1 of this Article applies to any state which during the Second World War has been an enemy of any signatory of the present Charter.

Article 54

The Security Council shall at all times be kept fully informed of activities undertaken or in contemplation under regional arrangements or by regional agencies for the maintenance of international peace and security.

CHAPTER IX

INTERNATIONAL ECONOMIC AND SOCIAL CO-OPERATION

Article 55

With a view to the creation of conditions of stability and well-being which are necessary for peaceful and friendly relations among nations based on respect for the principle of equal rights and self-determination of peoples, the United Nations shall promote:

  a. higher standards of living, full employment, and conditions of economic and social progress and development;
  b. solutions of international economic, social, health, and related problems; and international cultural and educational co-operation; and
  c. universal respect for, and observance of, human rights and fundamental freedoms for all without distinction as to race, sex, language, or religion.

Article 56

All Members pledge themselves to take joint and separate action in co-operation with the Organization for the achievement of the purposes set forth in Article 55.

Article 57

  1. The various specialized agencies, established by intergovernmental agreement and having wide international responsibilities, as defined in their basic instruments, in economic, social, cultural, educational, health, and related fields, shall be brought into relationship with the United Nations in accordance with the provisions of Article 63.
  2. Such agencies thus brought into relationship with the United Nations are hereinafter referred to as specialized agencies.

Article 58

The Organization shall make recommendations for the co-ordination of the policies and activities of the specialized agencies.

Article 59

The Organization shall, where appropriate, initiate negotiations among the states concerned for the creation of any new specialized agencies required for the accomplishment of the purposes set forth in Article 55.

Article 60

Responsibility for the discharge of the functions of the Organization set forth in this Chapter shall be vested in the General Assembly and, under the authority of the General Assembly, in the Economic and Social Council, which shall have for this purpose the powers set forth in Chapter X.

CHAPTER X

THE ECONOMIC AND SOCIAL COUNCIL

Composition

Article 61

1. The Economic and Social Council shall consist of fifty-four Members of the United Nations elected by the General Assembly.
2. Subject to the provisions of paragraph 3, eighteen members of the Economic and Social Council shall be elected each year for a term of three years. A retiring member shall be eligible for immediate re-election.
3. At the first election after the increase in the membership of the Economic and Social Council from twenty-seven to fifty-four members, in addition to the members elected in place of the nine members whose term of office expires at the end of that year, twenty-seven additional members shall be elected. Of these twenty-seven additional members, the term of office of nine members so elected shall expire at the end of one year, and of nine other members at the end of two years, in accordance with arrangements made by the General Assembly.
4. Each member of the Economic and Social Council shall have one representative.

Functions and Powers

Article 62

1. The Economic and Social Council may make or initiate studies and reports with respect to international economic, social, cultural, educational, health, and related matters and may make recommendations with respect to any such matters to the General Assembly, to the Members of the United Nations, and to the specialized agencies concerned.

2. It may make recommendations for the purpose of promoting respect for, and observance of, human rights and fundamental freedoms for all.

3. It may prepare draft conventions for submission to the General Assembly, with respect to matters falling within its competence.

4. It may call, in accordance with the rules described by the United Nations, international conferences on matters falling within its competence.

Article 63

1. The Economic and Social Council may enter into agreements with any of the agencies referred to in Article 57, defining the terms on which the agency concerned shall be brought into relationship with the United Nations. Such agreement shall be subject to approval by the General Assembly.

2. It may co-ordinate the activities of the specialized agencies through consultation with and recommendations to such agencies and through recommendations to the General Assembly and to the Members of the United Nations.

Article 64

1. The Economic and Social Council may take appropriate steps to obtain regular reports from the specialized agencies. It may make arrangements with the Members of the United Nations and with the specialized agencies to obtain reports

of the steps taken to give effect to its own recommendations and to recommendations on matters falling within its competency made by the General Assembly.

2. It may communicate its observations on these reports to the General Assembly.

Article 65

The Economic and Social Council may furnish information to the Security Council and shall assist the Security Council upon its request.

Article 66

1. The Economic and Social Council shall perform such functions as fall within its competence in connection with the carrying out of the recommendations of the General Assembly.
2. It may, with the approval of the General Assembly, perform services at the request of Members of the United Nations and at the request of specialized agencies.
3. It shall perform such other functions as are specified elsewhere in the present Charter or as may be assigned to it by the General Assembly.

Article 67

1. Each member of the Economic and Social Council shall have one vote.
2. Decisions of the Economic and Social Council shall be made by a majority of the members present and voting.

Article 68

The Economic and Social Council shall set up commissions in economic and social fields and for the promotion of human rights, and such other commissions as may be required for the performance of its functions.

Article 69

The Economic and Social Council shall invite any Member of the United Nations to participate, without vote, in its deliberations on any matter of particular concern to that Member.

Article 70

The Economic and Social Council may make arrangements for representatives of the specialized agencies to participate, without vote, in its deliberations and in those of the commissions established by it, and for its representatives to participate in the deliberations of the specialized agencies.

Article 71

The Economic and Social Council may make suitable arrangements for consultation with non-governmental organizations which are concerned with matters within its competence. Such arrangements may be made with international organizations and, where appropriate, with national organizations after consultation with the Member of the United Nations concerned.

Article 72

1. The Economic and Social Council shall adopt its own rules of procedure, including the method of selecting its President.
2. The Economic and Social Council shall meet as required in accordance with its rules, which shall include provision for the convening of meetings on the request of a majority of its members.

CHAPTER XI

DECLARATION REGARDING
NON-SELF GOVERNING TERRITORIES

Article 73

Members of the United Nations which have or assume responsibilities for the administration of territories whose peoples have not yet attained a full measure of self-government recognize the principle that the interests of the inhabitants of these territories are paramount, and accept as a sacred trust the obligation to promote to the utmost, within the system of international peace and security established by the present Charter, the well-being of the inhabitants of these territories and, to this end:

a. to ensure, with due respect for the culture of the peoples concerned, their political, economic, social, and educational advancement, their just treatment, and their protection against abuses;
b. to develop self-government, to take due account of the political aspirations of the peoples, and to assist them in the progressive development of their free political institutions, according to the particular circumstances of each territory and its peoples and their varying stages of advancement;
c. to further international peace and security;
d. to promote constructive measures of development, to encourage research, and to co-operate with one another and, when and where appropriate, with specialized international bodies with a view to the practical achievement of the social, economic, and scientific purposes set forth in this Article; and
e. to transmit regularly to the Secretary-General for information purposes, subject to such limitation as security and constitutional considerations may require, statistical and other information of a technical nature relating to economic, social, and educational conditions in the territories for which they are respectively responsible other than those territories to which Chapters XII and XIII apply.

Article 74

Members of the United Nations also agree that their policy in respect of the territories to which this Chapter applies, no less than in respect of their metropolitan areas, must be based on the general principle of good-neighbourliness, due account being taken of the interests and well-being of the rest of the world, in social, economic, and commercial matters.

CHAPTER XII

INTERNATIONAL TRUSTEESHIP SYSTEM

Article 75

The United Nations shall establish under its authority an international trusteeship system for the administration and supervision of such territories as may be placed thereunder by subsequent individual agreements. These territories are hereinafter referred to as trust territories.

Article 76

The basic objectives of the trusteeship system, in accordance with the Purposes of the United Nations laid down in Article I of the present Charter, shall be:

a. to further international peace and security;
b. to promote the political, economic, social, and educational advancement of the inhabitants of the trust territories, and their progressive development towards self-government or independence as may be appropriate to the particular circumstances of each territory and its peoples and the freely expressed wishes of the peoples concerned, and as may be provided by the terms of each trusteeship agreement;
c. to encourage respect for human rights and for fundamental freedoms for all without distinction as to race, sex, language, or religion, and to encourage recognition of the interdependence of the peoples of the world; and
d. to ensure equal treatment in social, economic, and commercial matters for all Members of the United Nations and their nationals, and also equal treatment for the latter in the administration of justice, without prejudice to the

attainment of the foregoing objectives and subject to the provisions of Article 80.

Article 77

1. The trusteeship system shall apply to such territories in the following categories as may be placed thereunder by means of trusteeship agreements:

   a. territories now held under mandate;
   b. territories which may be detached from enemy states as a result of the Second World War; and
   c. territories voluntarily placed under the system by states responsible for their administration.

2. It will be a matter for subsequent agreement as to which territories in the foregoing categories will be brought under the trusteeship system and upon what terms.

Article 78

The trusteeship system shall not apply to territories which have become Members of the United Nations, relationship among which shall be based on respect for the principle of sovereign equality.

Article 79

The terms of trusteeship for each territory to be placed under the trusteeship system, including any alteration or amendment, shall be agreed upon by the states directly concerned, including the mandatory power in the case of territories held under mandate by a Member of the United Nations, and shall be approved as provided for in Articles 83 and 85.

Article 80

1. Except as may be agreed upon in individual trusteeship agreements, made under Articles 77, 79 and 81, placing each territory under the trusteeship system, and until such agreements have been concluded, nothing in this Chapter

shall be construed in or of itself to alter in any manner the rights whatsoever of any states or any peoples or the terms of existing international instruments to which Members of the United Nations may respectively be parties.

2. Paragraph 1 of this Article shall not be interpreted as giving grounds for delay or postponement of the negotiation and conclusion of agreements for placing mandated and other territories under the trusteeship system as provided for in Article 77.

Article 81

The trusteeship agreement shall in each case include the terms under which the trust territory will be administered and designate the authority which will exercise the administration of the trust territory. Such authority, hereinafter called the administering authority, may be one or more states or the Organization itself.

Article 82

There may be designated, in any trusteeship agreement, a strategic area or areas which may include part or all of the trust territory to which the agreement applies, without prejudice to any special agreement or agreements made under Article 43.

Article 83

1. All functions of the United Nations relating to strategic areas, including the approval of the terms of the trusteeship agreements and of their alteration or amendment, shall be exercised by the Security Council.
2. The basic objectives set forth in Article 76 shall be applicable to the people of each strategic area.
3. The Security Council shall, subject to the provisions of the trusteeship agreements and without prejudice to security considerations, avail itself of the assistance of the Trusteeship Council to perform those functions of the United Nations under the trusteeship system relating to political, economic, social, and educational matters in the strategic areas.

Article 84

It shall be the duty of the administering authority to ensure that the trust territory shall play its part in the maintenance of international peace and security. To this end the administering authority may make use of volunteer forces, facilities, and assistance from the trust territory in carrying out the obligations towards the Security Council undertaken in this regard by the administering authority, as well as for local defence and the maintenance of law and order within the trust territory.

Article 85

1. The functions of the United Nations with regard to trusteeship agreements for all areas not designated as strategic, including the approval of the terms of the trusteeship agreements and of their alteration or amendment, shall be exercised by the General Assembly.
2. The Trusteeship Council, operating under the authority of the General Assembly, shall assist the General Assembly in carrying out these functions.

CHAPTER XIII

THE TRUSTEESHIP COUNCIL

Composition

Article 86

1. The Trusteeship Council shall consist of the following Members of the United Nations:
   a. those Members administering trust territories;
   b. such of those Members mentioned by name in Article 23 as are not administering trust territories; and
   c. as many other Members elected for three-year terms by the General Assembly as may be necessary to ensure that the total number of members of the Trusteeship Council is equally divided between those Members of the United

Nations which administer trust territories and those which do not.

2. Each member of the Trusteeship Council shall designate one specially qualified person to represent it therein.

Functions and Powers

Article 87

The General Assembly and, under its authority, the Trusteeship Council, in carrying out their functions, may:

a. consider reports submitted by the administering authority;
b. accept petitions and examine them in consultation with the administering authority;
c. provide for periodic visits to the respective trust territories at times agreed upon with the administering authority; and as previously
d. take these and other actions in conformity with the terms of the trusteeship agreements.

Article 88

The Trusteeship Council shall formulate a questionnaire on the political, economic, social, and educational advancement of the inhabitants of each trust territory, and the administering authority for each trust territory within the competence of the General Assembly shall make an annual report to the General Assembly upon the basis of such questionnaire.

Voting

Article 89

1. Each member of the Trusteeship Council shall have one vote.
2. Decisions of the Trusteeship Council shall be made by a majority of the members present and voting.

Procedure

Article 90

1. The Trusteeship Council shall adopt its own rules of procedure, including the method of selecting its President.
2. The Trusteeship Council shall meet as required in accordance with its rules, which shall include provision for the convening of meetings on the request of a majority of its members.

Article 91

The Trusteeship Council shall, when appropriate, avail itself of the assistance of the Economic and Social Council and of the specialized agencies in regard to matters with which they are respectively concerned.

CHAPTER XIV

THE INTERNATIONAL COURT OF JUSTICE

Article 92

The International Court of Justice shall be the principal judicial organ of the United Nations. It shall function in accordance with the annexed Statute, which is based upon the Statute of the Permanent Court of International Justice and forms an integral part of the present Charter.

Article 93

1. All Members of the United Nations are *ipso facto* parties to the Statute of the International Court of Justice.
2. A state which is not a Member of the United Nations may become a party to the Statute of the International Court of Justice on conditions to be determined in each case by the General Assembly upon the recommendation of the Security Council.

Article 94

1. Each Member of the United Nations undertakes to comply with the decision of the International Court of Justice in any case to which it is a party.
2. If any party to a case fails to perform the obligations incumbent upon it under a judgment rendered by the Court, the other party may have recourse to the Security Council, which may, if it deems necessary, make recommendations or decide upon measures to be taken to give effect to the judgment.

Article 95

Nothing in the present Charter shall prevent Members of the United Nations from entrusting the solution of their differences to other tribunals by virtue of agreements already in existence or which may be concluded in the future.

Article 96

1. The General Assembly or the Security Council may request the International Court of Justice to give an advisory opinion on any legal question.
2. Other organs of the United Nations and specialized agencies, which may at any time be so authorized by the General Assembly, may also request advisory opinions of the Court on legal questions arising within the scope of their activities.

CHAPTER XV

THE SECRETARIAT

Article 97

The Secretariat shall comprise a Secretary-General and such staff as the Organization may require. The Secretary-General shall be appointed by the General Assembly upon the recommendation of the Security Council. He shall be the chief administrative officer of the Organization.

Article 98

The Secretary-General shall act in that capacity in all meetings of the General Assembly, of the Security Council, of the Economic and Social Council, and of the Trusteeship Council, and shall perform such other functions as are entrusted to him by these organs. The Secretary-General shall make an annual report to the General Assembly on the work of the Organization.

Article 99

The Secretary-General may bring to the attention of the Security Council any matter which in his opinion may threaten the maintenance of international peace and security.

Article 100

1. In the performance of their duties the Secretary-General and the staff shall not seek or receive instructions from any government or from any other authority external to the Organization. They shall refrain from any action which might reflect on their position as international officials responsible only to the Organization.
2. Each Member of the United Nations undertakes to respect the exclusively international character of the responsibilities of the Secretary-General and the staff and not to seek to influence them in the discharge of their responsibilities.

Article 101

1. The staff shall be appointed by the Secretary-General under regulations established by the General Assembly.
2. Appropriate staffs shall be permanently assigned to the Economic and Social Council, the Trusteeship Council, and, as required, to other organs of the United Nations. These staffs shall form a part of the Secretariat.
3. The paramount consideration in the employment of the staff and in the determination of the conditions of service shall be the necessity of securing the highest standards of efficiency,

competence, and integrity. Due regard shall be paid to the importance of recruiting the staff on as wide a geographical basis as possible.

CHAPTER XVI

MISCELLANEOUS PROVISIONS

Article 102

1. Every treaty and every international agreement entered into by any Member of the United Nations after the present Charter comes into force shall as soon as possible be registered with the Secretariat and published by it.
2. No party to any such treaty or international agreement which has not been registered in accordance with the provisions of paragraph 1 of this Article may invoke that treaty or agreement before any organ of the United Nations.

Article 103

In the event of a conflict between the obligations of the Members of the United Nations under the present Charter and their obligations under any other international agreement, their obligations under the present Charter shall prevail.

Article 104

The Organization shall enjoy in the territory of each of its Members such legal capacity as may be necessary for the exercise of its functions and the fulfillment of its purposes.

Article 105

1. The Organization shall enjoy in the territory of each of its Members such privileges and immunities as are necessary for the fulfillment of its purposes.
2. Representatives of the Members of the United Nations and officials of the Organization shall similarly enjoy such privileges and immunities as are necessary for the

independent exercise of their functions in connection with the Organization.

3. The General Assembly may make recommendations with a view to determining the details of the application of paragraphs 1 and 2 of this Article or may propose conventions to the Members of the United Nations for this purpose.

CHAPTER XVII

TRANSITIONAL SECURITY ARRANGEMENTS

Article 106

Pending the coming into force of such special agreements referred to in Article 43 as in the opinion of the Security Council enable it to begin the exercise of its responsibilities under Article 42, the parties to the Four-Nation Declaration, signed at Moscow, 30 October 1943, and France, shall, in accordance with the provisions of paragraph 5 of that Declaration, consult with one another and as occasion requires with other Members of the United Nations with a view to such joint action on behalf of the Organization as may be necessary for the purpose of maintaining international peace and security.

Article 107

Nothing in the present Charter shall invalidate or preclude action, in relation to any state which during the Second World War has been an enemy of any signatory to the present Charter, taken or authorized as a result of that war by the Governments having responsibility for such action.

CHAPTER XVIII

AMENDMENTS

Article 108

Amendments to the present Charter shall come into force for all Members of the United Nations when they have been adopted by a vote of two thirds of the members of the General Assembly and ratified in accordance with their respective constitutional processes by two thirds of the Members of the United Nations including all the permanent members of the Security Council.

Article 109

1. A General Conference of the Members of the United Nations for the purpose of reviewing the present Charter may be held at a date and place to be fixed by a two-thirds vote of the members of the General Assembly and by a vote of any nine members of the Security Council. Each Member of the United Nations shall have one vote in the conference.

2. Any alteration of the present Charter recommended by a two-thirds vote of the conference shall take effect when ratified in accordance with their respective constitutional processes by two-thirds of the Members of the United Nations including all the permanent members of the Security Council.

3. If such a conference has not been held before the tenth annual session of the General Assembly following the coming into force of the present Charter, the proposal to call such a conference shall be placed on the agenda of that session of the General Assembly, and the conference shall be held if so decided by a majority vote of the members of the General Assembly and by a vote of any seven members of the Security Council.

CHAPTER XIX

RATIFICATION AND SIGNATURE

Article 110

1. The present Charter shall be ratified by the signatory states in accordance with their respective constitutional processes.

2. The ratifications shall be deposited with the Government of

the United States of America, which shall notify all the signatory states of each deposit as well as the Secretary-General of the Organization when he has been appointed.

3. The present Charter shall come into force upon the deposit of ratifications by the Republic of China, France, the Union of Soviet Socialist Republics, the United Kingdom of Great Britain and Northern Ireland and the United States of America, and by a majority of the other signatory states. A protocol of the ratifications deposited shall thereupon be drawn up by the Government of the United States of America which shall communicate copies thereof to all the signatory states.

4. The states signatory to the present Charter which ratify it after it has come into force will become original Members of the United Nations on the date of the deposit of their respective ratifications.

The present Charter, of which the Chinese, French, Russian, English, and Spanish texts are equally authentic, shall remain deposited in the archives of the Government of the United States of America. Duly certified copies thereof shall be transmitted by that Government to the Governments of the other signatory states.

IN FAITH WHEREOF the representatives of the Governments of the United Nations have signed the present Charter.

DONE at the city of San Francisco the twenty-sixth day of June, one thousand nine hundred and forty-five.

Notes

Chapter 1. The United Nations
and Its Membership

1. United Nations, *Everyone's United Nations*, p. 3. This is a comprehensive and authoritative source of information on the organization and functioning of the UN.
2. Shirley Hazzard, *Defeat of an Ideal*, p. 81.

Chapter 2. The General Assembly

1. Michael Akehurst, *A Modern Introduction to International Law*, pp. 23–42.

Chapter 3. The Security Council

1. Jack C. Plano and Robert E. Riggs, *Forging World War*, p. 251.

Chapter 4. Peacemaking
or Peacekeeping

1. A substantial recital of this history is to be found in United Nations, *The Blue Helmets: A Review of United Nations Peace-keeping*.
2. Ibid., p. 13.
3. Ibid., pp. 13–14.
4. Clyde Eagleton, *International Government*, pp. 541–45.
5. Ibid., pp. 542–43.
6. Ibid., pp. 543–44.
7. United Nations, *The Blue Helmets*, p. 43.
8. Ibid., p. 44.

9. Ibid., p. 45.

10. Max Harrelson, *Fires All Around the Horizon*, pp. 71–79.

11. United Nations, *The Blue Helmets*, pp. 46–47.

12. Ibid., p. 78.

13. Ibid., p. 228.

14. Ibid., p. 232.

15. Ibid., pp. 237–45.

16. Brian Urquhart, "For a UN Volunteer Military Force," *New York Review of Books*, June 10, 1993, pp. 3–4.

Chapter 5. The Secretary-General and the Secretariat

1. For numerous examples, see: Thomas M. Franck, *Nation Against Nation*, pp. 134–60.

2. Discussion of the problems involved in the selection and role of the secretary-general is found in Brian Urquhart and Erskine Childers, *A World in Need of Leadership: Tomorrow's United Nations*, available through the Ford Foundation in New York City. See especially p. 28.

3. Ibid., p. x.

4. *Yearbook of the United Nations 1991*, p. 891.

5. Hazzard, *Defeat of an Ideal*, passim.

6. *New York Times*, November 6, 1992.

7. Franck, *Nation Against Nation*, p. 94.

8. Ibid., p. 15.

9. Hazzard, *Defeat of an Ideal*, p. 65.

10. Franck, *Nation Against Nation*, p. 109.

11. Peter J. Fromuth, ed., *A Successor Vision: The United Nations of Tomorrow*, pp. 230–32.

12. Paul Taylor and A.J.R. Groom, eds., *Global Issues in the United Nations Framework*, p. 323.

Chapter 6. The Economic and Social Council and the Subsidiary Organs

1. The author must apologize for the tedious and varied information contained in the following pages. Yet the presentation should have the usefulness of impressing one with the variety and importance of the range of economic and social work in which the UN is involved. The procedures involving who reports to whom are surely not as fine-tuned as the classification used here implies; the structure is really not very tidy. But, for better or worse, the classification of the agencies that is followed here is approximately that used in the *Yearbook of the United Nations, 1991*.

2. United States Department of State, *United States Participation in the UN, 1990*, p. 226.

3. Ibid., p. 245.

4. Yves Beigbeder, *Management Problems in United Nations Organizations*, p. 159.

5. United States Department of State, *United States Participation in the UN*, passim.

Chapter 7. Financial Policy

1. Plano and Riggs, *Forging World Order*, pp. 189–91.

2. *New York Times*, November 28, 1989.

3. Franck, *Nation Against Nation*, pp. 85–86.

4. United States Department of State, *United States Participation in the UN, 1990*, p. 69.

Chapter 8. The International Court of Justice

1. United Nations, *Everyone's United Nations*, p. 370.

2. *New York Times*, April 9, 1993.

3. David P. Forsythe, ed., *The United Nations in the World Political Economy*, pp. 36–53.

4. Ibid.

5. *Amnesty Action, 1992*, published by Amnesty International USA, Winter 1993, p. 6.

Chapter 9. Colonies and the Trusteeship Council

1. United Nations, *Everyone's United Nations*, pp. 332–35.

Chapter 11. The Pattern and the Role of Technology

1. Wendell Gordon and John Adams, *Economics as Social Science*, pp. 11–12.

2. *The Houston Post*, July 16, 1994.

Chapter 12. Institutions

1. Gordon and Adams, *Economics as Social Science*, ch. 3.

2. Hazzard, *Defeat of an Ideal*, ch. 1.

3. Philip C. Jessup, *A Modern Law of Nations*, pp. 20–23.

4. Wendell Gordon, *The Economy of Latin America* (New York: Columbia University Press, 1950), p. 202.

5. United States Congress, House of Representatives, Committee on Banking and Currency, *Export-Import Bank Loan Guaranty Authority* (Washington, D.C.: Government Printing Office, 1949), p. 56, cited in Wendell C. Gordon, *International Trade: Goods, People, and Ideas* (New York: Alfred A. Knopf, 1958), pp. 497–98.

6. *Foreign Affairs* 71 (Winter 1992–93): pp. 79–88.

Chapter 13. The Environment

1. Erich W. Zimmermann, *World Resources and Industries*, esp. part I, unit 1.

2. T.T.B. Koh, "Negotiating a New World Order for the Sea," in Alan K. Henrikson, ed., *Negotiating World Order*, pp. 33–44.

3. Foreign Policy Association, *Great Decisions, 1992*, p. 54.

4. Al Gore, *Earth in the Balance*.

5. Ibid., p. 305.

6. Ibid., p. 352.

7. Ibid., p. 302.

8. Ibid.

Chapter 14. People

1. *New York Times*, April 30, 1992.

2. Foreign Policy Association, *Great Decisions, 1992*, p. 25.

3. *Houston Post*, May 14, 1992.

4. *New York Times*, December 18, 1992.

5. Lung-chu Chen, *An Introduction to Contemporary International Law*, pp. 191–92.

6. *New York Times*, May 28, 1992.

7. See, for example, "Haitian Leaders Object to U.N. Observer Plan," *New York Times*, January 29, 1993.

8. "Europe Warned on Ethnic Conflicts," *New York Times*, May 18, 1993.

Chapter 15. Reform of the United Nations

1. "At U.N. Compound, in Due Course, Marines Ride to Rescue, *New York Times*, January 4, 1993.

2. *New York Times*, December 31, 1992, op. ed. page.

3. Hazzard, *Defeat of an Ideal*. This idea is a theme of Hazzard's book.

Bibliography

Abbott, John. *Politics and Poverty: A Critique of the Food and Agriculture Organization of the United Nations*. London: Routledge, 1992.

Akehurst, Michael. *A Modern Introduction to International Law*, 6th ed. London: Allen and Unwin, 1987 (1970).

Angell, Sir Norman. *The Great Illusion*. New York: G.P. Putnam's Sons, 1911.

Bailey, Sydney D. *The Procedure of the United Nations Security Council*, 2nd ed. Oxford: Clarendon Press, 1988 (1975).

Baratta, Joseph P. *Strengthening the United Nations: A Bibliography*. New York: Greenwood, 1987.

Beigbeder, Yves. *Management Problems in United Nations Organizations: Reform or Decline*. New York: St. Martin's, 1987.

Birn, D.S. *The League of Nations, 1918–1945*. London, 1981.

Bloomfield, Lincoln P. *International Military Forces*. Boston: Little, Brown, 1964.

Chen, Lung-chu. *An Introduction to Contemporary International Law*. New Haven: Yale University Press, 1989.

Clark, Grenville, and Sohn, Louis B. *World Peace Through World Law*. Cambridge: Harvard University Press, 1958 (3rd ed., 1966).

Claude, Inis L., Jr. *Power and International Relations*. New York: Random House, 1962.

Cleveland, Harlan. *Birth of a New World: An Open Moment for International Leadership*. San Francisco: Jossey-Bass, 1993.

Coate, Roger A., ed., *U.S. Policy and the Future of the United Nations*. New York: Twentieth Century Fund Press, 1994.

Commission to Study the Organization of Peace. *Strengthening the United Nations*. New York: Harper, 1957.

Conwell-Evans, T. P. *The League Council in Action*. London: Oxford University Press, 1929.

Damrosch, Lori Fisler. *Enforcing Restraint: Collective Intervention in Internal Conflicts*. New York: Council on Foreign Relations Press, 1993.

Damrosch, Lori Fisler, and Scheffer, David J. *Law and Force in the New International Order*. Boulder, CO: Westview, 1991.

Davis, Harriet E., ed. *Pioneers in World Order: An American Appraisal of the League of Nations*. New York: Columbia University Press, 1945.

Dell, Sidney. *The United Nations and International Business.* Durham, NC: Duke University Press, 1990.

Eagleton, Clyde. *International Government,* 3rd ed. New York: Ronald, 1957.

Evatt, H. V. *The United Nations.* Cambridge: Harvard University Press, 1949.

Falk, Richard. *The End of World Order.* New York: Holmes and Meier, 1983.

Falk, Richard A. *A Study of Future Worlds.* New York: Free Press, 1975.

Falk, Richard A.; Kim, Samuel S.; and Mendlovitz, Saul H., eds. *The United Nations and a Just World Order.* Boulder, CO: Westview, 1991.

Finger, Seymour Maxwell. *American Ambassadors at the United Nations.* New York: Holmes and Meier, 1988.

Finkelstein, Lawrence A., ed. *Politics in the United Nations System.* Durham, NC: Duke University Press, 1988.

Foreign Policy Association, *Great Decisions 1992.* New York: Foreign Policy Association, 1992.

Forsythe, David P., ed. *The United Nations in the World Political Economy.* London: Macmillan, 1989.

Franck, Thomas M. *Nation Against Nation.* New York: Oxford University Press, 1985.

————. "The Emerging Right to Democratic Governance," *American Journal of International Law* 8, no. 1 (1992).

Fromuth, Peter J., ed. *A Successor Vision: The United Nations of Tomorrow.* Lanham, MD: University Press of America and UNA-USA, 1988.

Frye, William R. *A United Nations Peace Force.* New York: Oceana, 1957.

Gati, Toby Trister, ed. *The United States and the United Nations, and the Management of Global Change.* New York: New York University Press, 1983.

Glossop, Ronald J. *World Federation? A Critical Analysis of Federal World Government.* Jefferson, N.C.: McFarland, 1993.

Goodland, Robert; Daly, Herman; El Serafy, Salah; and von Droste, Bernd, eds. *Environmentally Sustainable Economic Development: Building on Brundtland.* Paris: UNESCO, 1991.

Goodrich, Leland M.; Hambro, Edvard; and Simons, Anne Patricia. *Charter of the United Nations,* 3rd ed. New York: Columbia University Press, 1969.

Gordon, Wendell, and Adams, John. *Economics as Social Science.* Westwood, MA: Riverdale Company, 1989.

Gore, Al. *Earth in the Balance: Ecology and the Human Spirit.* Boston: Houghton Mifflin, 1992.

Gottlieb, Gidon. *Nation Against State: A New Approach to Ethnic Conflicts and the Decline of Sovereignty.* New York: Council on Foreign Relations Press, 1993.

Halderman, John W. *The Political Role of the United Nations—Advancing the World Community.* New York: Praeger, 1981.

Harrelson, Max. *Fires All Around the Horizon: The UN's Uphill Battle to Preserve the Peace.* New York: Praeger, 1989.

Harrod, Jeffrey, and Schrijver, Nico. *The United Nations under Attack.* Aldershot: Gower, 1988.

Hazzard, Shirley. *Defeat of an Ideal: A Study of the Self-Destruction of the United Nations.* Boston: Little, Brown, 1973.

Henkin, Louis, et al. *Right v. Might: International Law and the Use of Force,* 2nd ed. New York: Council on Foreign Relations Press, 1991.

Henrikson, Alan K., ed. *Negotiating World Order.* Wilmington, DE: Scholarly Resources, 1986.

Hill, Martin. *The United Nations System: Coordinating Its Economic and Social Work.* Cambridge, UK: Cambridge University Press, 1978.

Hoffman, Walter, ed. *A New World Order: Essays on Restructuring the United Nations.* Washington, DC: World Federalist Association, 1991.

Hollins, Harry B., et al. *The Conquest of War: Alternative Strategies for Global Security.* Boulder, CO: Westview, 1989.

Hudson, Manley O. *International Tribunals.* London, 1944.

Independent Advisory Group on United Nations Financing, *Financing an Effective United Nations.* New York: Ford Foundation, 1993.

Independent Commission on Disarmament and Security Issues (Palme Commission). *Common Security: A Blueprint for Survival.* New York: Simon and Schuster, 1982.

James, Alan. *Sovereign Statehood: The Basis of International Society.* London: Allen and Unwin, 1986.

Jessup, Philip C. *A Modern Law of Nations.* New York: Macmillan, 1948.

Joyce, James Avery. *Broken Star. The Story of the League of Nations, 1919–1939.* Swansea, 1978.

Juyal, Shreesh, and Babu, B. Ramesh, eds. *The United Nations and World Peace.* New York: Facet Book International, 1990.

Luard, Evan. *A History of the United Nations,* 2 vols. New York: St. Martin's, 1982.

Mackinlay, John. *The Peacekeepers: An Assessment of Peacekeeping Operations at the Arab-Israel Interface.* London: Unwin Hyman, 1989.

MacPherson, Bryan F. *An International Criminal Court: Applying World Law to Individuals.* Washington, DC: Center for UN Reform Education, 1992.

Mitchell, George J. *World on Fire, Saving an Endangered Earth.* New York: Scribner's, 1991.

Murray, Gilbert. *From League to United Nations.* London, 1948.

Northedge, F. S. *The League of Nations: Its Life and Times, 1920–1946.* New York: Holmes and Meier, 1986.

Palme Commission. *See* Independent Commission on Disarmament and Security Issues.

Patil, Aiyali V. *The UN Veto in World Affairs, 1946–1990.* Sarasota, FL: Unifo-Marshall, 1992.

Perez de Cuellar, Javier. *Anarchy or Order—Annual Reports 1982–1991.* New York: United Nations, 1991.

Plano, Jack C., and Riggs, Robert E. *Forging World Order: The Politics of International Organization.* New York: Macmillan, 1967.

Renninger, John P., ed. *The Future Role of the United Nations in an Interdependent World.* Boston: Martinus Nijhoff, 1989.

Rochester, J. Martin. *Waiting for the Millennium: The United Nations and the Future of World Order*. Columbia, SC: University of South Carolina Press, 1993.

Russell, Ruth B. *United Nations Experience with Military Forces*. Washington, DC: Brookings, 1964.

Sandler, Todd. "After the Cold War, Secure the Global Commons," *Challenge* 35 (July 1992): pp. 16–29.

Scott, George. *The Rise and Fall of the League of Nations*. London: Hutchinson of London, 1973.

Streit, Clarence K. *Union Now*. New York: Harper, 1939.

Streit, Clarence K.; Roberts, Owen J.; and Schmidt, John F. *The New Federalist*. New York: Harper, 1946.

Taylor, Paul, and Groom, A.J.R., eds. *Global Issues in the United Nations Framework*. London: Macmillan, 1989.

United Nations. *The Blue Helmets: A Review of United Nations Peace-Keeping*. New York: United Nations, 1990.

————. *Everyone's United Nations: A Handbook of the Work of the United Nations*, 10th ed. New York: United Nations, 1986.

————. *Some Reflections on Reform of the United Nations*. Geneva: United Nations Joint Inspection Unit on Personnel Problems in the United Nations, 1971–72.

————. *A Study of the Capacity of the United Nations Development System*. New York: United Nations, 1969.

————. *World Court: What It Is and How It Works*. New York: United Nations, 1989.

————. *Yearbook of the United Nations, 1986*. New York: United Nations, 1990.

United Nations Association. *See* Fromuth, Peter J.

UN Chronicle. A quarterly publication.

United Nations Conference on Environment and Development. *The Global Partnership for Environment and Development: A Guide to Agenda 21*. Geneva: UNCED, 1992.

United States Department of State. *United States Participation in the UN, 1990*. Washington, DC: Government Printing Office, 1991.

Urquhart, Brian. "For a UN Voluntary Military Force." *New York Review of Books* (June 10, 1993): pp. 3–4.

Urquhart, Brian, and Childers, Erskine. *A World in Need of Leadership: Tomorrow's United Nations*. Uppsala, Sweden: Dag Hammarskjold Foundation and Ford Foundation, 1990.

Wainhouse, David W. *International Peace Observation*. Baltimore: Johns Hopkins University Press, 1966.

Williams, Douglas. *The Specialized Agencies and the United Nations: The System in Crisis*. New York: St. Martin's, 1987.

World Commission on Environment and Development. *Our Common Future*. New York: Oxford University Press, 1987.

Zimmermann, Erich W. *World Resources and Industries*, rev. ed. New York: Harper, 1951 (1933).

Index

About the Author

Wendell Chaffee Gordon was born October 9, 1916, in Birmingham, Alabama. His parents were Gertrude Mills Gordon and Dugald Gordon. He graduated from Rice Institute and obtained an M.A. at American University in Washington, DC. He received his Ph.D. in 1940 at New York University, having written his dissertation in political science/international relations under Professor Clyde Eagleton. The topic was *The Expropriation of Foreign-Owned Property in Mexico*. He has also studied at the Sorbonne, the National University of Mexico, and the University of Havana. He taught from 1940 to 1984 in the Department of Economics at the University of Texas. He has also taught at the University of Buenos Aires and at the University of the Americas in Mexico. He served in the United States Army from 1942–45 in North Africa, Sicily, southern Italy, France, and southern Germany. His publications include: *The Political Economy of Latin America, International Trade: Goods, People, and Ideas; Institutional Economics—The Changing System*; and *Economics as Social Science: An Evolutionary Approach*. He has been retired since 1984 and is living in Houston.